114,-
111,92

Harry Seidler   Four Decades of Architecture

Four Decades of Architecture

Harry Seidler

Kenneth Frampton
Philip Drew

Thames and Hudson

First published in Great Britain in 1992 by
Thames and Hudson Ltd, London

First published in the United States of America
in 1992 by Thames and Hudson Inc.,
500 Fifth Avenue, New York, New York 10110

Copyright © 1992 by Harry Seidler
Texts copyright © Kenneth Frampton and
Philip Drew

Library of Congress Catalog Card Number: 92–80804

All Rights Reserved. No part of this publication may be
reproduced or transmitted in any form or by any means,
electronic or mechanical, including photocopy, recording,
or any other information storage and retrieval system,
without prior permission in writing from the publisher.

Design
Harry Williamson
Mark Edwards Butler

Typeset in Frutiger

Printed and bound
Dai Nippon, Japan

Contents

8	Introduction by William H Jordy	202	Offices and Apartments, Kuala Lumpur, Malaysia, 1980
		204	Hong Kong–Shanghai Bank, Hong Kong, 1979
13	**The Migration of an Idea 1945–1976** by Philip Drew	206	Hong Kong Club and Office Building, Hong Kong, 1980–84
32	Three Houses –	218	Waverley Civic Centre, Melbourne, 1982–84
34	Rose Seidler House, Turramurra, 1948–50	226	L. Basser House, Castle Cove, 1980–81
42	Rose House, Turramurra, 1949–50	230	Merson House, Palm Beach, 1981–83
46	Marcus Seidler House, Turramurra, 1949–51	232	Bland House, Rose Bay, 1981–83
48	T. Meller House, Castlecrag, 1950	234	Hannes House, Cammeray, 1983–84
50	Williamson House, Mosman, 1951	240	Grosvenor Place, Sydney, 1982–88
52	Hutter House, Turramurra, 1952	254	IEL Tenancy
54	Muller House, Port Hacking, 1963	258	Riverside Development Stage 1, Brisbane, 1983–86
56	Ski Lodge, Thredbo, 1962		
60	Harry and Penelope Seidler House, Killara, 1966–67	276	Riverside Development Stage 2, Brisbane, 1988
68	Gissing House, Wahroonga, 1971–72	278	Hilton Hotel, Brisbane, 1984–86
70	McMahons Point Development, North Sydney, 1957	282	Capita Centre, Sydney, 1984–89
72	Blues Point Tower Apartments, North Sydney, 1959–61	296	Shell Headquarters, Melbourne, 1985–89
		310	Landmark Tower, Brisbane, 1985
74	Rushcutters Bay Apartments, 1963–65	312	Phoenix Tower, Sydney, 1987
76	NSW Housing Commission Apartments, Rosebery, 1964–67	316	Casino and Hotel Competition, Darling Harbour, 1986
78	Garran Group Housing, Canberra, 1964–68	322	Harry Seidler Offices, Milsons Point, 1971–73
80	Arlington Apartments, Edgecliff, 1965–66	326	Office Extension and Penthouse Apartment, Milsons Point, 1986–88
82	Condominium Apartments, Acapulco, Mexico, 1969–70		
		336	QV1 Office Tower, Perth, 1987–91
85	**Isostatic Architecture 1965–1991** by Kenneth Frampton	354	Australia–Israel Friendship Forest Memorial, Israel, 1988
		356	Waverley Cultural Centre, Melbourne, 1988
		357	Waverley Art Gallery, Melbourne
112	Australia Square, Sydney, 1961–67	360	Grand Central, Melbourne, 1989
124	Exhibition Pavilion, Hyde Park, Sydney, 1970–72	366	Hamilton House, Vaucluse, 1989–91
126	Trade Group Offices, Canberra, 1970–74	372	ABC Apartments, Darlinghurst, 1990
134	Tuggeranong Offices, Canberra, 1974–76		
140	MLC Centre, Sydney, 1972–78	377	**Planning and Architecture at the End of our Century** by Harry Seidler
154	The Australian Embassy, Quai Branly, Paris 15, 1973–77		
172	Barranduda Town Centre, Albury–Wodonga, 1976–78		
176	Ringwood Cultural Centre, Melbourne, 1978–80	387	**Biographical Chronology**
180	Hillside Housing, Kooralbyn, Queensland, 1979–82		
188	Yarralumla Group Houses, Canberra, 1982–84	426	**Selected Bibliography**
192	Australian Parliament House Competition, Canberra, 1979	430	**Credits**
194	Navy Weapons Workshop, Garden Island, Sydney, 1980–85	431	**Collaborators**

Introduction

by William H Jordy

It is of Seidler's towers I would speak, leaving for consideration elsewhere his prolific and distinguished achievement in other areas. Even on these, this is no more than a synopsis with a thesis for what follows. Seidler's continuous exploration of the skyscraper through a number of examples is certainly among his principal contributions to architecture. These towers, moreover, provide a convenient means of positioning him in his point of view. The sequence begins with Australia Square (1961–67), his first large-scale commission, which is (paradoxically) a cylindrical tower, but centred in a plaza which organises an entire city block (the 'Square') in downtown Sydney.

In evaluating this and the towers that follow, history will surely count Harry Seidler among that group of architects who held to the principal convictions of Modern architecture in its original sense, confirming their validity while expanding their possibilities. He would be pleased with this verdict. He has worked directly out of the particular situation and time in Modern architecture in which he found himself at the start of his professional career in the aftermath of the Second World War. Although thoroughly cosmopolitan in outlook and alert to developments, he has not needed any radical realignment of his point of view along the way. So the baseline for his professional career needs but a quick summary.

Seidler determined the direction his architecture would take after a long journey which took him from Vienna at the age of 15, via England and Canada, to Harvard's Graduate School of Design where he received advanced architectural training under Walter Gropius and Marcel Breuer in 1946. While there he also spent a memorable summer with Josef Albers at Black Mountain College, and afterward a year and a half in Breuer's New York office. Add to this close-knit nexus of influence a tropical touch. En route to Australia for a first 'visit' there to his parents, where they had eventually emigrated, he stopped over in Brazil to examine the work and office of Oscar Niemeyer. He was one of the few architects within Seidler's immediate reach who had done a substantial volume of Modern work. This sojourn in a tropical place may also have set him to thinking about the problems of adapting modern architecture to the relatively benign climates of Australia as compared to those he had known in New England and New York (let alone Canada, where he had received his original professional training). Not until his later work, however, did the haunting memory of his Brazilian interlude seem to have returned with special intensity. And finally, a little later, to this compact bundle of seminal influences add one more: Pier Luigi Nervi. He became a collaborator on Australia Square and subsequently on other Seidler buildings.

The isolated tower tube of Australia Square, rising sheer in open space, its parapet sharply clipped, is a cardinal image both for historical Modernism and for the majority of Seidler's towers. He has specifically opposed, as unreal to modern conditions, the popular Post-Modern urban ideal of the walled street. True, his plazas tend to be framed at the street line with lower buildings – sometimes a mix of older buildings nearby left standing and extended by new construction, sometimes wholly new. They are all widely open to access and typically, the pavements of his multi-level plazas, as here, are embedded with radiating designs which resonate the centrifugal-centripetal movement of pedestrians to and from the commanding focus.

The circular tube of Australia Square became its own paradigm for variations on similarly compact towers, each centred in an elevator and utility core – the tower for the MLC Centre in Sydney takes its overall shape from a polygon with a wide face alternating with a narrow face; Riverside Centre in Brisbane, a triangle with rounded corners. The shape of the towers tends to be derived from a tight pack of basic shapes – a Baroque sort of packing. The QV1 Tower in Perth, for example, has a fan-shaped arc bowed as a convex curvex (for the stack of office floors), tangent to a small segment of the arch (for the service core), with the residual angular intervals infilled with pie-shaped wedges (for more office space). Hence the long continuous curve of the tower wall in one direction becomes undulant in the opposite.

The core-tower paradigm, which began so literally at Australia Square, can be further elaborated. The stacks of office floors can assume a certain independence of the core. Grosvenor Place in Sydney consists of two offset arcs, bowed in opposed directions, their inside corners lightly touching, the core occupying the space between like the pointed pit of a peach. In the Kuala Lumpur project in Malaysia the stacks of offices and apartments are ribboned as two elongated S-shapes, again lightly touching an offset configuration, with the pit at the centre now undulant too. In the Shell Tower in Melbourne a more free-form service core to fit an irregular lot, presents a curved face off which the office floor unfurls like a flag, to accommodate to an elongated site with views mostly toward one orientation.

In almost every instance basic geometric shapes account for both tower and core (sometimes as echoing, sometimes as contrasting shapes). The clipped parapets, which screen all rooftop mechanical equipment, emphasise the elemental geometry of the shapes. The beautiful forms are the primary forms as in Le Corbusier's familiar coda for early Modernism. Seidler deplores the Neo-Modern skyscraper with its arbitrary setbacks and, possibly even more, the Neo-Academic skyscraper with its piling of building-block temples and monuments to Lysicrates, by means of which so many late 20th century skyscrapers clamour for urban 'identity'. Nor does he favour purely fanciful shaping by curves and slices by which much mirror-glass treatment seeks uniqueness. For him, elemental geometry suffices for individual identity – a differently shaped tower for each of his skyscrapers. Perhaps the theme of the tower-in-space has, at least in part, encouraged the concentrated nature of his typical tower. Many were the tallest or most conspicuous when built in their downtowns as the eruptive 'Stadtkrone' of their metropoli – although, of course, it is in the nature of competitive urbanism that every 'Stadtkrone' begets another.

This early Modern preference for unitary, elemental geometric form was reinforced by Seidler's summer experience with Albers, although he prizes the experience for sharpening his visual acuity in more subtle ways. No architect has used minimal painting and sculpture more subtly in relation to his buildings than he, and none has learned more about form from studying it.

He also adheres to a second position of historic Modernism, which was in the 1920s and 1930s perhaps more honoured in slogan than in fact: architectural form should be an expression of structure and function. The underlying reasons for his core-and-perimeter tower are practical. From Australia Square onward, in most of his towers the core is ideally positioned to stiffen the tower and to concentrate circulation. By the spoking of identical floor beams from core to perimeter both fabrication and construction are faster and cheaper (and even if the perimeter is unrolled from its core, wall-to-wall spans can be identical). Most of the towers are in reinforced concrete and the shapes lend themselves to easy forming, although they also facilitate framing in steel.

The commission of Australia Square at the beginning of the 1960s also occurred at a time when there was considerable architectural interest in the possibility of creating a more sculptural and hence more monumental Modernism. A major source of course for this interest was the sculptural inventiveness of Le Corbusier, with its potential to bring forth work as profound as (say) Louis Kahn's on the one hand, or the huffing and puffing of much superficial 'New Brutalist' form on the other. Another source of inspiration at the time for building form which was both sculptural and monumental occurred with the architectural discovery, in a flurry of publications on the work of the great 20th century engineers in reinforced concrete from Robert Maillart onward. Seidler's sympathies were instinctively on the side of the engineers at the time. Inevitably perhaps, he was especially attracted to Nervi's collaboration with Breuer on the UNESCO Building in Paris (1953–58). Seidler called on Nervi too, for free span, concrete panels in 'ferro-cement' (Nervi's term) to circle the first two floors of Australia Square, in which the sculptured ceiling pattern reflected the placement of the steel reinforcing to counteract the structural forces operating in the plane. These were to be exhibition floors, and hence might be heavily loaded. Nervi also calculated the changing cross-section for the taper of the ring of projecting supports from ground to parapet which received the spoked floor beams from their hub to the periphery.

Perhaps, too, Australia Square was meant to be a distant translation, in a different building technology, of the simple unitary shape and illusory taper of the walls of Burnham & Root's venerable Monadnock Building (1884–85) in Chicago. It, too, was among the revived icons in the longing for plastic monumentality around 1960.

From his limited and dichotomous use of reinforced concrete in Australia Square for the plastic expression of its structural capabilities, Seidler continued this quest within a building type which is intrinsically resistant to such effects. In a subsequent building, the MLC Tower, also with projected supports, these now act as curved buttresses at the ground, and twist as they rise to become a tapered column which melds into the parapet, more Monadnock than ever.

Meanwhile, Seidler explored the full range of Nervi's technology (frequently calling on Nervi's assistance, up to the time of his death). In a series of buildings, beginning with the Milsons Point offices, the spoked floor beams curve downward at their centres and taper to compactness at either end to make visible the structural forces of tension versus compression and shear acting on them, and to reduce dead load in the process. These sculptural beams are flared into Ts to fuse with the floor slab. When fitted together the opposed flaring creates elongated bowls in the ceiling below against which to diffuse hung fluorescent fixtures. Seidler's extensive experiments with exterior sun baffles against heat and glare in Australia's semi-tropical environment tend to be treated less as applied fixtures and more as sculptural entities integral with the building. In a few buildings the sun louvres become mammoth planes spanning the whole of their elevations between giant supports at the corners, each plane warped to resist bending moments. The curved and tilted or fanned shaping of supports at the ground, and especially at entrances, when extended upward make undulant hollows of the walls immediately above. Suspended within these hollows as entrance shelters, cones or tents of metal and glass provide a billowing counterpoint. And in a few towers, where there is reason to connect several floors, this provides the excuse for stairs as a suspended vortex at the core of the multistorey space.

Such sensuous curvature seems to bring back the interlude with Niemeyer, not as a superficial souvenir of his too often merely bravura effects, but as the reward for the hard-won exploration of the curvilinear possibilities inherent in architectural structure. These memories are joined by Seidler's exploration of the Baroque masters.

This increasingly sculptural expression of structure in reinforced concrete is extended by a series of three towers done between 1984 and 1987 – Capita, Landmark and Phoenix – which employ a different structural approach, that of exposed tubular steel frames with giant membering as their support system. An influence is Mies van der Rohe's use of exposed steel in his late work, but in standard building profiles rather than tubes.

Two of Seidler's towers, the Capita and the Phoenix, occupy crowded sites and would seem to be necessary exceptions to his Modernist predilection for the tower-in-space. Seidler lifts Capita and Phoenix above the ground so that virtually the entire site becomes a plaza. Capita, located mid-block and pressed by relatively tall buildings on three sides, is in effect a tower turned inside out as a light well, with floors ingeniously stepped in banks on opposite walls to permit a diagonal shaft all the way to the plaza. Seidler compensates for the unequal loading of this hollow tube with a mega-truss on end at the street elevation. Of the building, but perceived as a little in front of it, it makes its own monument to structure and height. For Phoenix, the tower is lifted above a rectangular site which fills the end of a city block, its plaza therefore opening on three sides to streets (with a wall for elevators and utilities closing the fourth against its neighbours). Here bridging at two levels by V-shaped cords stabilised the frame across its width.

At Landmark the bridging variously links and braces at four levels pairs of vertical tubular supports which are centred on each face of the building. Set backs occur and may seem an exception to Seidler's predilection for the sheer tower with centred core – although of course this is to be understood merely as a generative theme for his work which seems linked to sympathies born in his past, not a strait-jacket; not even perhaps rationalised beyond its practical implications, but instinctively embraced. Even so, the contradiction is more apparent than fundamental. Landmark originates in a square core within a square office perimeter. As the elevators progressively fall away in the upper storeys, the core changes shape, like the reduction of the perimeter, in squared increments. But the exposed vertical supports are positioned to the width of the core, and on two sides they rise the full height of the building, as though to make visible the invisible core and hold the composition together with the image of the sheer rise of a compact tower. Across the roof a tilted frame binds the supports. Here the frame is another stabilising diagonal, pitched as a solar panel to reduce energy costs in the building.

It is part of the critique of historic Modernism by those who have 'taken it on' in various ways since the 1960s that its logical and abstract bias nullifies the mythopoetic in architecture – a stricture only partially true, as proved by those who use early Modernist motifs and images in a nostalgic vein, but certainly true in part. As Seidler increasingly explores the plasticity of Baroque curvilinear form, however, the ecstasy which is potential in these freer forms will surely augment the logic.

For an unbuilt casino project in Sydney, the hotel floors again unfurl from their utility spindle, this time in more forceful undulation as a broad slab. The parapet is now radically stepped in concert with a tall base stretched over two roads, which is itself stepped with terracing and heaving in curved profile. So the building takes on landscape qualities. In a similar vein, for a sizeable development on the Sydney Harbour a cluster of curved towers (again slabs) step down toward the water, their roofs freely curved planes as an architectural swell.

If such forms owe something to Le Corbusier's famous project for Algiers (1930 *et seq.*), it is less as a source of inspiration than as a point of return after a long development. Their true source is closer to home. This is Sydney, and such expression seems to respond to the city's signifying landmarks: the great arch of the Sydney Harbour Bridge (1932) which crosses Seidler's office window on Milsons Point, and the telescoped shells of Jørn Utzon's Opera House (1957–73).

So Seidler's career demonstrates his life-long commitment both to the ideals and many of the formal themes of Modernism as these had evolved up to the decade after the Second World War. Undeflected from his early convictions by succeeding waves of Anti- and Post-Modernism, he has 'stayed the course'. Yet he has also steadily enlarged on his inheritance by structural, sculptural and geometric innovation, until his most recent buildings – even those in the hard-bitten, 'bottom line' realm of skyscraper development – increasingly open to lyrical allusions. Seriousness of purpose and variety of possibility characterise Seidler's quest out of what Modern architecture once was, and might continue to be in an augmented future.

W.H.J. *Providence R.I.*

1945–1976   The Migration of an Idea

by Philip Drew

Part 1
Early Years

It is early morning on 13 March 1938. In the thin, watery light, huge red flags, vertical slashes of colour, displaying the swastika on a white ground, deck the street facades of building after building. In a matter of days, Vienna had been translated into a magnificent Wagnerian opera set (1, 2). Emerging from the Westbahnhof station, Harry Seidler made his way along the quiet cobblestone streets, his skis slung over his shoulder. Only then, did the full import of Anschluss suggest itself to him.

Anschluss will shatter his life, disperse the Seidler family, and begin a journey lasting 10 years which only ends when the family is once again reunited in distant Sydney.

It is difficult to know precisely how much of Vienna Harry Seidler took with him. He was very young when all this happened, a boy of 14 living a comfortable middle-class existence. Yet there is much about his approach to life and architecture, not so much the details, rather, in the emphasis given to certain things, the discipline and importance attached to geometry, the juxtaposition of formal rectilinear elements with the Baroque, the will to permanence, a belief in the importance of culture, a cluster of attitudes which underpin his activities as a designer, all of which recall Vienna. Even the Viennese tendency to see life in terms of theatre[1] found expression in the way Seidler later dramatised the conflict between Modern architecture in Australia and local councils, inasmuch as the courtroom served as a kind of theatre for the vindication, and ultimate triumph, of Modernism.

Seidler brought the idea of Modern architecture to Australia. What mattered was the idea and procedure, rather than the style. He was inspired by an ideal conception of architecture as being essentially contemporary and constructed out of the materials and experiences of the 20th century, a conception which was not fixed, but rather one which was fluid and capable of reinterpretation.

But for the thoroughness and rigour with which Seidler set about realising the ideal, which was unmatched in Australia at that time, it might have been called a hypothetical architecture. There was about Seidler in the early years an air of the missionary, a mixture of *conquistador* and apostle,[2] of one who was determined to convert an entire society to the new art and architecture. If Modern architecture resembled a religion, the architect was its messenger and defender. Sigfried Giedion observed of Seidler in 1945 that he was 'a fighter for his and our generation'.[3] Giedion would have been surprised at how accurate his premonition was to prove later.

In Australia, the Rose Seidler House at Turramurra in 1950 had a similar impact on Australians as did Seidler's Viennese bicycle, with its big tyres, gears and heavy frame, on his English school friends at Cambridge a decade earlier.[4] It was precisely because of the cultural contrast more than the technical, which represented a distinct set of values worked through and applied with great thoroughness, which stunned his audience. The sheer novelty of it. Australians were unable to imagine anything so different.

Seidler did not introduce Modern architecture to Australia – it reached Australia well ahead of him in the mid-1930s.[5] Modern architecture was not new. It was Seidler's mixture of American Modernism, his closeness to the fountainhead, to Gropius and Breuer, his studies under Albers and later contact with Niemeyer, the lack of any Australian or colonial inflexions and absence of compromise, which shocked and excited Australians. Its foreignness. The purity of his forms was undiluted by historical residues or other stylistic impurities. The work possessed a Futuristic quality. It seemed to many that they were seeing the future.[6] It was not quite real, like travelling in time. Australians were astonished, nonplussed.

Seidler's experiences at Harvard, what he learned in 1945–46 under Walter Gropius and Marcel Breuer, were central to his development. They overlaid and built on the foundation memories from a Vienna childhood which was urban and classical in its make-up. All that had gone before, led up to, and predisposed Seidler. The year at Harvard, Black Mountain, and later New York, fixed the direction his architecture was to take.

Seidler's conversion to Modern architecture was a profound experience. It determined his future, and established a commitment to a set of ideas and approaches from which, in later life, he rarely strayed. The remarkable thing about all this is the flexibility of Seidler's mature years. In others, such a strong commitment would have wasted itself in a sterile repetition of the old formulas, but in Seidler, if anything, the work has grown freer and more confident with time, more able to take risks, less constrained by the dogmas.

No other architect in Australia has created such a body of high-quality work of comparable integrity spanning over four decades from 1949, which illustrates the ideas of Modern architecture as a unique synthesis of technology, society, and the visual imagery of this century. That the work was done in Australia, it will become apparent, was an accident of history.

Seidler has always been an internationalist, his references, his collaborators, the artists whose work he selects, have overwhelmingly been from outside Australia. He is an Austrian who learned his profession in America and practised in Australia. His architecture is East Coast Modern, the American version of the Bauhaus idea restated by Breuer, which is identified more with the USA, than it is with Australia. Having lost his natural homeland, Seidler replaced it with the '*Republik der Geister*'.[7]

Until he was 10 years old, Seidler's parents (3) occupied an apartment on the topmost level of a handsome corner block at 1 Grundlgasse, Vienna IX (5).[8] Prior to this, Max and Rose Seidler lived in the poor 20th district. In 1933, the Seidlers moved to a spacious apartment in 68 Peterjordan Strasse in the 19th Cottage district, farther out, and northwest of the city, which his mother commissioned Fritz Reichl,[9] a former student and assistant of Josef Hoffman, to redecorate in a fussy Art Deco idiom.

Seidler attended the Bundesgymnasium Vienna IX, known as the Wasagymnasium because of its location in Wasagasse (6).[10] Run like a military academy, it had a reputation for preparing youths to enter the professions (notably medicine) with a constant diet of Latin and Greek. Freud's house at 19 Berggasse was only a few blocks distant. The Voltivkirche, designed in 1853, in the Gothic style by Heinrich Fertstel, is a near neighbour.

Seidler grew up surrounded by buildings. He was accustomed to city living. As a youth, he discovered the tall steel and glass Hochhaus (7) on the way to piano lessons,[11] and heard the shooting from the siege of the Karl Marx Hof housing in 1934 (8).[12]

For all its apparent solidity, Austria was tottering on the brink. Hitler's annexation played out the final scene. The half-hidden disintegration of the Austro–Hungarian Empire, defeated on the battlefield by Prussia at Koeniggratz in 1866, torn by Balkan nationalism and devastated by the bank crash of 1873 produced a strange simultaneity, a tension running through Austrian society and expressed as ambivalence, hysteria and neurosis.[13] At the same time that it was said that things never looked better they had never been worse.

Born on 25 June 1923, Harry was the younger of two sons of Max Seidler and Rose Schwarz. His father, who came to Vienna seeking work as a youth, fought on the Isonzo in the First World War (4), and afterwards developed a successful textile business. They were an upwardly mobile, middle-class, Viennese family.

Hitler's annexation of Austria changed this. Seidler's schooling ended abruptly in June 1938, and by September he had left via Aachen and Ostende for England ahead of his parents, whose factory was taken over by the Nazis (9).[14] There his brother Marcel arranged through the Society of Friends for him to stay with Lady Edith MacAlister and her sister in Cambridge. He was enrolled in the Cambridge Polytechnic School and stayed with the MacAlister sisters until his internment (10).

6

7

8

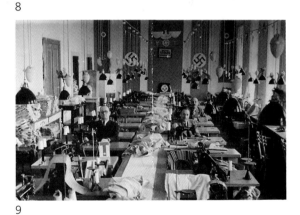
9

10

Cambridge gave Seidler his confident use of English, an ability to say what he meant forcefully and with precision, a facility that proved its worth in publicising his views, and the trades background and skill in drawing, together with his Harvard training, made him an indispensable assistant to Marcel Breuer.

On 10 May 1940, Winston Churchill was called to the premiership as head of an all party administration. Two days later, all enemy aliens, including refugees from the Nazis like Seidler, were interned. Thus began 16 months of internment from 12 May 1940, to 4 October 1941. It was a time of considerable strain and uncertainty, made all the more stressful because it was indefinite. 'I am continually nervous,' he wrote.[15]

13

Seidler was moved from one camp to another, mixed in with Nazi prisoners of war, at Liverpool and the Isle of Man, before being transported by ship to Quebec, thence to Sherbrooke in Canada (11, 12).[16] One of the three ships was sunk on the journey. The kind of individual who emerges from the internment diary is a sensitive and deeply concerned young man struggling to come to terms with the injustice of his imprisonment, who was at the same time, aware of the sufferings of his fellow internees.

14

Release came in the form of acceptance to study architecture at the University of Manitoba, Winnipeg (13). On completing his Bachelor of Architecture degree with first-class honours in 1944, Seidler moved to Toronto where he worked for a year on military hospitals and services[17] before winning a scholarship to Harvard's Graduate School of Design from which he graduated in May 1946. Gropius' Master class in 1946 included some exceptional talents, men like I.M. Pei, Ulrich Franzen, Henry Cobb, Donald Olsen, and John Parkin (14).[18] Although not in his year, Paul Rudolph and Ed Barnes were his contemporaries.

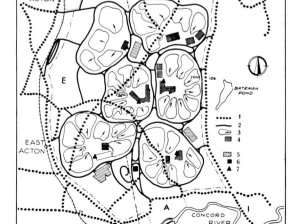

15 16

Harvard was an exciting place in the autumn of 1945. The feeling existed that the new graduates were destined to transform the visual man-made world. There was revolution in the air. This was also Marcel Breuer's last year as a teacher. Breuer was more effervescent than Gropius, and frequently introduced his own ideas in competitions with the older and more experienced students.[19] Gropius, who had been appointed in 1937, admonished students not to copy his designs or other precedent. He sought instead to foster independence of thought. Gropius made it clear that he did not want a 'Gropius architecture'. In a brief statement to the Harvard Club in Boston, he explained: 'My intention is . . . to introduce a method of approach which allows one to tackle a problem according to its peculiar conditions . . . It is not so much a ready-made dogma that I want to teach, but an attitude to the problems of our generation which is unbiased, original and elastic.'[20]

Seidler welcomed this open approach, by implementing the idea, rather than the style. Gropius was a unique figure in that he integrated a high ethical purpose in architecture with the new aesthetics of Modernism and, for this reason, refused to see Modern architecture as just another style. Associated with this was a desire to improve the lot of ordinary people by the provision of modern, well-designed housing. In one of the proposed schemes for six new townships near Concord outside Boston (1945–46), Seidler contributed the planning of one neighbourhood and a design for five-storey slab apartments adjoining the town centre (15, 16). The planning of Campbelltown in 1969 is a belated implementation of the Concord ideas, as too, is Seidler's proposal for redeveloping McMahons Point, Sydney, in 1957, which visualised housing people in slab and tower blocks to achieve a density of 370 people per hectare, and the 1959 apartment scheme at Camperdown (a development of the Concord housing type). The Blues Point Tower (1961), comprising 168 apartments rising from the end of McMahons Point, is a survival from this ambitious, but unrealised, proposal.

At Gropius' suggestion, Seidler attended Josef Albers' summer course in 1946 at Black Mountain College, North Carolina (17).[21] This was a modest translation of the Bauhaus Itten–Albers–Moholy–Vorkurs introduction to basic design. The reason for Gropius' suggestion was simple: in his architectural training Seidler had missed out on such instruction which Gropius considered was essential. It is clear from the course notes, that the instruction given by Albers was quite elementary. Nevertheless, Albers' approach inclined Seidler towards Minimalism as exemplified by Norman Carlberg whose quadrant sculptures Albers showed him in 1965, Charles Perry, Frank Stella whose influence is later, and Alexander Calder, artists whose art, if not a direct extension of Albers' ideas, demonstrates a concern for the essentials of geometric structure, along with a more detached aesthetic orientation.

One principle in particular continued to be influential; this is the principle of tensional composition, defined as the balance of unequals, and the exploitation of strong visual contrasts or visual counterpoint (18, 19). Seidler later recalled that Black Mountain was one of the most influential experiences of his life, inasmuch as Albers inculcated an awareness of the nature of perception: 'He [Albers] made us understand just how our eyes react in predictable ways to visual phenomena and which ones are of particular interest to 20th century man.'[22]

Seidler commenced work in Breuer's first New York office on 88th Street in September, and stayed until March 1948, when he left for Australia on what was intended to be a short visit to execute a house for his parents in Sydney.

In 1946 the office comprised of Breuer and Seidler; Seidler of necessity became the office factotum, doing the drawing, assisting with supervision, and even caring for Breuer when he was ill. Seidler worked on a number of houses, including the Geller House, New York (1945) which was then nearing completion. He subsequently designed the guest wing and prepared all the drawings for the Thompson House, Ligonier, Pennsylvania (1946), and was heavily involved in the Robinson House, Williamstown, Massachusetts (1947) (20), and Breuer's own Cantilever House, New Canaan, Connecticut (1947) (21).[23]

17

18

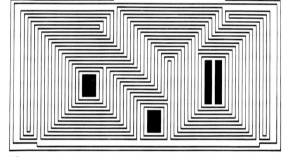

19

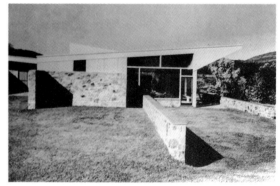

20

21

22

23

24

The Thompson House, in particular, was influential, if only indirectly, on Seidler's Australian debut. The Thompsons occupied a family estate consisting of several houses grouped apart, but related to one another in a marvellous landscape. Seidler became friends with the son, Rolland Thompson, and in association with Thompson, who was employed on a casual basis by Breuer in 1947, designed a three-bedroom family house at Foxborough, Massachusetts, overlooking a lake. This hypothetical house, worked out in considerable detail, was published in the January 1948 edition of *Arts and Architecture*[24] two months before he left Breuer's office. It is substantially the Rose Seidler House of 1948. So similar were they, the model of the 1947 scheme was used to illustrate the Rose Seidler House (32).

Besides housing, there was no Modern architecture worthy of the name in North America in 1946, and this was mostly designed for individual clients. Seidler visited the Gropius residence at Lincoln (1937) (22), Breuer's first house nearby, completed two years later, the Chamberlain Residence, Wyland, Massachusetts (1940), and the Hagerty Residence, Cohasset, Massachusetts (1938).[25] He was especially impressed by the sculptural expressiveness of the Gropius House and its contrasting relationship with the arcadian New England landscape.

Seidler's early Australian domestic work, as one would expect, continued the New England idiom of Breuer's light North American timber houses. But despite their obvious similarity, the repetition of cantilevered sun awnings and rough masonry walls, Seidler's early Australian houses were never obvious imitations of the Breuer idiom. They were constructed, in the main, of timber clad with vertical boards, and employed in-line, hollow square, ring, or bi-nuclear plans. The main floor was usually lifted up and isolated from the ground on columns or rubble stone walls. The roofs were flat, or as in Breuer's 1949 Exhibition House at the Museum of Modern Art (23), introduced a novel butterfly profile drained internally which soon became synonymous with the Seidler name in Australia.

These early American houses of Breuer's respected the character of the region by their generous use of texturally rich materials, such as wood and rubble, and by paying attention to the landscape and topography of each site. Breuer, in keeping with his outgoing personality, preferred to make his buildings from many different elements and to systematise the details. By comparison, Seidler restricted his choice to a few basic elements. His Australian houses repeated Breuer's New England idiom with few concessions to the Sydney region.

Breuer was interested in sun control and perfected a variety of novel details (24). Seidler followed his lead which was fortunate given the hot Sydney summer. Conditions in Australia differed markedly from North America. Seidler's early clients came from a broad cross-section of Australian society. In the 1950s Australians were innocent and uncomplicated. Many quite ordinary people responded to the clarity and rationalism of Modernism as Seidler presented it to them. They were predominantly Europeans, like himself. Few of them could be called wealthy. There was one common denominator: they all had limited means, and this fact enforced a degree of economy and austerity in the planning of his houses not encountered in the American work.

It is an oft-repeated truism that behind every good building is a good client. G.J. Dusseldorp, a Dutch engineer who came to Australia in 1950 as the representative of Bredero Bouwbedrijf of Utrecht, and later established Civil & Civic Contractors, was just such a good client who always demanded the best.[26] It was Dusseldorp who supplied the drive and vision which made Australia Square a reality.

The building industry in Australia suffered from a wide range of material restrictions after the Second World War and lacked the technical sophistication of the Americans. There was no Modernist furniture, fabrics, light fittings, or sliding doors. This compelled Seidler to improvise, and in the case of his parents' house, to bring the required items with him from New York.[27]

En route to Sydney in March 1948, Seidler spent

over three months (from April to June) in Brazil. There he met and worked with Oscar Niemeyer [centre], (26). The inspiration of Niemeyer's flamboyant use of modern technology and sense of colour made a lasting impression. From Rio de Janeiro, Seidler travelled across to the Pacific coast and up to Los Angeles where he met John Entenza, the editor/publisher of *Arts and Architecture* magazine (later Head of the influential Graham Foundation), before flying on to Sydney.

Nowhere else in the world, at that time, could one see so much genuine Modern architecture as in Brazil. There was, for one thing, the Ministry of Education and Health (25), inspired by Le Corbusier's visit in 1936, and numerous works by Sergio Bernades and M. Roberto, and not neglecting Niemeyer, the housing for an aeronautical technical centre at Sao José dos Campos (27). What impressed him most was the 'flair and exuberance of expression displayed by the Brazilians',[28] which struck him as immensely appealing. The double shell roof of the Williamson house at Mosman (1951) is an obvious reminder of Seidler's Brazilian sojourn, and of Niemeyer's Church of Pampulha (1943) in particular (28, 29).

The same was not true of Australia. The Rose Seidler House at Turramurra marked a watershed in Australian culture which announced in unmistakable terms the rising wave of popular American influence (30). It was an ideas house lacking any suggestion of compromise. Therein lay its power. Its apparent lack of compromise.

It recalled Le Corbusier's Villa Savoie, Poissy (31), not so much in its specific forms, as the establishment of similar spatial relationships between the living area and the terrace, and the terrace to centre stair, as well as the garaging of the motor car, though Seidler stopped short of repeating Corbusier's Futurist solution at ground level. In the past, insufficient attention has been paid to the fusion of Breuer language with Le Corbusian motifs which make it difficult, at times, to disentangle individual influences. The Rose Seidler House is not a simple work but a complex interleaving of

25

26

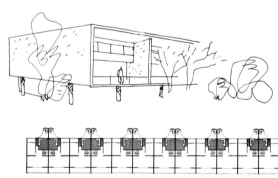
27

28

29

30

31

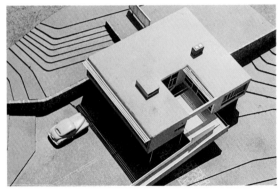
32

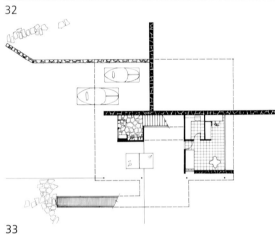
33

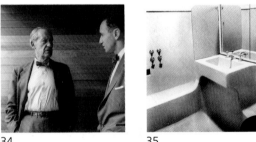
34 35

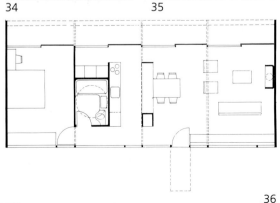
36

ideas from several sources, fused at high temperature. Like the Villa Savoie, it is an ideal house, even though the radiating stone walls say otherwise.

Seidler made only minor changes to the 1947 scheme for Foxborough (32) other than to rotate the plan through 90 degrees: the window fenestration pattern of vertical mullions gave way to an Elementarist pinwheel arrangement of radiating vertical and horizontal members which echoed the plan *parti*; horizontal sun louvres shading the south-facing bedroom windows were repositioned on the north wall jutting out above the glass wall of the living area; while the cubelike skylight over the bathroom was modified to a skillion roof. The fireplace, which originally opened to the dining and living areas, now faced one way onto the living area. The ramp (reminiscent of the external stair at Le Corbusier and Jeanneret's Villa Stein, Garches, 1927) which connected the outdoor living area to the lakeside was retained, but it makes less sense at Turramurra without the lake. A shared swimming pool was planned but failed to materialise. A coat storage cupboard separating the children's playroom from the dining area was omitted altogether, freeing up the centre space around the stair. Nearly all the changes were improvements. It is remarkable, in retrospect, that Seidler managed to find a site so similar to Foxborough which entailed so few alterations to the first scheme.

The centripetal spatial arrangement of the main floor was repeated in the composition of the rough stone wall elements at ground level. The isolation of the Villa Savoie has been reduced in Seidler's scheme by the presence of these radiating walls which extend out from the house core across the site. The ramp reinforced the connection between the dwelling and its environment (33).

The thing that most impressed people about the house was its completeness.[29] All the walls were light grey with a mid-grey carpet, intersected by black wall cabinets, desks and kitchen benches. Red, yellow and blue were introduced on the doors and curtains. The Purist intention of the colour scheme was extended to the furniture.

Seidler brought with him from New York, Hardoy chairs, 1945 Eames dining and lounge chairs, and Knoll 'Grasshopper chairs' by Saarinen.

The Rose Seidler House is central to an understanding of Seidler's later work because the leading motifs are already clearly articulated: the ramp connecting with the environment, the large outdoor space in front; the building form as an elevated radiating presence; restrained austere expression, strong geometrical composition echoed in the parts; transparency; the strange simultaneity of rectilinear and curvilinear themes; along with the homage to art in some outdoor or prominent entry location of artworks can be found in his buildings from this, a small dwelling, to the largest city tower blocks such as the MLC Centre or Grosvenor Place. That is what makes Seidler such a fascinating architect, the consistent elaboration of a set of themes which are stated at the outset.

The reuse of an earlier scheme is not at all unusual for Seidler because important themes are continually being elaborated and carried forward into new projects, especially if the first scheme is unrealised. On the same 6.5 hectare site, Seidler completed the Marcus Seidler House (1949–50) and the Rose Seidler House (1950), originally designed for his brother Marcell close by his mother's house. In effect, Harry Seidler was following the contemporary New England, USA, model of the family estate which he merged with Modern urban theory and communal housing.[30]

Seidler was welcomed by his contemporaries in the late 1940s – Sydney Ancher, Arthur Baldwinson, and designer Doug Snelling.[31] He was also in demand for opening art exhibitions. His early reputation was founded on an extraordinary range of domestic designs before 1954, climaxed by the 'House of the Future' Exhibition at the Sydney Town Hall, opened by Walter Gropius (34), for which Seidler contributed a model prefabricated dwelling made from 1 mm-thick zinc annealed interlocking wall and roof panels based on four equal 3.353 m bays. This featured prototypes of prefabricated bathroom and kitchen units (35, 36).

In 1958 Seidler married Penelope Evatt (37), the younger daughter of Clive Raleigh Evatt, the eminent Sydney barrister and former New South Wales Minister for Education and then Housing in the years 1941 to 1954.[32] Penelope Seidler, who subsequently completed an architecture degree, provided an entrée to Australian political life. The pair attracted a good deal of publicity. They epitomised for the media the up-to-the-minute modern couple. Penelope charmed rather than confronted people, and these social skills proved invaluable in establishing and maintaining broad social contacts.

37

Part 2
Foundations

The basic plan types introduced in the mid-century Modern houses of Seidler had their origin in two plan types favoured by Breuer; the long in-line plan (38), rectangular, economical to construct and simple to expand; and the 'bi-nuclear' plan (39). In either its 'H' or 'U' (indented square) permutations the bi-nuclear plan formed private patios between the wings of the house and clearly separated the day and night-time areas (40). Both plan types are reiterated in Breuer's 1940s American houses; in the Cantilever House (1947) (43), and Breuer's second house with its long or in-line plan. His third house (1951) has a U-shaped bi-nuclear plan, while the Robinson House, which Seidler worked on, and surely knew in minute detail, is a classic H-shaped bi-nuclear plan type (44).

Seidler incorporated the in-line plan in private dwellings – Rose Seidler House, Turramurra (1950); Meller House, Castlecrag (1950); Sussman House, Kurrajong Heights (1950); the Exhibition House, Town Hall, Sydney (1953–54), and in multi-storey housing where the linear arrangement proved especially economical (41) – apartments at Camperdown (1959); Rushcutters Bay (1959). Seidler's House for his parents at Turramurra (1948–50) was originally conceived in the bi-nuclear form with an extra wing. A fully fledged H-shaped bi-nuclear plan type was proposed in the Hutter House, Turramurra (1952), and the unrealised Rubenson House, Quirindi (1951), where an elaborate brief encouraged a

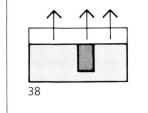
38

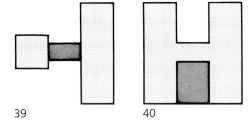
39 40

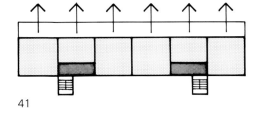
41

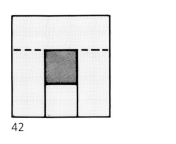
42

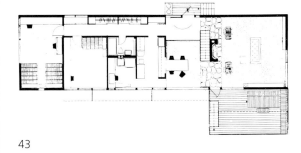
43

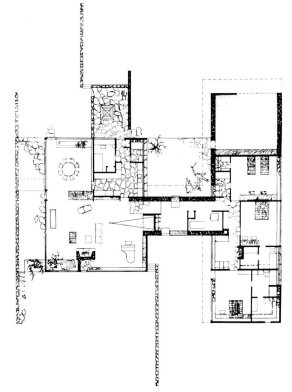
44

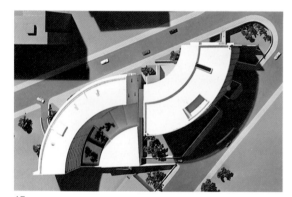

45

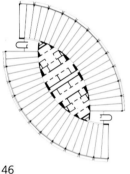

46

47

48

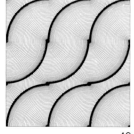
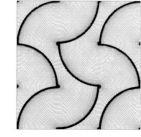

49

more distinct and articulated character to develop between the sleeping and living wings of the house.

The ring plan (42) found application in the Marcus Seidler House, Turramurra (1949–51), and was the forerunner of such high-rise projects as the Blues Point Tower Apartments, NSW (rectangular), the Australia Square (polygonal), and MLC (irregular octagon) Towers. The Trade Group Offices, Canberra, ACT (1970–74), is a variation of the ring plan not all that different from the Blues Point Tower Apartments, however, in this instance, the core of the ring is omitted to leave a hollow centre.

By the mid-1960s Seidler had begun to experiment with circular, elliptical and curvilinear geometries. Sometimes he took only part of the system such as a quadrant, and when this occurred, the principles of reverse symmetry and self-reversal were introduced to enhance the tension between the opposed forms. The selection of a circular plan shape for the Australia Square Tower (1963–67) marked an important departure from the existing repertoire of rectilinear forms which had dominated until then. It was the end result, interestingly enough, of a progressive assessment of square, octagonal, and polygonal forms. The immediate advantage of the circular plan was uniform floor beams, shortened circulation distances, and a compact economical vertical core. In later schemes, notably the Trade Centre, Milsons Point, NSW (1968–69), the Chevron Development, Melbourne (1969), and the Paris Embassy (1973–77), floor geometries based on the quadrant were adopted to minimise the ratio of circulation and service core area to office space, and to standardise the span of floor decks and beams. In the Paris Embassy (45), and later, the Grosvenor Place tower (46), there was the further advantage that the radial geometry produced the greatest exposure to the view. Quadrant auditoriums occur in the Trade Group Offices, the Paris Embassy, and the Ringwood Cultural Centre Theatre (47).

The strange simultaneity of complex undulating curvilinear surfaces in Seidler's architecture is most easily explained by reference to the Baroque, which to some degree was sanctioned in *Space, Time and Architecture* by Sigfried Giedion, whose lectures Seidler attended at Harvard in the autumn semester of 1945.[33] But, in addition, it goes back to Seidler's Viennese inheritance, to the kind of furniture his mother selected for their apartment, to the love of richness and elaboration which is such a fundamental component of the Viennese attitude to form.

No less significant, from this viewpoint, were the dazzling compositions of Frank Stella (48) and the sculptural screens of Norman Carlberg (49). The brilliant self-reversing forms of Charles Perry offered Seidler a model of intellectual simplicity, capable of generating a bewildering multiplicity of seductive sculptural shapes. Variety spawned by standard forms. The secret, in each instance, was geometry.

Seidler introduced a free form and part-elliptical geometry for a children's playground at Rosebery for the Housing Commission (1964–67) (50), and two years later, he based his Memorial to Martyrs, Rookwood, on a composition of ellipses and part-ellipses.

Linear and quadrant systems were sometimes combined, as in the Conzinc Riotinto Development for Melbourne (1972–75), and the Trade Group Offices, Canberra. These examples were far from exceptional. In 1975, the architect applied the principle of reverse symmetry inspired by Josef Albers' 'vice versa' composition, to an office project for Kuala Lumpur, and the Town Centre at Albury–Wodonga.

The exploration of non-rectilinear geometries was actuated by a combination of practical, structural and sculptural, not to mention aesthetic considerations. The unequal arc lengths of the quadrant forms offered several advantages over linear planning. The serpentine offices of the Tuggeranong project, Bushey Park Housing, Singapore (1973) (51), and the Parliament House Scheme, Canberra (1979), are effectively curvilinear serial applications of the in-line house type. To a considerable extent the curvilinear is the result of Seidler's insistence on buildings being a camera-on-the-view.

Ideas in Seidler's architecture are never casual, a momentary flirtation quickly dropped. The split-level section is just such an idea which made its appearance in the 1950 Meller House, Castlecrag (52), which was elaborated in his early houses, and even occurs in much grander designs such as the competition scheme for the National Art Gallery, Canberra (1968) (53). The three floors of the Meller House are connected by a double ramp. The attraction of the split-level, which in effect expressed the floors of a building as a stair with the floor decks reading as enlarged landings, was to open up and fuse the interior into a single space continuum.

The origin of the split-level, which over the years became a Seidler signature, can be traced to Le Corbusier's M. Errazuriz House, Chile (1930) (54).[34] Deliberately rustic in its materials, the house's mezzanine level was linked to the ground floor by means of a double ramp. This opening up of the interior expanded the interior space horizontally, while it simultaneously fused it vertically. It did so in a manner calculated to excite the pulled-apart floors so they interact more dynamically. Instead of the house consisting of isolated static cells, the ramps released the individual spaces and set them ricochetting into one another.

The ramp was an important device for connecting the parts of a design, whether they are the house and its surrounds, as in the Rose Seidler House, or the different floor levels as in the Meller House, Castlecrag (1950), completed about the same time. The ramp is a source of continuity. The two floors of the Waks I House, Northbridge (1950) were related by a two-storey open well at the centre. Seidler repeated the same split-level section in his multistorey and high-rise housing. The split-level arrangement of apartments with staggered longitudinal corridor access in the Arlington Apartments, Edgecliff (1965–66) (55), enabled Seidler to face all the living rooms towards the desirable views and sunny aspect.

50

51

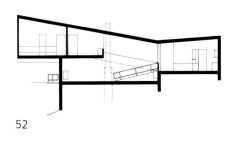
52

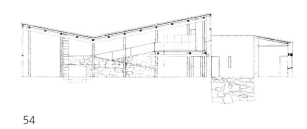
54

53

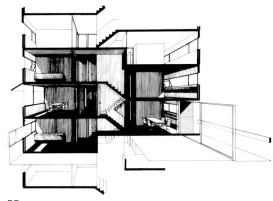
55

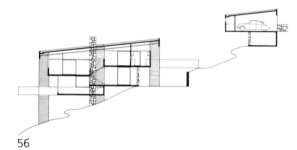

56

57

58

The most spectacular application is undoubtedly Seidler's own house at Killara (1967) (57) with its echoes of Wright's *Falling Water* (58), not least in the magnificent choice of site. Here, Seidler separated the four floors by an open well at the centre, and this results in the fusion of the various levels (56), which enhances the continuity of the interior in a way that subtly suggests the Baroque.

Structure, with geometry and painting, is an important strand running through the architecture. The dominance of structural, and avoidance of overtly historical motifs is still further evidence of his rational bias. The structural language is limited in its range and can be categorised as the cantilevered box section, the channel-section beam, the Nervi interlocking rib-floor, and the precast T-beam with structurally expressive changing section from bending moments to shear. Seidler likes to consider each and every building element as a structure whose design is determined by its load-carrying role. There can be no slackers, every part must be seen to do a job. Thus, the garage at the architect's home at Killara was conceived as a thin-walled cantilevered concrete box (56). The 15.5 m-long pedestrian ramp at the Ski Lodge Thredbo (1962), which was designed as a stiff plywood truss – the same detail appeared in Seidler's house for his parents – is another.

It is impossible sometimes to decide what is structure, and what is pure sculpture. The J. Rose House, Turramurra (59), is a case in point. The first floor deck was suspended from four steel masts by means of diagonal rod stays much like a bridge deck. The house is a bridge building, a form lightly suspended above its surroundings. The formal theme for the house is derived from the tensile skeleton. Expression and structure are inseparable. Using this simple stayed mast motif, Seidler initiated a formal theme of lightly suspended horizontal planes and diagonals. The floor and roof elements were emphasised by setting back the north facade behind a generous balcony. The diagonal motif was mimicked by the triangulated external stair balustrade.

The pursuit of total structural solutions frequently leads to beautiful forms, which combine the rational and the aesthetic. Nervi presided as midwife over the gestation of many of the post-1960 Seidler innovations in concrete.

The lobby ceilings of the Australia Square and MLC Towers and the Theatre Royal Lobby were designed in collaboration with Nervi (60) and constructed with very beautiful interlocking systems of ribs. In the Australia Square and MLC Towers these ribs resist heavy floor loads and stiffen the central core. The sculptural precast T-beams used in the Trade Group Offices, Seidler's own office at Milsons Point, and the Paris Embassy, were developed in conjunction with Nervi. The concept originated from a proposal by the Sydney structural engineer, Peter Miller,[35] to vary the section of the floor beams of the Trade Group Offices to accommodate the change from maximum bending moments at the centre of the span to maximum shear stresses at the supports. The shape of the beams was obtained by giving them a curved transitional profile which expressed this altered stress condition. The concourse beams of the Sydney Opera House are a more complex application of the same structural idea.[36]

In the decade prior to 1960 Seidler was occupied designing houses. Lend Lease House (1961) was his first substantial commercial commission. It was followed by other important projects such as Australia Square (1961–67), the Trade Group Offices for the Australian Government in Canberra (1970–74), the architect's own offices at Milsons Point, Sydney (1971–73), and the magnificent new Australian Embassy in Paris (1973), in every respect, the crowning achievement of Seidler's long career. In the 1960s there was a shift away from designing single residences for private clients in the northern suburbs of Sydney around the harbour, to work on high-rise and group housing for a variety of private speculative and governmental authorities.

Against this, after more than a quarter of a century spent designing houses for others, Seidler settled down with his wife, Penelope, to design a house for his own family at Killara (1966–67)

59

(57). The result justified the wait. The romantic bush setting with its creek and sandstone rock ledges was the Australian equivalent of Bear Run in western Pennsylvania. Seidler's house broke with the past in favouring board-formed concrete and concrete block, permanent masonry in lieu of the Harvard timber idiom he pursued in the 1950s. Low-maintenance monumental materials ensured that the house was a durable presence in the landscape.

Seidler's love of strongly expressive forms and fluid space – space running up and down the hillside, tucking under at the base, and splashing out at the sides – was given free rein. It is a large house, not in overly ostentatious ways so much as in its serious embodiment of all that Seidler believed in, both artistically and intellectually. It represents a physical summary of his ideas for the 20th century house.

The house is more a cave than a pavilion, more sheltering and protective, in the same way that Walter Burley Griffin's houses fortify themselves against the landscape. Inside the masonry shell, the spaces interlock and slide over one another. There are strong connections to the outside, especially where the north balcony alights on a grassed shelf. The tilted roof element spells shelter. It is rather like a salute, a hand pressed across the brow in recognition of the landscape – an iconic gesture. Through such oppositions and deliberate formal contrasts, the clash of different characters, the concrete wall and floor planes resemble an abstract egg crate, rising up from the monumental sandstone ledges and shelves, to impose itself on the bush setting.

This is a Brutalist *Falling Water*, more American, more late Breuer in its strong forms, and Viennese in its will to permanence, in its hard Norwegian quartzite floors and determination to impose an aesthetic on the Australian bush. Inside, surrounded by Albers' paintings and Perry sculptures, the visitor returns luxuriously to New England, to an American cultural ambience.

Blues Point Tower (1961) (61), on the tip of McMahons Point opposite the Sydney Harbour Bridge, is exposed and assertive. Seidler placed the 24-storey apartment tower on the fingerlike sandstone promontory. Its facade is a syncopated composition of solids and voids, a salute to Josef Albers' 'The City' (1928) composition (62),[37] high above the blue harbour. The rhythm of the openings resulted from the clever alternation of differently sized two-bedroom apartments at each corner, so placed that their main glass areas face in different directions on successive floors. This ensured that a high percentage of apartments enjoy views in two directions as well as being cross-ventilated. The staggered balconies also satisfied the fire separation requirement by imposing a vertical masonry wall between the floors, inasmuch as there is a solid wall above and below each glazed balcony.

Seidler's commitment to improving the quality of housing led him to speak out in public to attack the unthinking application of rows of cheap cheek-by-jowl speculative flats in Sydney. He designed many group housing projects at considerably higher densities and with an urban atmosphere that Australians were generally accustomed to. Kings Cross in the 1950s and 1960s was the only community in Sydney which possessed such a quality of cosmopolitan variety and energy. No doubt his Viennese childhood, as much as arguments about the efficient use of urban land, encouraged Seidler to pursue such solutions.

The two parallel multistorey blocks in a low-cost project at Rosebery (1964–67) were staggered to avoid any feeling of congestion associated with densities of 740 people per hectare. A sense of openness which was enhanced by lightening the bridge connection between the two blocks (63).

In order to ensure privacy and minimise the length of public circulation space, each apartment was accessed by galleries on every second floor. A central double elevator tower with bridges suspended from it by high-tensile steel hangers connected with the galleries. The playful amoeboid serpentine walls and earth mounds of the children's playground

60

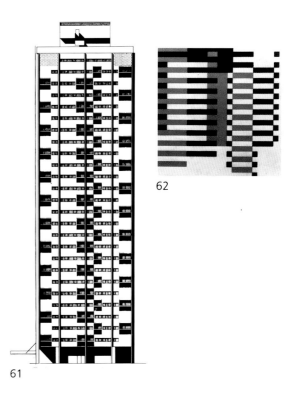
62

61

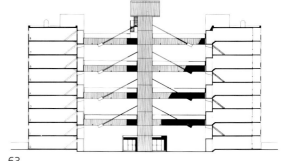
63

offered a visual contrast with the strict order of the rectilinear industrial forms of the housing block.

Roslyn Towers Apartments (1963–65) (64, 65), overlooks a park beside Rushcutters Bay in Sydney Harbour, so named because some convicts cutting rushes there had once been speared to death by Aborigines. The block of 80 rental apartments repeated the system of split-level planning with access galleries every second floor. On this occasion, the system was justified by the concern that every apartment face the harbour. From the access gallery half flights led up and down to pairs of units. A highly sculptural effect resulted with the upper bedrooms projecting out over to shade the external galleries. The integrity and rhythm of the concrete frame was enhanced by isolating the elevator and fire stair shafts from the main block so that they now straddle the curved access bridge.

The same split-level system was repeated in the Arlington Apartments at Edgecliff (1965–66). Here, however, the limitation of the building height, and the need to take advantage of the view, dictated a staggered arrangement of the two blocks, one of four storeys, the other of eight. Once again, the building elevations were skilfully contrasted patterns of solid and void, light and shadow, projections and recessions. The window fenestration varied according to the differing room functions and plan arrangements. Seidler contrived a Mondrian-like random compositional effect from the exposed concrete frame with its down-turn beams and varying floor heights.

By the mid-1960s Seidler was working in Canberra. The Group Housing at Garran, ACT (1964–68) (66), evolved from the expression of repetitive planning and building sections. The staggered arrangement of the two house types with opposing sloping roofs produced a vibrant parrying of roof forms. Using ordinary materials and sensible plans for the houses, Harry Seidler succeeded in extracting the maximum of architectonic interest while achieving a medium density of 86 people per hectare, in what was a low-cost development to house University Fellows and research students on a sloping site in the Woden Valley.

Lend Lease House (67) was the first of a long series of office buildings by the architect. Prior to its construction in 1961, Sydney, and other Australian cities, had endured a rash of glass curtain wall towers. This clean-cut 19-storey tower was fitted out with a system of adjustable horizontal aluminium louvres to shade the main east and west facades from the low-angle morning and afternoon sun. The offices looked strangely South American. There was a touch of Niemeyer flamboyance about the animated facades with their independently adjustable louvres, and rippling inflexions of light and shadow.

Australia Square was a crucial marker in Seidler's career, a high water mark of sorts, for the Tower with its wonderful plaza (a haven for lunch-time crowds insulated from the bustle, fumes, and noise of the city streets) was the climax which announced his maturity. It was a slow work which evolved gradually over some four years through a variety of shapes before the 20-sided polygonal plan shape, and elegant tapered column fins, with their brilliant precast column casing was agreed upon. The importance of the evolution of the design, the painful testing of alternatives, and the moving on to a better solution, was crucial to the quality of the final outcome. Only when the early proposals are reviewed, does it become apparent how far the design progressed, and what a great advance it represented for Seidler.

Australia Square was inserted in the centre of Sydney's business district not far from Circular Quay, and, straddling, on the east boundary, the famous Tank Stream whose location occasioned the V-pilotis of the lower office building. The site encompassed an entire block which previously had been divided into 30 separate properties and a number of narrow internal streets, all of which were amalgamated to create the site for the tower. A 13-storey building was built first on Pitt Street to serve as a portico to the open plaza ahead of the main tower before the remainder of the site became available.

The cylindrical form of the tower was arrived at by a process of elimination. Early on, the Columbia Broadcasting System Building (1962–64), on Sixth Avenue and 52nd Street, New York (68), was studied as a possible paradigm for the tower, and the uniform ribbed expression of the Australia Square tower, even in its white quartz final version (70), owes a debt to the simple elegance of the Saarinen concept. Seidler worked on a preliminary design in association with I.M. Pei in 1960 (69, 71).[38]

The analysis of rectangular building footprints parallel to the street pattern, and square or rectangular buildings on the diagonal, pointed to the advantage of a cylindrical shape which, it was quickly recognised, created more desirable relationships toward adjacent properties and avoided objectionable canyon-like residual spaces. The mandatory building setbacks permitted, at best, a maximum allowable rectangular tower of 1114 m^2 compared with 1300 m^2 for a circular-shaped tower. This conveniently coincided with the limit of 25 per cent coverage of the site.

The circular plan also lent itself to an economical stiff tower structure constructed out of uniform length floor beams, avoiding the anomaly of the corner encountered in a square tower. It was an ideal shape for resisting imposed wind loads. Each floor beam spanned 11 m from the perimeter to the core, giving the tower a diameter of 41 m. Within the core were two interlocking scissor-type fire stairs, air-conditioning ducts, goods elevators, and toilets. The polygonal floor shape with its circular core produced an economical ratio of less than 20 per cent for service space to 80 per cent usable office space. The circular plan shape was not difficult to subdivide as many people anticipated, mainly because of its large diameter.

The early model for the ribbed cylindrical tower lacked the structural expressiveness of the final design (72). It is rather dull in retrospect. Pier Luigi Nervi articulated the columns and beams so the loads visibly flow through them, and the observer senses immediately how the structure carries its loads to the ground. Nervi transformed an inert, unexpressive tower into a structure which is delicate and strong, and a sculpturally satisfying urban object.[39]

Nervi also contributed the design for the ribbed floor system for the first two floors of the tower and the procedure of using precast tapered external columns. The curvature, taper, and variation in width of the interlocking floor ribs trace the alignment of the stresses in the floor and simultaneously act as a beautifully articulated ceiling lobby. Structure and expression are united. The column casings and the component forms for the ground floor ceiling ribs were precast and acted as an integral formwork for the *in situ* concrete. Tapered external columns graphically express the cumulative transfer of floor loads, stacked one on top of the other, to the footings.

Almost the entire site was given over to a pedestrian plaza which extended on the lower side from under the 'gathered' V-columns of the lower office building, into the circular shopping arcade tucked under the upper plaza, which encircled the entrance lobby of the tower. A number of curved screen walls, planting beds and fountains sheltered the plaza precinct from the city and rendered it more intimate (73).

This was the single most significant achievement of the project – the creation of the first socially viable plaza in Sydney for people where they were safe and protected.

Architects like to talk about people as if they mattered, but in practice, achieving an outdoor space people actually do like, which they choose to be in, is a hit-and-miss affair which requires more than just good intentions. It depends on a feeling for intangible qualities, a cultivated urbanism that stimulates and nurtures human activities. The Australia Square plaza got it right. The plaza is always alive with movement. It is invariably filled with the excitement of people meeting and conversing.

One of Seidler's most attractive works, certainly the most memorable in terms of its setting and

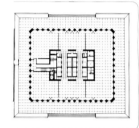
68

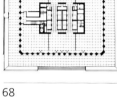
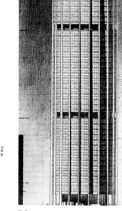
69 70

71 72

73

74

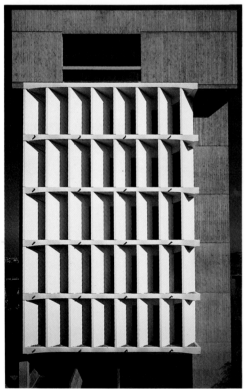

75

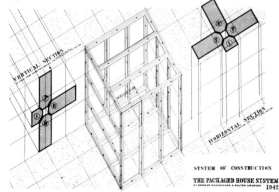

76

proximity to the Sydney Harbour Bridge which towers over it, was the offices Seidler designed for himself in 1971–73 (74, 75). Overlooking defunct Luna Park, the five-storey office block was a nodal presence on Milsons Point and a catalyst for later development of the area. A mixture of board-finished *in situ* concrete and precast T-beams, the expression of the building is enhanced immeasurably by the contrast between the *in situ* grey concrete frame and the large white precast *brise-soleil* units on the east and west faces.

Undoubtedly one of Seidler's most successful works, the floor decks were assembled from 2.4 m-wide precast floor elements which span 11 m from the concrete core, containing the vertical circulation and mechanical services on the north, and an open framework of beams and columns on the south. The beam section was varied from a T-profile at the mid-span, to resist the maximum bending moments, to a flat plate at the support to resist shear. Similar shaped beams, post-stressed and cast using smooth steel forms, were incorporated in the Trade Group Offices in Canberra.

The profile of the T-beams allowed the environmental services to be exposed and integrated with the structure. The open office space was subdivided with free-standing storage and furniture caseworks. Seidler's own office on the fifth floor is a double-height space with a mezzanine level overlooking the drafting office, and a bridge spanning to a sheltered garden terrace. It was used for the architect's office in the 1988 ABC television production of Robert Drewe's *The Bodysurfer*.

The industrialisation of the building process was a leading objective of Modernism, and although not strictly the same thing, the Meccano-like procedure adopted in the assembly of the Trade Group Offices (1970–74) from a few standard structural elements was a convincing exercise in rational building. Its success is in marked contrast to the irrational-rationalism of the Cameron Offices.

At the time when Seidler was studying at Harvard, Gropius was engrossed in the General Panel System of prefabricated dwelling construction (76) which he had developed with Konrad Wachsmann in the years from 1943 to 1945.[40] This made a lasting impression on Seidler, who saw standardisation as a necessary discipline in working with industry, if the architect was to extract the maximum result in terms of quality and performance.

Seidler saw the need, as also did Gropius, to avoid the attendant monotony which so often results from the mechanical repetition of identical elements. When he arrived in Australia, Seidler quickly ascertained that the local building industry lacked the sophisticated capability of the North Americans, but to compensate for this deficiency, the temperate climate enabled precast concrete to be produced economically out-of-doors, a procedure followed by the engineers, Arups, in fabricating the Sydney Opera House roof-ribs.

The solution to the problem of creating formal variety from a few standard components had already been investigated by Josef Albers and the young American sculptors, Norman Carlberg and Charles Perry, who studied under Albers at Yale when Albers taught there in the 1950s.

The trick to achieving greater variety from standard shapes lay in the initial choice of a geometry. Again and again, Carlberg and Perry were able to demonstrate how easy it was to generate intriguing sculptural configurations from standard forms. Perry's yellow 'S' sculpture for the upper MLC plaza is an outstanding instance, inasmuch as there are 16 different outcomes which can be generated using the same standard elements (77). The investigations of Albers, Perry and Carlberg on three-dimensional form generation undoubtedly influenced Seidler's adoption of quadrant systems in his most notable work, the Australian Embassy, Paris.

The quadrant theme was implemented in the glass entry lobbies and the free-standing conference hall of the Trade Group Offices (78). The deliberate contrast of the rectilinear office wings with their standard floor decks supported between the cylindrical access cores was extended to the courtyard paving pattern of opposing quadrants, the fountain, and Norman Carlberg sculptures.

The open courtyard arrangement of office floor decks, sandwiched between the access cores, was predicated on the client's requirement for flexible office areas which could easily be expanded should the need arise. This led to the adoption of a long span structure with 24.4 m by 15.25 m bays. The vertical circulation and mechanical services were grouped in cylindrical cores which rise five storeys at the end of every second floor bay, every 48.8 m.

Standard 15.25 m-long prestressed T-shaped floor planks, similar to the Milsons Point Office beams, were fabricated for the project. Three-legged travelling gantries mounted on rails (designed to rotate at the corners) were used to lift the facade beams, weighing 81.6 tonnes, and the floor elements of 11.2 tonnes, into position.

The Trade Group was sited on the Kings Avenue axis of the proposed New Parliament House. This meant that it had to be designed as a low horizontal form so as not to obstruct the Parliament House when it was completed. Three Commonwealth Government departments were to occupy the complex, making a total of two thousand, for the first stage, and another, of one thousand, for the second stage.

Part 3
Relations to the Third Generation

In the 1950s a third generation of Modern architects swung into action. This new generation revised and extended Modern architecture. Included among its membership were Paul Rudolph, Jørn Utzon, Kevin Roche, Robert Venturi, Kiyonori Kikutake, Arata Isozaki, Noriaki Kurokawa and Moshe Safdie.[41] Harry Seidler belongs to the more conservative wing, with architects such as Pei who extended Modern architecture. A Late Modernist, Seidler was an unwavering solid personality whose commitment to the new architecture continued and enlarged upon the

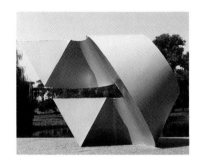

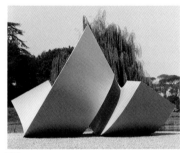

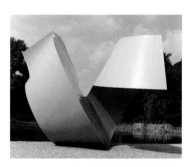

77

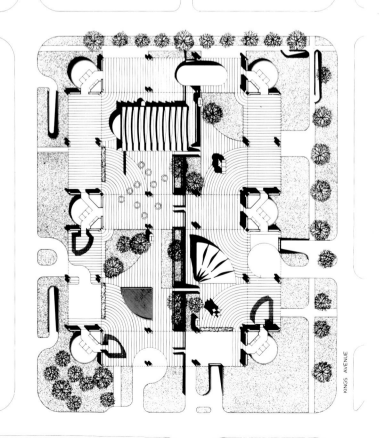

79

80

81

traditional precepts of Modern architecture.⁴²

One of the leading characteristics of this generation, according to Sigfried Giedion writing in 1966, was the establishment of a relation to the past. In the case of Seidler, contact with the past meant a revivification of the Baroque, in terms of visual oppositions and contrast.⁴³

Seidler, unlike Utzon who epitomised the third generation for Giedion,⁴⁴ showed little regional awareness. Utzon responded with extraordinary sensitivity to the poetry of place (79).

Henry Kissinger once quipped: 'And where is Australia on the way to?' He had a point. Australia is very isolated. It is on the way to nowhere if the truth be known. Seidler, unlike Utzon, was isolated in remote, far-away Australia. There is a feeling of isolation, a continual drawing on the stored reservoirs of fat built up at Harvard and New York. A continuing tension, almost fear, of losing touch with the centre.

Seidler cultivated his early connections with New York, with Breuer, and later Nervi, and with New York Minimalism in art. Both I.M. Pei and Seidler were to remain faithful to their early training and Pei's triumphs with the East Wing (80) and Louvre (81) projects strengthened Seidler's resolve to give no quarter in responding to post-Modern attacks, which were, in any case, inevitable in the 1980s. Seidler's devotion to the ideas of Modern architecture made it inevitable that he would oppose post-Modernism and the direction taken by Michael Graves.

His was an anxious internationalism. This was not so much anti-regional as a strained internationalism, which because it was isolated and vulnerable, and so often under attack, sought spiritual reinforcement by identifying itself with other strongholds of Late Modernism, and by repeated returns to the important creative centres in Europe and America.

There remains the problem of Seidler's relationship to Australian culture. There is none, simply because Seidler is dismissive of Australian culture and art. Bernard Smith contended in his 1980 Boyer Lectures

that, 'A culture cannot live upon other people's universals. It requires moral values born of its own historical experience, values which are continually tested against successive challenges to its history'.⁴⁵ The fact is that the universals which animate Seidler's work are European not Australian, in so far as he is a Late Modernist trained at Harvard. One only has to recall the circumstances which led Seidler to come to Australia to appreciate that. The price of sticking to the task of faithfully enlarging Modernism was the exclusion of Australian content.

Seidler's stature can only be estimated by comparing him with architects outside Australia such as the class of '46 at Harvard, to architects, who in the main, accepted the challenge to extend Modern architecture. In these terms, Seidler measures up exceedingly well, both as regards consistency, quality, and the sheer quantity of outstanding building he accomplished. Seidler's architecture is a solid achievement by whatever standard is applied to it. Australia in a great many ways was not a favourable location for Seidler. There were severe constraints on what he could attempt, and hostility from many quarters. Yet, in spite of this, the work continued to be done. The pressures in Australia to try something new, to stay ahead may have been less, and isolation may have had its benefits. That in many ways has been his greatest achievement, to survive as a dedicated Modern architect in Australia. And for all his loyalty to the ideas he showed remarkable imagination and powers of invention in applying the spirit, rather than the letter of Modern doctrine.

One can but marvel at the prophetic grasp of Sigfried Giedion all those years ago, when he foretold that Seidler would become the fighter for his and Giedion's generation of Modern architects. Perhaps, after all, it is the individual, not anonymous historical forces, who ultimately decides the future. One should not be surprised by what Seidler has achieved in the four decades after 1950 because the will to form was never in any doubt, only the circumstance leading to its application.

Notes

1. Hermann Bahr once said that for the Viennese life begins at the theatre. Repeatedly, in Viennese writing and thought, it is the polarity between the rational and the mystical, between to clarify the order, or to ornament and embellish in art, which emerges as the dominant strain. The same strange simultaneity can be detected at work in Seidler's architecture, especially after 1980.
2. Keith Newman, in 'Another K.O. By Young Fighter', *Sydney Morning Herald*, Sat., 22 March 1952, p. 2, wrote: 'For this personable young bachelor does not practise architecture merely to make money (although after a few uphill years, he is probably doing well enough there). His fervour is that of a crusader horror stricken at the mess men have made of Sydney . . .' *People* magazine, October 1950, called Seidler the 'High Priest of the Twentieth Century'.
3. Dedication from the hand of the historian on the title page of Seidler's copy of the 1944 edition of *Space, Time & Architecture*. It reads in full: 'Mr Harry Seidler from Canada to be destined as a fighter for his and our Generation,' Giedion, November 45.
4. The incident of Seidler's bicycle is recounted in Janis Wilton, *Transcripts of recorded recollections of Mr Harry Seidler, 15 January 1982*, for the Oral Histories Project of the Ethnic Affairs Commission of NSW, p. 13. The Wilton interviews cover the period of Seidler's life from his childhood to his arrival in Australia and is more personal than other materials.
5. J.M. Freeland, *Architecture in Australia*. Ringwood: Penguin, 1968, p. 253, dates the advent of Modern architecture from 1934 with Mewton & Grounds residence at 72 Halifax St, Brighton, Victoria. Edward Billson's Sanitarium Health Food Company, Warburton (1936), was another landmark of pre-war Australian Modernism, as also was Sydney Ancher's Kambala Road House at Bellevue Hill, Sydney (1937). John Rivett's Constructivist 'Caringal' flats at 3 Tahara Road, Melbourne (1948) was at least the equal of the Rose Seidler House, though it received less publicity. 'Stanhill' flats at 34 Queens Road, Melbourne City, by Frederick Romberg in 1949, was an extraordinary accomplishment in Modern maritime imagery and reinforced concrete expression.
6. *The Australian Women's Weekly*, 5 May 1954, p. 32, labelled it 'Home of the Future', and other popular descriptions included: 'houseful of sunshine', 'modernistic house', 'ultra-modern', 'futuristic house', 'shape of home to come'.
7. Ise Gropius in a letter to Seidler dated 17 October 1976 suggested that Seidler, like her husband, had replaced his natural homeland, which he too had lost, with the 'Republik der Geister'.
8. Wilton, *op. cit.*, p. 2.
9. *Harry Seidler*: De Berg Tapes, Nr. 565, National Library of Australia, Canberra, 13 January 1972, p. 2.
10. Seidler's recollections of the school and its regimented teaching methods are in Wilton, *op. cit.*, s. 2, p. 9.
11. De Berg Tapes, *op. cit.*, s.1, pp. 1–2.
12. Wilton, *op. cit.*, s. 2, p. 9.
13. See Vienna 1900: *Art, Architecture & Design*, New York: MOMA, Exhibition catalogue 3 July–21 October 1986, pp. 1, 16, for an analysis of the paradoxical and unstable character of Vienna's cultural achievement at the beginning of the 20th century.
14. Seidler decided quite independently to leave Vienna in September, Wilton, *op. cit.*, s. 2, p. 9.
15. From *Harry Seidler Diary 12 May 1940–4 October 1941*. The entry was for Tuesday, 23 June 1941.
16. See Janis Wilton (ed.), *Internment. The Diaries of Harry Seidler May 1940–October 1941*, Judith Winternitz, trans., Sydney: Allen & Unwin, 1986. This is a shorter abridged version of the original diaries.
17. De Berg Tapes, *op. cit.*, 565 [1], p. 5
18. *idem*.
19. See Reginald Isaacs, *Gropius at Harvard*, Berlin: Bauhaus-Archives, 18 May 1983, p. 17.
20. *ibid.*, p. 4. First recorded in the *Architectural Record*, May 1937, from Gropius' address to the Harvard University Overseers' Committee on 30 March 1937 at the Harvard Club, Boston.
21. See Mary Emma Harris, *The Arts at Black Mountain College*, 1987, and the De Berg Tapes, *op. cit.* 565 [1], p. 6.
22. *ibid.* 565 [1], p. 7.
23. Stated to the author in 1980.
24. 'Project – Harry Seidler, Architect; Rolland Thompson, Associate', *Arts and Architecture*, 64, January 1948, pp. 32–3.
25. Stated to the author in 1980.
26. See Mary Murphy, *Challenges of Change: The Lend Lease Story*, Sydney: Lend Lease, 1984, for an account of the establishment of this important construction company and the pivotal role played by G.J. Dusseldorp.
27. 'Seidler Chair Quartet', *Newsletter: Historic Houses Trust of New South Wales*, 13, 1987–3, p. 1.
28. De Berg Tapes, *op. cit.*, p. 8.
29. For an exhaustive treatment of the subject and arguments concerning the house's historic significance see Peter Emmett, *Mid Century Modern: Rose Seidler House, Wahroonga 1948–50*. Sydney: Historic Houses Trust Conservation Plan, November 1989.
30. *ibid.*, pp. 18–19.
31. *ibid.*, p. 96.
32. The Evatts were originally landowners in Kent and Leicestershire, England, who arrived in Australia by way of India. They are an important family, comparable to the Boyds and Lindsays, whose contribution has been to the judiciary and left-wing political life, but they have also evinced a strong interest in Australian art. See Robert Drewe, 'Australia's most remarkable family', *The Bulletin*, 30 August 1975, pp. 30–4.
33. De Berg Tapes, *op. cit.*, p. 5. Seidler recalled: 'I did a lot of reading in those days [1945–46], and the book that influenced me most was probably *Space, Time & Architecture*, by Sigfried Giedion which had just been published. It stimulated me, having read about the Bauhaus and Gropius, to apply to study under Gropius at Harvard . . .', 'He [Giedion] was, of course, a friend of Gropius and he came as a visiting critic for one programme . . .'
34. Stated to the author in 1980. See Philip Drew, 'Ethic and Form', *Space Design* (Tokyo), 197, February 1981, p. 87, fig. 88.
35. *ibid.*, p. 87.
36. *Sydney Opera House: a paper on its design and construction* by Sir Ove Arup and Jack Zunz. Sydney Opera House Reprint Series, 1, 1988, p. 8, fig. 13.
37. By Josef Albers, The City, 1928, in the Kunsthaus, Zurich, is customarily given as the reference for Blues Point Tower, however, some of Piet Mondrian's images would be equally applicable in this context.
38. See Murphy, *op. cit.*, p. 82.
39. Peter Blake, *Architecture for the new world: The Work of Harry Seidler*, Sydney: Horwitz Australia, 1973, p. 9, comments: 'Certainly, one of Seidler's many lucky breaks, in this regard, was his meeting with Pier Luigi Nervi . . .'
40. Drew, *op. cit.*, p. 81.
41. See Philip Drew, Third Generation: *The Changing Meaning of Architecture*, New York: Praeger, 1972, for an account of the range of interests encompassed by the third generation in the 1960s.
42. Ise Gropius, in a letter to Seidler, *op. cit.*, praised Seidler's constancy in the following terms: 'It must be your European heritage which enabled you to withstand all the temptations for momentary eccentricity and to develop instead a solid, step-by-step process which unfolded gradually and has now found inexhaustible means of expression'.
43. The attraction of the Baroque and Borromini in Seidler's architecture may be explained by a love of opposition from which a synthesis is expected to emerge. This is the basis of Borromini's attraction in the 20th century, as one who, in the words of Anthony Blunt, *Borromini*. London: Allen Lane, 1979, p. 222, observed: 'We appreciate a struggle between opposites, not, as the Romantics did, in the expectation of defeat, but in the hope that a synthesis will be achieved. To us the struggle in *Borromini* between imaginative energy and intellectual control can be more attractive than the easy achievement of Benini's rhetoric'.
44. See 'Jørn Utzon and the Third Generation', in the 1966 5th edition of *Space, Time & Architecture*, pp. 668–95.
45. Bernard Smith, *The Spectre of Truganini*, 1980 Boyer Lectures, Sydney: Australian Broadcasting Commission, 1980, p. 11.

Three Houses

The first task Seidler set himself after his arrival in Sydney was to find a suitable, large tract of land on which to build his parents' house. He located 6.5 ha of sloping bushland on the northern fringes of Sydney adjoining and overlooking a long broad valley of the public reserve, Kuring-gai Chase. Just as he had experienced in the eastern USA, he planned a group of houses for relatives or friends, far enough apart to be visually private from each other but sharing a common access road and a future swimming pool.

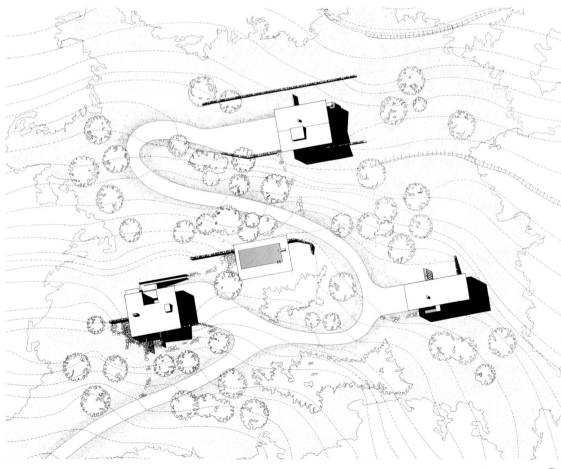

Rose Seidler House
Turramurra, 1948–50

The first house to be completed was for his parents. The ample site and a desire for maximum interior spatial interplay resulted in a hollowed out square plan freely exposed on all sides but opening the living space and sheltered terrace to the preferred northern orientation and valley view. Living and sleeping areas are separate, joined by a central family room, which can be joined with the alcove-type bedrooms or made part of the living space by a dividing curtain.

The rectangular mass of the building is hollowed by the open central terrace and the adjacent two-storey-high well piercing the building vertically, allowing light to penetrate into the otherwise dark centre.

From the rectangular structure 'tentacles' reach out and anchor it into the surrounding land, the stone retaining walls, the ramp leading to the garden (and future pool) and the louvre fence shielding the drying yard.

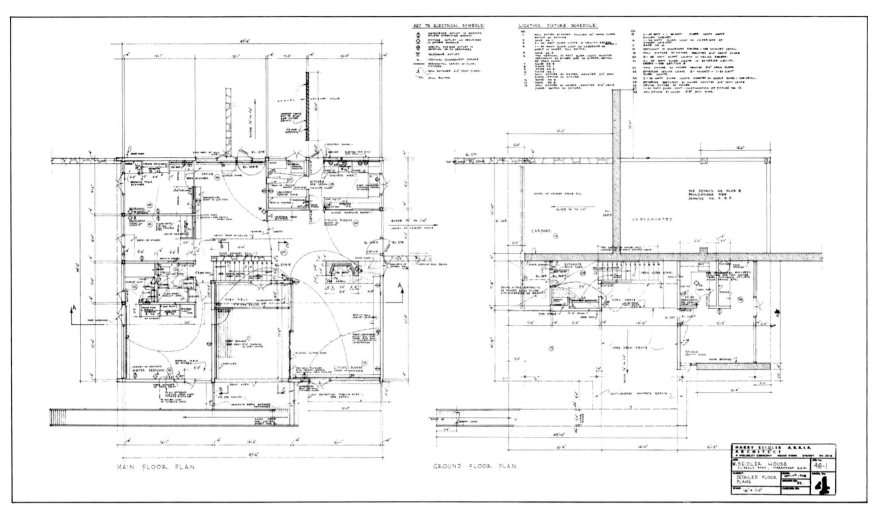
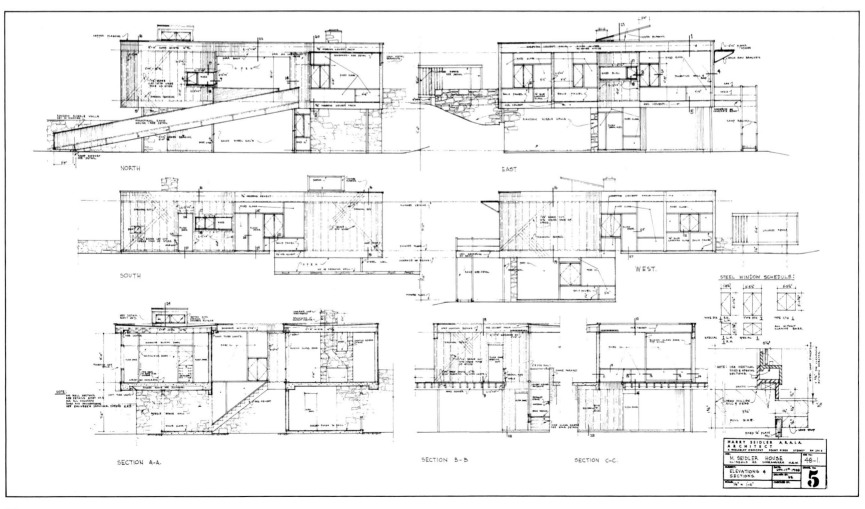

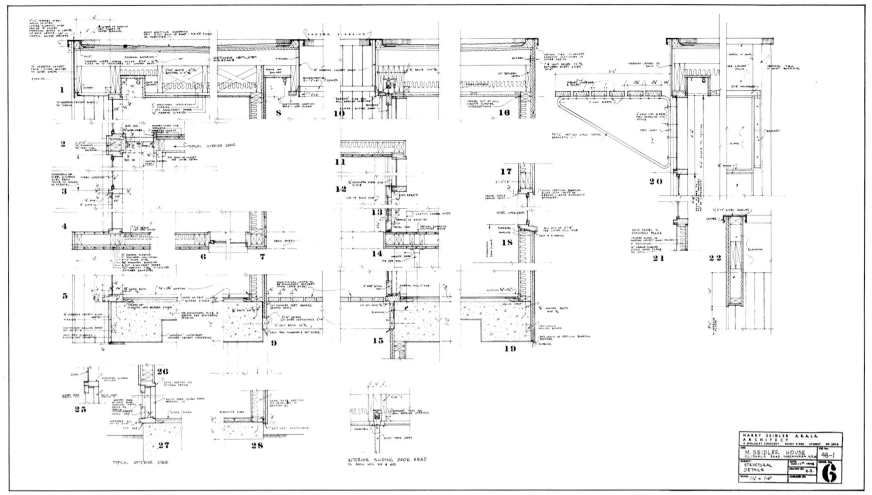

Courtesy Mitchell Library, Sydney.

'... These are the first drawings I made in Australia, in November 1948, just after moving into the Point Piper studio on the waterfront...'

The floor of the house is of concrete, supported by the sandstone walls and steel pipe columns. The superstructure is of standard American timber framing with two layers of exterior boarding. The glass walls are in timber frames with steel opening casements. The details show American profile window sills which are substituted by Australian standards.

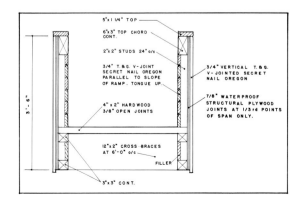

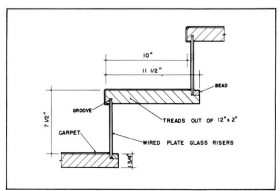

37

To maximise the spatial flow, colours in the house play off opposing hues and textures; smooth cold blue curtains against rough warm coloured sandstone, white against yellow curtains or brown walls. The bright colours of the mural wall, painted by the architect, are recalled on solid exterior doors, on accent cushions, etc.

All chairs (by Eames and Saarinen) and light fittings were brought from New York in 1948.

In 1988 the house was acquired by the Historic Houses Trust of NSW and opened to the public in its original furnished condition.

'... There can be no more captive client than a mother! The local council rejected the plans at first, misunderstanding that the central bathroom's window was above the roof.

'Mother agreed to sell all her Viennese furniture, but refused to part with her elaborately decorated silver cutlery. Whenever I came to dinner, only the Russel Wright stainless steel flatware I brought from New York was allowed to be seen. Now that she is dead, we prefer to use her Viennese silver in our Killara house...'

Rose House
Turramurra, 1949–50

The second house in the group is a weekend retreat built for friends. The minimal structural steel frame stands on four columns 10 m x 10 m apart from which diagonal hangers give support to the 20 m x 8 m raised floor which projects 5 m at each end.

The in-line arrangement faces all rooms to the northern view, shaded by a continuous terrace.

The structural frame is exposed both inside and out. Contrasting with the rectilinear building form are the diagonal lines of the suspension members which find their counterpoint in the expressed slope of both exterior stairs; solid on the 'void' north side and projecting on the more solid south side.

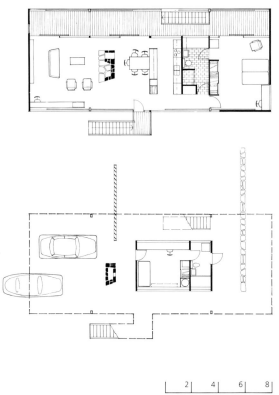

'... Just before completion of the house a tradesman came to weld the northern terrace handrail into place. He pointed his acetylene torch onto the steel diagonal tension member supporting the cantilevered end of the house and watched in amazement as the steel pipe became longer and longer and thinner and thinner... He stopped only when he heard the loud noise of the glass behind him exploding. If he had continued the house would have collapsed! It was soon put right by jacking up the deflected end of the house and repairing the tension member...'

Marcus Seidler House
Turramurra, 1949–51

The third house in the group, built for a relative, is placed on the sloping land below the others. It has an elevated floor of 110 m², arranged in a 'ring' plan without any circulation spaces around a central kitchen with an overhead skylight. The living area and its continuous northern terrace overlook the valley view. The west-facing bedroom window is equipped with movable vertical sun louvres (based on Brazilian prototypes).

The structure consists of steel pipe columns and beams with timber joists supported between them.

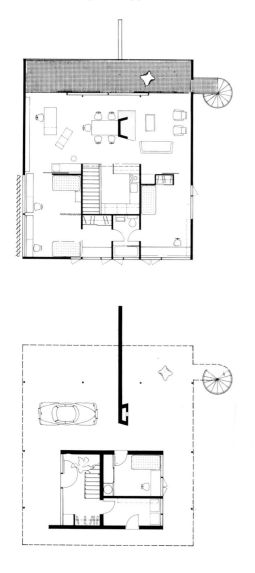

'... After working with Niemeyer I was still full of enthusiasm from my Brazilian experience, especially the work of Portinari and Burle Marx. Their influence made me paint this second mural after the one in my parents' house. Later on I did not paint any more, but the forms came back to me and re-emerged on plans of urban spaces in later years...'

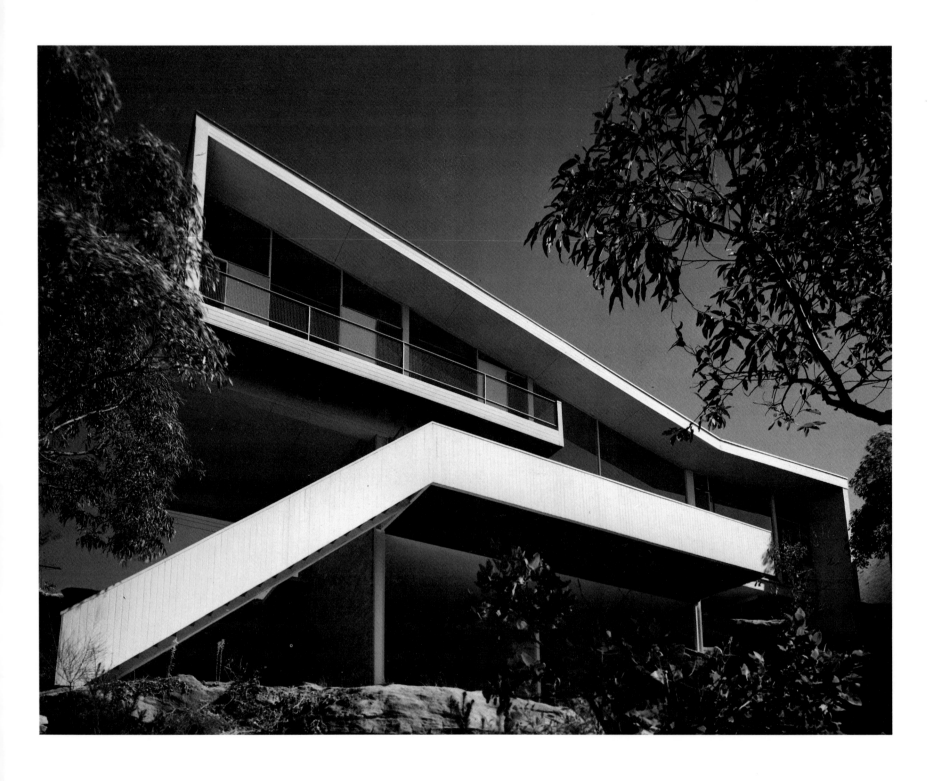

T. Meller House
Castlecrag, 1950

'... Built for a Viennese friend of the family – not only did the Council object to the design, but the local covenant, prohibiting any material other than masonry, was invoked by Nicholls, a one-time assistant to Walter Burley Griffin (the American designer of Canberra) who controlled the sub-division. The timber-clad overhanging section offended. Only the original authors of the covenant could alter its provisions. My phone call to Chicago pleading with 82-year-old Marion Mahoney Griffin finally resulted in her relenting to change the rules...'

The long side of this steeply sloping rocky site faces north-east toward Sydney Harbour. The 160 m² house maximises this outlook by exposing every room's glass wall and terrace to the view and arranging them in three longitudinally split-level floors connected by ramps. The resulting horizontal spaciousness is amplified by the vertical openness which penetrates all levels. The opposing roof slopes impart a dynamic quality to the building's profile which expresses the different floor levels. Construction is of cavity brick walls and steel beams supporting timber floors. The upper floor is cantilevered over a huge rock boulder which remains untouched.

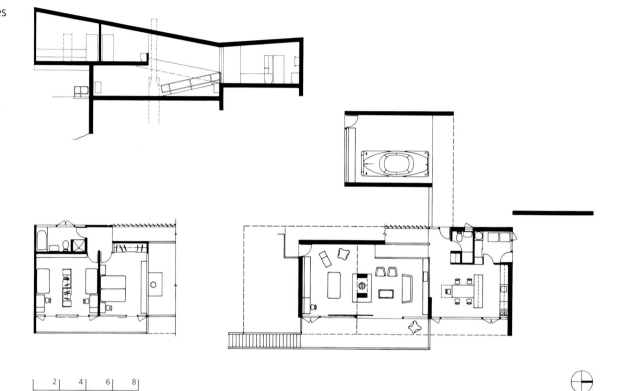

Williamson House
Mosman, 1951

'... The highly visible "Igloo House" attracted much attention. The structural engineer, Peter Miller, helped me make this minimal statement of a concrete sandwich. Construction was slow – by a brave solicitor owner-builder, in a period of shortages and delays...'

The precipitously sloping rocky site commands panoramic views over Middle Harbour coinciding with an ideal north-east orientation. The only structure considered feasible was a flat concrete slab 15 cm thick and roof supported by five regularly spaced (5 m) bays of internally exposed columns cantilevering front and back of the house. This enabled an in-line plan to face all rooms toward the view. Recessed terraces provide shade for the full glass walls.

A bridge leads to the roof-top garage which is covered by two concrete vaults. These induce largely horizontal loads in the roof, creating tension rather than bending in the slab. Lightweight masonry walls further reduce weight on the suspended structure.

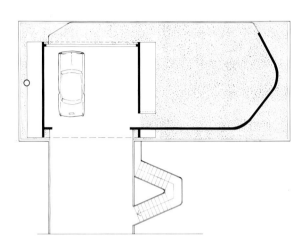

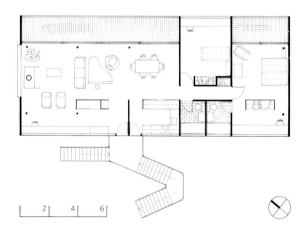

Hutter House
Turramurra, 1952

Built on a large slightly sloping site, the plan of this house is bi-nuclear. Living and bedroom wings are separate and joined by an entrance-ramped link. The carport is a third element, joined by a covered walkway. Between the different wings courtyards are created for entry, living and service. The slope of the roof is parallel to the ground but changes direction over the living wing to open the space toward the lower garden. The materials used are white painted brickwork, sandstone and natural cedar boarding.

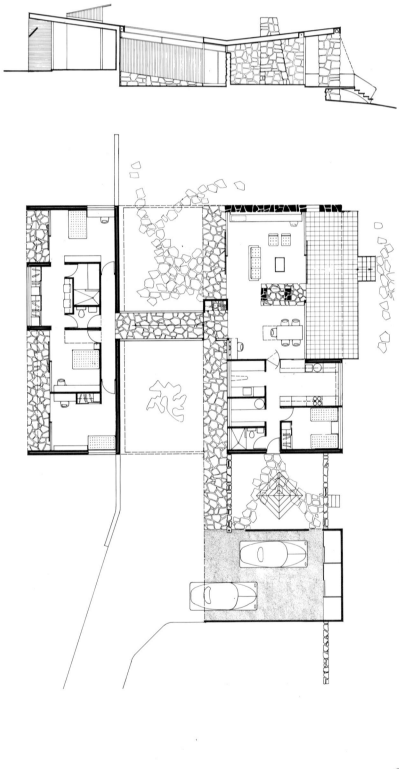

'... The middle-aged, cultured couple had nostalgic recollections of their large property in Austria and wanted to establish an orchard in this serenely beautiful setting. It was the first of many houses built by Peter Cussel during the following 15 years. He was an excellent builder, who was trained in Germany...'

Muller House
Port Hacking, 1963

Built on a steeply sloping waterfront site this house faces an inlet from the sea, south of Sydney. All major rooms face the water view. The upper level is for the owner's use – living, dining, kitchen and main bedroom suite. The lower floor contains guest bedrooms, playroom (for visiting grandchildren) and an outdoor covered area for barbecues.

The garage is at the top of the site and steps lead down to the main part of the house. The living room is on a lower level and given importance, not only by its increased height but also by its relation to outdoor living areas, the large suspended terrace facing the water and a shady patio on the approach side.

Construction and use of materials are closely related. The walls are of white concrete blocks forming evenly spaced 3 m-wide bays. The reinforced piers act as structural support and protection against horizontal sun. Floors are of concrete with the cantilevered terrace supported by upturned rails.

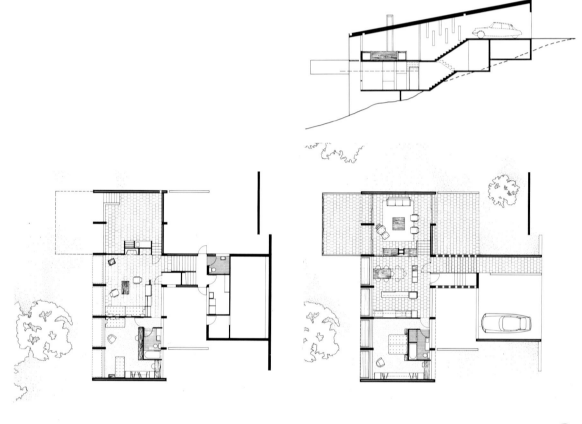

Ski Lodge
Thredbo, 1962

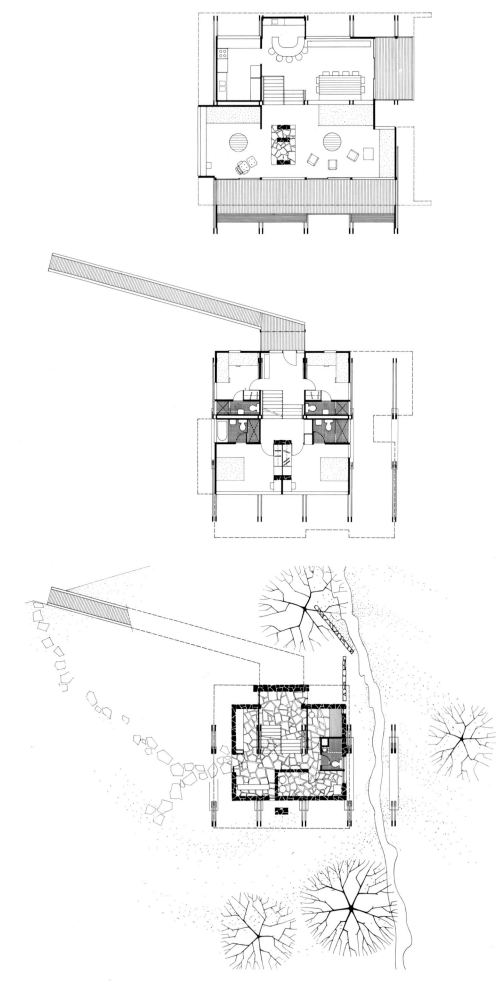

This mountain lodge is built at the edge of a ski resort village in the Snowy Mountains about 400 km south-west of Sydney. The sloping site, directly over a mountain creek, offered a good view of the ski slopes and the chair lifts to the north. The approach is from the east.

The shape of the compact, multilevel timber building was determined by the requirements. There are six half-levels connected by a centrally placed stair. The ski room, sauna, washing and drying rooms occupy a small space contained within a stone-walled bottom level (snow can pile up against this lowest level). The two double bedrooms and two four-bunk rooms on the part-centre floors are between this and the entertaining space; the lounge, den and dining areas with their terraces are on the top levels.

The floor areas increase toward the top and the resulting shape of the building becomes larger toward the upper levels. The structure is supported by five equally spaced, 3 m apart, vertical timber trusses with floors of increasing width hung between them. A free spanning U-shaped plywood truss ramp gives pedestrian access into the central stair.

The trusses consist of bolted, spaced double-timber members, stained black. The infill walls are of rough-sawn local ash boards and battens.

The freely planned space of the top living floors extends out onto terraces through sliding glass doors. A central skylight admits northern sun into the upper level and the freestanding two-way stone fireplace forms the focal point of the space. To allow a view down onto the running water under the building, a section of the living area floor, suspended over the creek, is of armoured plate glass.

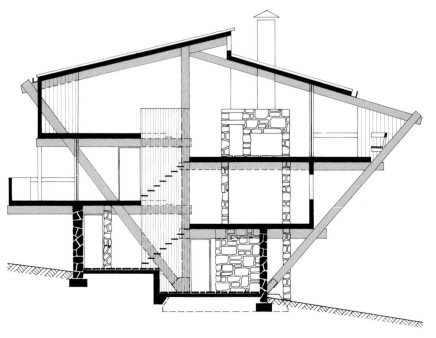

'... The skiing village was acquired by Dusseldorp's Lend Lease Corporation and he set a seemingly impossible tight construction schedule – four months total, so that his large family could all go skiing during the school holidays. It was pre-cut, fabricated and put up by a skilled Dutch carpenter, Bill Manten. We did it and there was a big house-warming party when, after some drinks, everyone jumped on the glass portion of the floor over the running creek below. I was worried but they couldn't break it. The best thing about that job were my supervision trips every weekend – Saturday on the job and on Sunday I skied ...'

Harry and Penelope Seidler House
Killara, 1966–67

'... Our years-long search for a site ended immediately when we stood looking down through beautiful trees to the waterfall – a mere 12 km from the centre of Sydney. We built a tough house...'

Although the site for this house is located in an established suburb it has no neighbours as it is surrounded by a natural bush reserve which assures privacy. The ruggedness of the site provided scope for a 'vertical' dimension, not only in the siting and approach of the house but also in the interior due to the resulting multi-level arrangement which follows the contours. The land slopes down from east to west, with the sunny northern orientation facing parallel to the street and the contours.

Being below the street the area is secluded with outlook only onto unspoilt nature and a creek – which turns into a gushing waterfall during rainy periods – running along the bottom of the site.

The garage was designed at the top, directly off the street, allowing space for visitors' cars. So as not to disturb a large rock ledge, the whole structure is suspended over it without visible support, leaving the rock exposed and unspoilt. The approach is over a suspended entrance bridge which springs from the top of a ledge across into the top one of the four half-levels of the house. The different levels not only accommodate various uses but they also make the house fit naturally into the slope of the ground.

The rectangular outline of the plan is divided into a sunny northern part for 'daytime active uses' and a shady southern part for 'quiet, passive uses'. The division is formed by the central half-flights of steps connecting the various levels.

The construction of the house is of maintenance-free materials, off-formed concrete and rubble stone. The three rows of vertical supports consist of reinforced concrete block piers (made of white cement), their varying lengths adjusting the building to the rugged terrain. They support suspended and cantilevered concrete floors, stiffened by rail-height parapets which make possible the long projections. Similar stiffening elements are provided for the concrete roof in the form of sun protection downturns, shielding the glass areas.

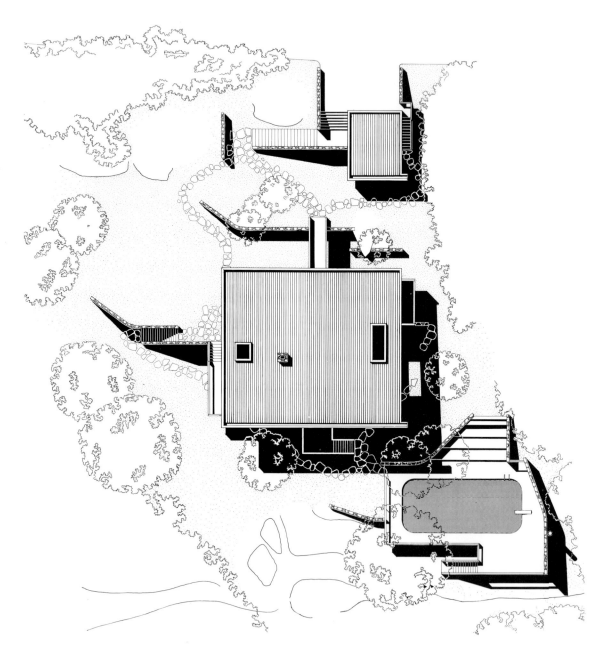

The main aesthetic aim of the house is not only to have horizontal freedom of space but by fusing and opening the various levels into each other and by 'pulling them apart' and thereby creating a two-and-a-half-storey-high open shaft between them, to add a vertical interplay of space.

A swimming pool was built below the house some years after it was completed.

The top level on the north accommodates the kitchen and dining room, on the south the library–study. The entrance hall serves as a gallery for artworks. The second level down, on the north contains the living area and on the south, the master bedroom suite. The third level down, on the north is the children's play room and on the east and south, three children's bedrooms. This is the only floor which is level with and has direct access onto the ground. The bottom level contains a studio on the north, the utility room and a self-contained guest or housekeeper's suite.

'... You arrive by a high road, you put the car in the garage, and then descend, going down, diving among the treetops, which reach the height of the garage, down along their trunks and down to the roots: and from all the great windows of the house, from all its openings, you see the same marvellous green, a fairytale colour humid and pure; and light, for the virgin woods of Australia are not the terrifying forests accursed and menacing with hidden death, but are innocent, maidenly, friendly woods ... it is not enough for the architect to create admirable spaces, lines and volumes – but also he must imagine, or discover, or suggest choices about a way of life, marvellous refuges – not so much distant, maybe, but passed over – to the friends who put their trust in him. That is why I admire Seidler, whose works I have visited ...'
Gio Ponti
Domus, Aug. 1968

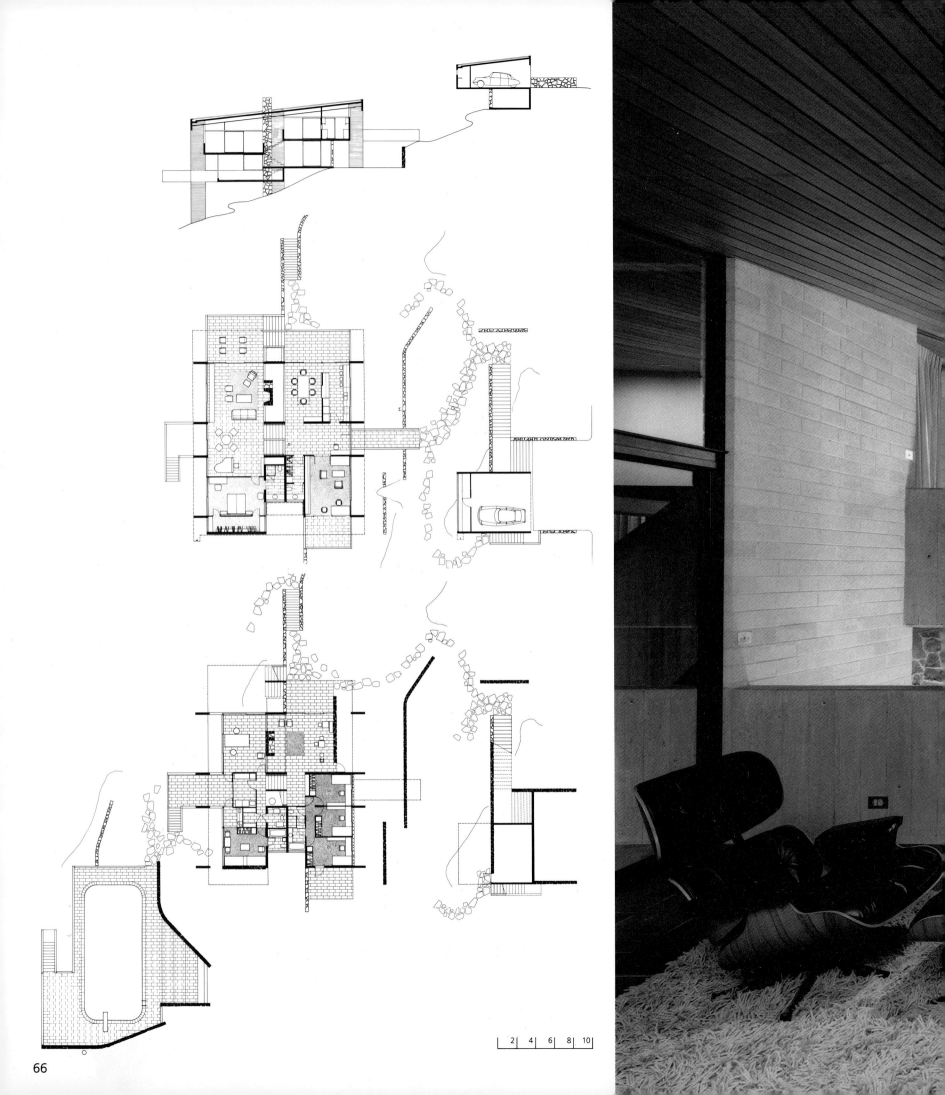

Gissing House
Wahroonga, 1971–72

Built for a family of five, this house is surrounded by mature gardens with high trees. The house is orientated to the sun, facing north with the living area opening onto a paved terrace around a swimming pool. The gentle ground slope was used to create a lower ground floor (with kitchen, dining and family rooms) and above it, a bedroom level. The three levels are connected by centrally placed half-flights of stairs. At the meeting of the levels, the section of the house is 'open' to create a void which spatially connects the different parts and creates changing vistas from one to another as one moves through the house.

Recurring circular elements contrast with the rectangular outline of the plan and its screen wall projections. Construction is of hollow, concrete block piers vertically reinforced, evenly spaced 3 m apart, supporting concrete floors and roof.

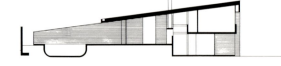

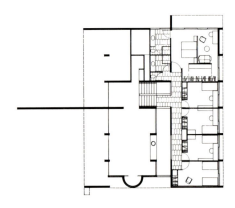

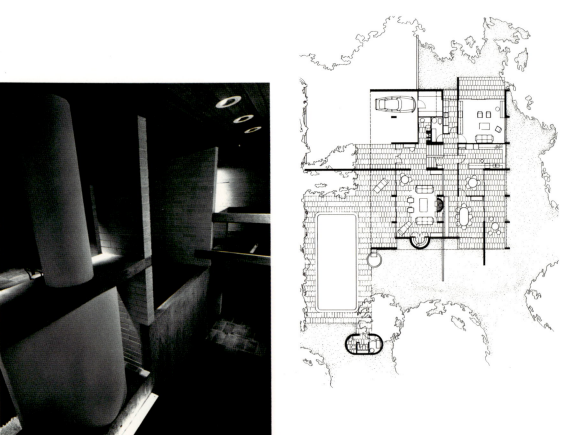

'... One of Penelope's schoolfriends visited us in our new house and wanted theirs to have that kind of feel...'

McMahons Point Development
North Sydney, 1957

This early planning scheme, for one of Sydney Harbour's peninsulas, illustrates the principle of tiered development; low buildings on the water's edge, medium height on the slopes in staggered groupings and high-rise towers on the crest. Only 13 years later was this zoning principle adopted by authorities in some areas to protect harbour views along the foreshores.

This purely diagrammatic scheme was prepared to demonstrate to the Planning Authorities who intended implementing an industrial zoning, that the area should be developed as high-density housing, being only a short ferry ride from the centre of Sydney. The plan shows the potential for an increase to housing densities in inner area waterfront suburbs (up to 370 people per hectare). Ample open space, permanent outlook and related building forms result, provided that comprehensive three-dimensional controls are adopted at an early stage for an entire district.

Unfortunately, only one apartment building on the promontory was realised. (See Blues Point Tower.) This location was intended for a tourist hotel. Progressive height zoning came into power only years later after much damage had already been done, the very opposite to what this scheme envisaged; waterfront towers blatantly blocking out views behind and low buildings instead of towers built along the ridge.

'... Hearing of the proposed industrial zoning, the local Progress Association asked me to help. Together with a number of young architects, we produced this "ideal" plan and model. An empty shop in the area was made available for our work – I met Penelope there...'

Blues Point Tower Apartments, North Sydney, 1959–1961

This is the only building which followed the planning scheme shown on the previous pages. The 0.8 ha site adjoins a park reserve which forms a promontory of steep sandstone cliffs to the water's edge. This parkland becomes part of the site, producing an area which is surrounded on three sides by water.

The 24-storey building contains 168 apartments, seven per floor. The siting is diagonal to avoid direct west or east orientations and to make it possible for a high percentage of apartments to have views in two directions as well as cross-ventilation. The four corners of the building contain different sizes of two-bedroom apartments arranged in such a way that their main glass areas, which are actually small 'french' balconies, are located to face alternate orientations on successive floors. This flexibility or choice of orientation and view is increased by plan reversal making possible further combinations of different size units facing any orientation. The staggering of balconies also overcomes the problem posed by the regulation requirement of vertical fire separation of masonry between floors since there is always a solid wall above and below every glazed balcony.

There are only four plumbing and mechanical equipment ducts. An isolated core houses two elevators, service risers and the incinerator.

The structure is of concrete. Cross-walls act both as structural support, wind-bracing element and soundproof division between apartments. The floors are of flat slab design and the shafts around stairs and elevators are vertically poured hollow tubes. The exterior infill walls are cavity brickwork.

'... Highly visible on the Sydney skyline, the tower has been much maligned as well as praised by the public. I still like its scintillating facades...'

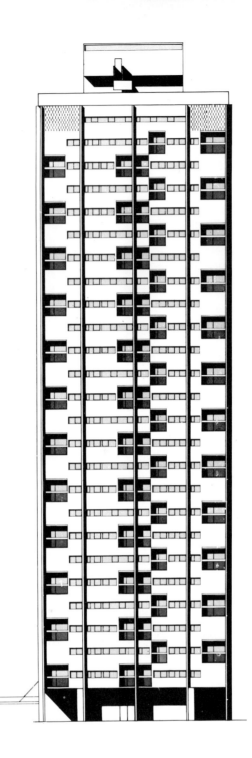
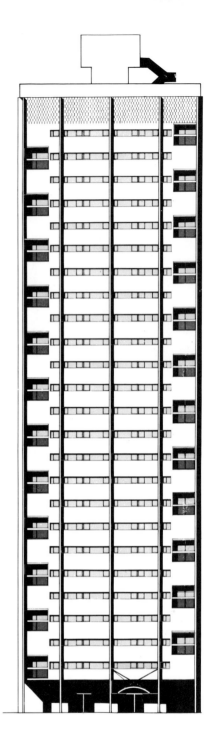
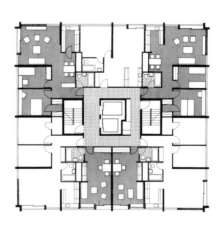
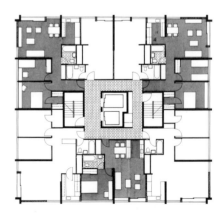

Rushcutters Bay Apartments
1963–65

'... The idea for the section came to me during a concert – how to place bedrooms on the off-view side and keep kitchen windows without interrupting access galleries ...'

The site for this block of 80 rental apartments is located at the bottom of a rock cliff 6 m below the street. The site is level and overlooks a park on the edge of the harbour. The building contains 60 small bed-sitting room units and 20 with separate bedrooms.

To face every apartment to the view (within the 10-storey height limit) a split-level plan was adopted with external access galleries every second floor. From these, half-level flights lead up and down to pairs of units. One of the upper units has a bedroom projecting over the galleries, which thereby does not obstruct the required kitchen window.

Two elevators and a firestair are contained in vertical shafts separated from the main building so as not to destroy its regular structure and planning. A curved pedestrian access bridge resolves the angled placing of the building to the street frontage and leads through the second floor of the access tower.

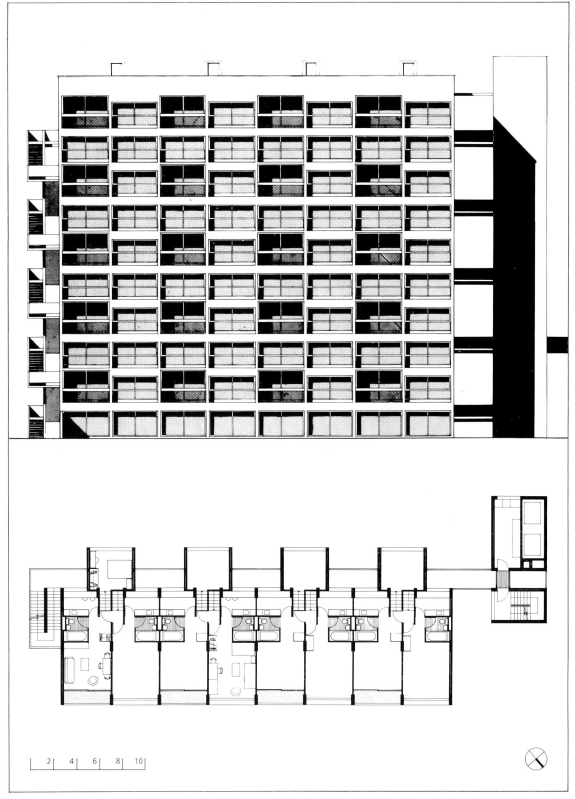

NSW Housing Commission Apartments
Rosebery, 1964–67

'... The challenge was to pare down housing to absolute essentials, develop a simple and fast construction cycle and yet build with lasting materials. The lowest cost ever achieved: £3500 per unit ...'

This low-cost State housing project, built on a 1 ha site, contains 226 apartments which represents a density of 740 people per hectare. To avoid a feeling of congestion, usual for such densities, two parallel but staggered blocks were planned facing the long boundaries. This resulted in a sense of openness which is maintained by the transparent bridge connection between the two blocks.

The planning of the apartment wings is repetitive and the method of construction was largely prefabricated. Apartments are planned across the long blocks for through-ventilation and economy of repetitive small-span (3 m to 4 m) cross-wall construction. External access galleries every second level occur between floors and apartments are reached by steps up and down. This reduces the amount of public space and assures privacy to all windows on the approach side (usually the disadvantage of gallery approach planning).

The cross-walls were built by the tilt-slab method, whereby they are poured horizontally and tilted up by hydraulic jacks. They then become the support for the next of the floors which are economical one-way flat slabs.

Ground-floor apartments have screened patios, and curvilinear children's playgrounds occupy the public spaces.

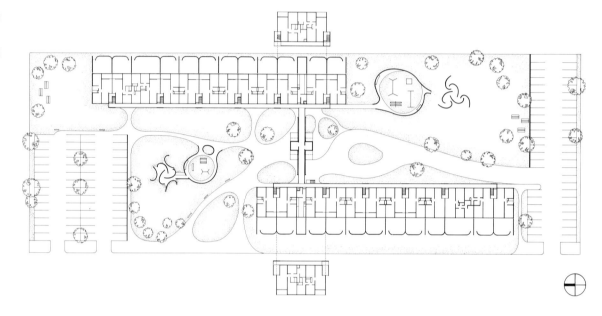

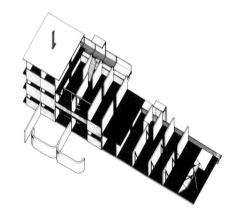

Garran Group Housing
Canberra, 1964–68

'... Ever since designing neighbourhood plans in Gropius' class, I welcomed this chance to show that medium-density housing could have most of the advantages of individual houses at lower cost and far less land usage ...'

This medium-density housing scheme (89 people per hectare) was built on a sloping site in beautiful rolling country of the Woden Valley. Views of distant hills, large trees, an existing school below the site and a nearby shopping centre made it an ideal housing location.

58 two-bedroom and 43 three-bedroom houses for families of University fellows and research scholars had to be built at low cost.

To avoid through traffic, the site plan consists of cul-de-sac access streets with staggered rows of houses in pairs, all with enclosed courtyards for privacy and safety of children. From every house the school is accessible without crossing any streets. A children's playground between the houses forms a focal point in the public space.

The houses are identical for each type, with opposing roof slopes for two- and three-bedroom houses. Internal planning employs a split-level system with approach to the houses possible both from the north and the south, depending on their street frontage and carport location.

The staggered arrangement of pairs of houses is dictated by the location of bathroom and study windows in the end walls. The stepped placing of groups along the contours of the site and the alternating roof slopes to preserve views, all help to vary street vistas and spaces and minimise any sense of regimentation of what are, actually, identical houses.

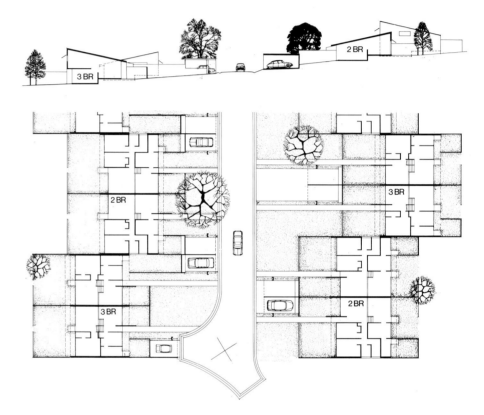

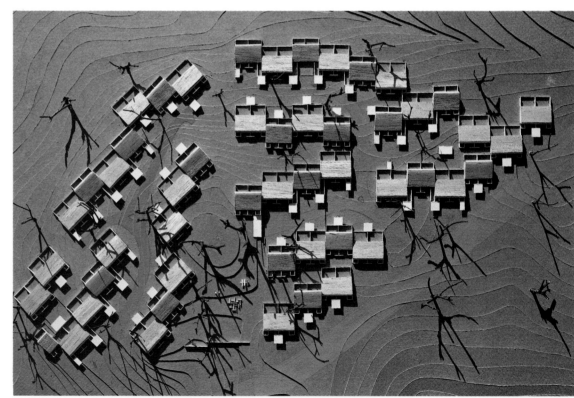

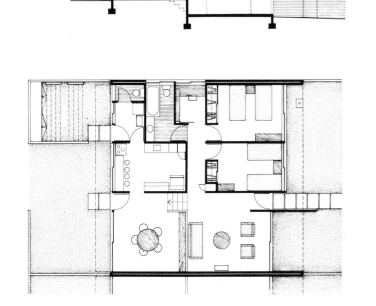

Arlington Apartments
Edgecliff, 1965–66

'... To have apartments cross over and under access corridors, lets all living rooms face the view – a system I later used in the Paris Embassy ...'

These apartments stand in a large old garden consisting of sloping land below street level with mature trees between old stone retaining walls. There are fine views of the harbour to the north.

A height limit of two floors above the access street was applied. As a result an eight-storey block was located on the lower section of the land and a four-storey block near the road. They are staggered so as not to obstruct views. To face the living areas of practically all units to the north and the harbour, split-level planning was adopted which also keeps public access space to a minimum (three corridors in an eight-storey building).

The four-storey south block contains two layers of maisonettes, directly approached over two ramps from the access road.

The main entrance is in the centre of the eight-storey building vertically and is reached by a footbridge. All apartments open from access galleries every two and a half floors. Within the apartments a half-flight connects the living level with the bedrooms. Some apartments without stairs open directly off the galleries.

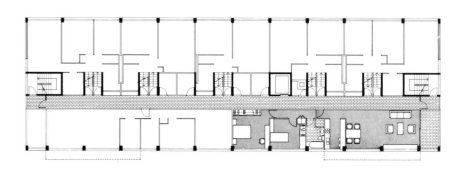

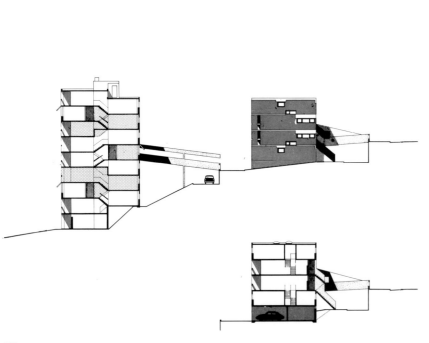

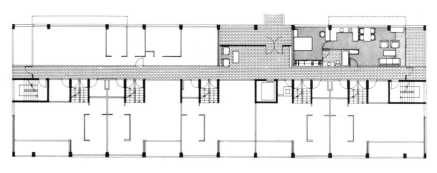

Condominium Apartments
Acapulco, Mexico, 1969–70

'... Exposure to the rich culture of Mexico made me respond for the first time with curved baroque-like forms. Julius Shulman, who produced the powerful images of Richard Neutra's work, came from Los Angeles to photograph this building ...'

The climate in the seaside resort town of Acapulco is tropical, buildings are usually white, and there is an exuberance in the character of many new structures. Labour is inexpensive, which allows architects to employ methods and forms not normally possible in high labour cost countries. Specially constructed timber formwork for expressive concrete profiles is readily possible.

The design of this 14-storey holiday apartment block takes these local characteristics into consideration. Although of regular layout and structure, the use of quadrant and elliptical free-form elements adds a deliberate sense of flamboyance to an otherwise rectilinear building. The structure is located back from the beach with a large golf course between, which forms a landscaped foreground.

Since the area is subject to earthquakes the expressed concrete frame of the building is heavy and rigid. The elongated curved columns are expressed on the exterior and reduce in size in the upper part of the building. The moulding of the expressed beam structure, inside and outside the building, produces the necessary stiffness at intersections between horizontals and verticals.

The exterior is finished in rough, throw-on, white render, typical for many Mexican buildings. The floor of the open ground level is covered with interlocking terracotta tiles which were handmade by local artisans. Floors throughout the rest of the building are of terrazzo. All apartments are air-conditioned.

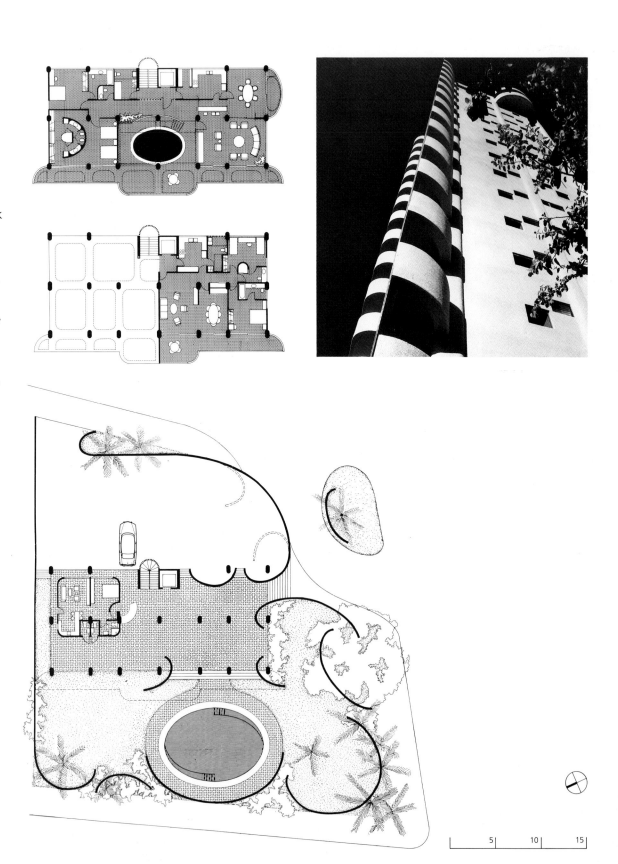

82

1965–1991   Isostatic Architecture

by Kenneth Frampton

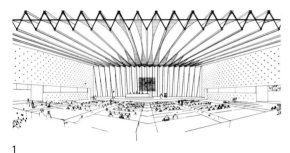

1

2

3

Let us state the conditions in the plainest manner. Briefly, they are these: offices are necessary for the transaction of business; the invention and perfection of the high-speed elevator makes vertical travel, that was once tedious and painful, now easy and comfortable; development of steel manufacture has shown the way to safe, rigid, economical conditions, rising to great height; continued growth of population in great cities, consequent congestation of centres and rise in value of ground, stimulate an increase in number of stories; these successfully piled one upon another, react on ground values – and so on, by action and reaction, interaction and interreaction. Thus has come about that form of lofty construction called the 'modern office building'. It has come in answer to a call, for in it a new grouping of social conditions has found a habitation and a name . . . How shall we impart to this sterile pile, this crude, harsh, brutal agglomeration, this stark, starving exclamation of eternal strife, the graciousness of those higher forms of sensibility and culture that rest on lower and fiercer passions? How shall we proclaim from the dizzy height of this strange, weird, modern housetop, the peaceful evangel of sentiment, of beauty, the cult of a higher life?
Louis Sullivan 1896[1]

Part 1
From Isostatic to Isomorphic

Harry Seidler's later career may be characterised as isostatic on three counts. In the first place, the term alludes to the isostatic structures that appear in his architecture from the mid-1960s onwards; in the second, it refers to the generally heightened level of plasticity that accompanies this use of laminated structure. While free curvilinear expression has an earlier origin in Seidler's career, above all in the brief apprenticeship that he served with Oscar Niemeyer, the term isostatic also alludes to the woven, layered quality of Seidler's later site planning as it shifts away from the normative open city model evident in his McMahons Point plan of 1957.

Shortly after the 1964 monograph devoted to his early career, *Harry Seidler 1955–63: Houses, Buildings and Projects*,[2] Seidler's architecture entered a new phase, not only in terms of the scale of the commissions he received but also in terms of the fundamental paradigms that governed the work. Indeed Seidler's own system of typological classification acknowledges this shift in distinguishing between the bi-nuclear and split level formats of his early domestic architecture and the quadrant and curvilinear mass forms that govern his later public work. This conceptual break is related to a similar rupture in the career of Marcel Breuer that occurs with Breuer's UNESCO Headquarters of 1954 designed in collaboration with Bernard Zehrfuss and Pier Luigi Nervi, Nervi being the common catalytic figure who played a decisive role in the careers of both Seidler and Breuer.

Seidler first worked with Nervi on his own account while designing the Australia Square Tower. Built in downtown Sydney in 1967, this work inaugurated their long collaboration which lasted until Nervi's death in 1979. Indeed, because this engineering input has since been provided by others who were trained by Nervi (above all by Nervi's former partner Mario Desideri) we may claim that Nervi continues to influence Seidler's architecture. Thus the origin of Seidler's isostatic architecture remains the canonical UNESCO Headquarters not only for the tripartite curvilinear plan form but also for the folded slab roof spanning over the adjacent auditorium (1). This primary influence is augmented by Seidler's experience of the Brazilian Modern movement in its prime, above all the seminal Ministry of Education of 1943, and the later rhythmic works of Niemeyer dating from the 1960s. These are still the 'after-images', so to speak, that appear in Seidler's Rocks Development, projected for Sydney in 1962 (2) or in the curvilinear wings of his entry for the Canberra Parliament Building, dating from 1976 (3).

Australia Square Tower, 1961–67
Aside from its tectonic order and its monumental presence within the skyline of Sydney (4), Australia Square Tower was a significant achievement in terms

of the technical methods employed. It pioneered permanent precast concrete formwork not only for the 20 tapering reinforced concrete columns running around its perimeter, but also for the spandrel beams carrying each floor. Nervi's isostatic structure is most evident perhaps in the exposed waffle slabs of the lobby and first floors, where, appropriately enough, reticulated structural soffits span across the monumental volumes of the principal public levels (5). Elsewhere, the standard office floors are supported by radial concrete beams spanning between the cylindrical service core and the outer circumference (6). This all too practical but nonetheless subtle differentiation between rental space on the one hand and public space on the other recalls Eugene Viollet-le-Duc's didactic observation that great civilisations manifest themselves in great public spaces, the monumental status of which is declared by the heroic scale of their spans (7). Of his initial collaboration with Nervi, Seidler has written:

My first experience of working with Nervi in 1963 remains vividly in my mind. After he expressed his interest in collaborating on the round office tower in Australia Square, I went to Rome with an engineer from Sydney. Nervi liked the repetitive constructional system ideas that a round tower offered; only one type of beam, only one type of column and one type of core unit. When discussing the need for the special, very heavily loaded two lowest exhibition floors, he soon suggested the use of curved interlocking ribs. With a somewhat shaky hand he sketched their intertwining pattern, during the first half-hour of our meeting . . . He not only gave the problem beautiful form but he also showed us how to build it – how to use ferro-cement and precast exterior forms for the tapered changing section columns that logically diminish in size as they rise; a system that has since been used on many high-rise buildings in Sydney.[3]

In the early 1970s Seidler's resurgent tectonic sensibility was complemented by the realisation of a little-known temporary pavilion erected in Hyde Park, Sydney (8). This diminutive structure (50.63 m long, 15.25 m wide and 9.15 m high) assumed the form of a partially buried frustrum lying on its side. In

4

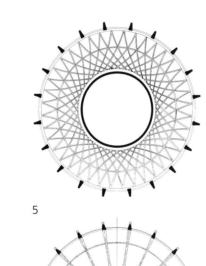
5

7

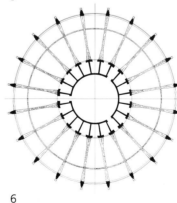
6

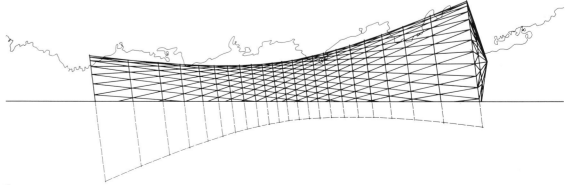
8

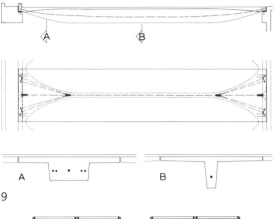
9

10

structural terms it comprised a hyperbolic catenary structure, covered by a translucent stressed skin. Designed in collaboration with the engineer, John Ferris, this work is significant since it shows the extent of Seidler's commitment to the structural basis of architectural form. The same period saw his first complete use of precast, prestressed, T-section floor planks. These were applied to the 11.0 m transverse span employed in his own offices built at Milsons Point, Sydney, in 1972 (9, 10).

Trade Group Offices, Canberra, 1970–74
The assimilation of the Nervi approach into Australian engineering practice came with Seidler's Trade Group Offices, constructed in Canberra between 1973 and 1974 (11, 12, 13). Designed with the Australian engineer, Peter Miller, this low-rise office complex was a brilliant demonstration of Nervi's precast technique, with T-sectioned, prestressed planks spanning 15.25 m across column-free office space to gain their edge support off 24.4 m span post-tensioned spandrel beams. Transforming their section within the span, these spandrels went from an I-section at mid-span to a rectangular section at the support, this last being necessary for the resistance of shear stress. This technical and tectonic articulation was further enriched by the metal covers of the prestressing anchors that punctuated the spandrel web at regular intervals; a classic instance of ornamenting a structure through the articulation of an expressive joint. Aside from this the planks curving upwards at their anchorage impart an expressive profile to the underbelly of the long span, while providing an appropriate frame for panoramic views over Canberra. Moreover, these bridgeforms, reminiscent in some respects of Kenzo Tange's Yamanashi Communications Centre (14), serve to define the limits of the paved podium that embodies the quadrangular campus of the site.

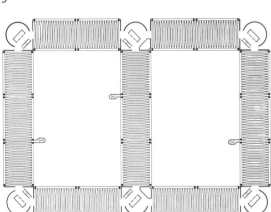
11

12

The 1974 design of the unbuilt Tuggeranong Offices seems to have arisen out of a further development of the structural system employed in the Canberra complex (15). By virtue of tapering the T-shaped floor planks in plan, the Tuggeranong office slabs were projected as free shapes thereby enclosing

13 14

an undulating rustic volume within the centre of the scheme. Related to Seidler's Baranduda proposal, this modified Radburn layout is the first full expression of what we may call Seidler's 'baroque' manner. While the particular *marriage de contour* adopted here owes much to the Brazilian Modern movement, the reiterative geometric means employed, the quadrants and the arcs, also indicate the influence of American Minimalist art.

With his adoption of prestressed, T-sectioned elements (16) Seidler strove to integrate the essential services within the depth of the structural section. The fact that he chose to achieve this without any kind of suspended ceiling was to put him among that small group of late Modernists for whom the concealment of structure was an anathema. In this respect he was close to the spirit of the late Louis Kahn, for whom a room could hardly be said to exist without the over-arching form of its containing vault or folded slab (17). Thus where the Trade Group Offices deployed a modified suspended ceiling, hung between the downstands of the planks, Tuggeranong, like Milsons Point, envisaged the suspension of air-conditioning tubes and lighting strips beneath the precast elements (18).

MLC Centre Tower, Sydney, 1972–78

The 67-storey MLC Centre in Sydney (the highest concrete structure in the world at the time of its completion) was the second high-rise that Seidler designed in collaboration with Nervi (19). The achievement in this instance, however, went beyond the probity of the structural form, for Seidler interpreted the commission as an occasion for creating a semi-public realm within the commercial fabric of downtown Sydney. Situated on the southern edge of an L-shaped interstitial site (20), the entry foyer to the tower gave onto a public plaza that in turn fed into a two-storey shopping concourse beneath the podium. In intent, the MLC Centre is reminiscent of Rockefeller Plaza in New York and it is this preoccupation with 'cities in miniature' that has characterised almost all of Seidler's subsequent centre-city developments. Of these the MLC is perhaps the most civic to date since unlike all his other high-rises it accommodates

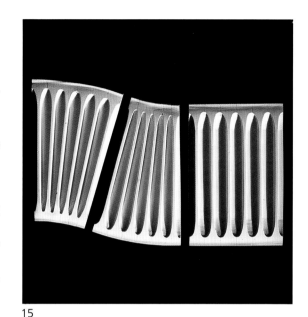

15

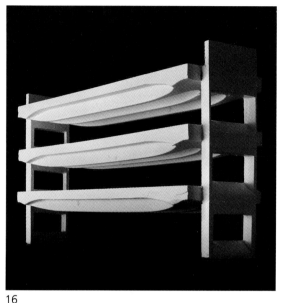

16

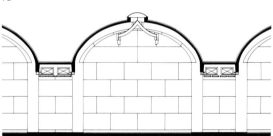

17

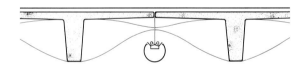

18

19

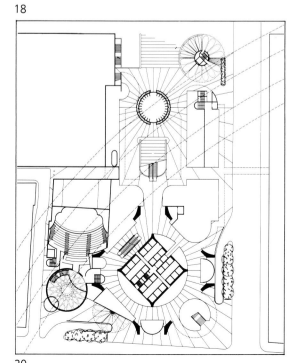

20

21

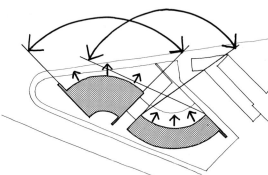

22

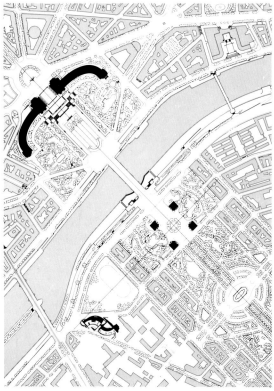

23

within its terrain a full-scale public institution set against the western boundary of the site, the New Theatre Royal (20).

Arising from the necessity of avoiding subway tunnels, the uneven sided, octagonal footprint of the tower yields a series of alternating short and long spans that are linked together in order to constitute the perimeter of the building (20). These alternating spans of varying section, together with the upward tapering columns, afford the felicitous effect of diminishing the apparent thickness of the tower, without reducing its monumental character. Once again, the expressive isostatic ribbed forms are reserved for the soffits of the public spaces.

Seidler's general adoption of this isostatic method has meant that almost all of his later structures have been a constructional *tour de force*, involving considerable ingenuity on the part of all concerned. Some idea of the problems that have been encountered in the erection of such large, precast concrete structures may be gleaned from an account of the interim support system that proved essential to the production of the principal spandrels (21).

The 19 m beams have a dead load of 76.5 tonnes and the design of the beam is such that it can only just support its own dead load plus that of a beam above when 28 days old. When the beam is four days old, it cannot even support itself. This meant that any form of conventional propping and repropping of the spandrel beams was unworkable. The solution to the problem was to use a spandrel support truss that could carry the loads of a new beam and distribute that load directly to the column faces. By using three levels of spandrel support trusses, no beam would have to carry its own load until it was eight days old and it would have no further loads imposed on it from above.[4]

Australian Embassy, Paris, 1973–77

Seidler's most honorific work to date is the Australian Embassy in Paris. The building was commissioned in 1973 and completed four years later, at about the same time as the topping out of the MLC Centre. Taken together, these two works establish the typological and expressive range of Seidler's isostatic architecture extending from the specifics of the tectonic invention, to the overriding rationality of the geometric *parti*. As a two-part composition on a very prominent but atypical site, Seidler's Australian Embassy accords a certain priority to the topography without jeopardising the tectonic probity of the work.

The principle of duality pervades the overall concept of this work at every level from the interaction of minimalist form with a clear typological order, to the 'yin yang' interplay of reversed quadrants that serve to govern the overall mass of the complex (22). Through the adoption of a subtly modulated sculptural form Seidler was able to accommodate a highly differentiated program while answering the all too stringent requirements imposed by the city, namely a maximum site coverage of 50 per cent and a height of no more than 31 m. Apart from meeting these exacting conditions Seidler's dyadic assembly is inflected so as to respond to the surrounding pattern of topographic axes and monumental forms; that is to say to the Neo-Baroque of the Palais de Chaillot, axially aligned with the radial geometry of the Eiffel Tower, and the intersecting cross axes of the Champ de Mars with the Seine. The Seine widens sharply at this point between the Pont de Bir-Hakeim and the Allée des Cygnes, and the Embassy deflects, as it were, towards the corresponding displacement of the Quai de Grenelle (23). This formal vector and the overall block height serve to reinforce the boundary that divides the boulevard fabric of Hausmann's Paris from the postwar, freestanding slab formation of the Front Seine. At the same time the quadrant theme enables Seidler to resolve the converging vectors of the rue de la Fédération and the rue Jean Rey without resorting to the traditional Hausmannian formula of a *bâtiment d'angle*. The dyadic composition of two quadrants also serves to differentiate between the Chancery approach on rue Jean Rey and the residential access taken from the rue de la Fédération (24).

A similar dialogical interplay theme is carried over into the detailing. It reappears in the twin windows facing north-east over the Quai Branly and above all in the *béton brut* fan-shaped piloti that are used to support the outer circumference of the respective quadrants. Rendered in two different versions these fan-shaped, hyperbolic pilotis are cast from timber formwork (25). These Brutalist supports not only derive from Breuer's UNESCO building but also from Le Corbusier's Unité d'Habitation at Marseille. With the building of the Embassy Seidler was able to bring his plastic syntax to a new level of metaphorical complexity, the split piloti supporting the Chancery entry being a case in point where the divided form seems to correspond to the ostrich and the kangaroo of the Australian Coat of Arms (25). Moreover, here as elsewhere, the prestressed, down-stand T-beams bestow an honorific status on the volumes they encompass. Both the Chancery foyer and exhibition hall are covered by such 'monumental' spans whereas the Embassy apartments are built of prefabricated flat slabs, cast on site and raised into position according to the so-called *prédalles* system. A brief technical description of this system testifies once again to the use of ever more ingenious and efficient methods for the appropriate prefabrication of concrete structures. Of the *prédalles* system we read:

This construction technique consists of the precasting of the bottom 5 cm to 6 cm thickness of all flat slab concrete floors on a steel platform at ground level, using minimal reinforcing. The upper surface is left very rough and the panels, up to 50 m² in area, are then picked up by crane using a unique, equalising load multiple pulley device which assures that the thin slabs do not crack. They are deposited on minimal central formwork and supported by precast facade elements and internal columns. Reinforcement is placed and the balance of the concrete slab is then poured in place, leaving a smooth paintable surface below, eliminating the need for plastering.[5]

Ringwood Cultural Centre and Kooralbyn Housing, 1978–82

The late 1970s and early 1980s brought change of scale and pace in the scope of Seidler's practice and for a brief while the commissions stemmed from ex-urbia. Seidler designed the Ringwood Cultural Centre in 1978 for a 40,000-strong middle-class enclave on the outskirts of Melbourne (26, 27), and later, a residential neighbourhood in Kooralbyn (28, 29), 100 km south-west of Brisbane, Queensland, completed in 1982. Demonstrative of the ways in which formal inflection may be used to characterise different cultural situations, Ringwood and Kooralbyn address themselves to different settings. Thus for all the plasticity of its immediate appearance Ringwood is geometric and public, whereas Kooralbyn evokes the organic irregularity of Mediterranean form. The two works seem to allude in a surprising way to the two distinct phases of Seidler's career with the latter alluding to the split-level domestic typology that dominated Seidler's work up to 1963 and the former deriving from the curvilinear geometry employed in his later public work. As Philip Drew has pointed out, Ringwood Cultural Centre is a direct manifestation of this last with its shifting quadrants recalling the form of the Australian Embassy. Drew's analysis of this permutational play merits citing in full:

The Ringwood composition is reminiscent of the Australian Embassy, Paris, but whereas the axes of the two quadrants forming the Embassy complex are parallel and opposite, resulting in a rhythmical alteration of convex and concave, in the Ringwood arrangement the axes intersect at right angles. Thus the two curved faces are opposed so as to face in opposite directions, one towards the ceremonial entrance, the other towards the main public approach.

In place of the rhythmic alignment of the two quadrants of the Paris Embassy, the Ringwood quadrants are relatively independent, at no point can the two curved faces be seen together, consequently, the curved face of one quadrant is always juxtaposed against the squared faces of the other.[5]

24

25

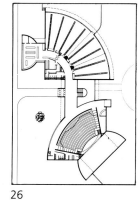 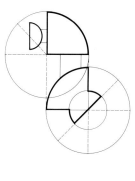

26 27

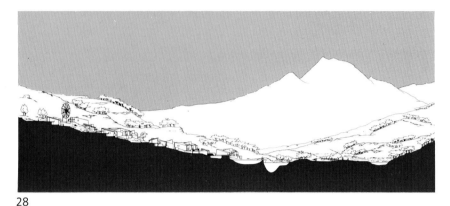

28

30

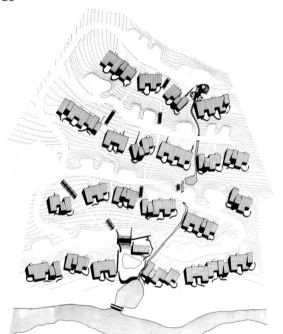

29

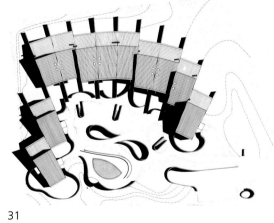

31

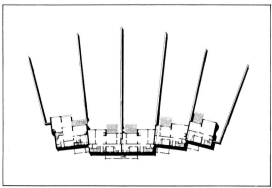

32

33

Seidler's Kooralbyn resort village, on the other hand, reverts to the pragmatic irregularities of the split-level ranch house and is driven more by the program than by the exigencies of form. This does not mean that its formal order has not been carefully considered and equally well orchestrated. Indeed the breaking, syncopated rhythm of the loosely clustered cross-wall units reminds one of Seidler's Broadbeach Apartments, completed at Broadbeach, Queensland, about two years before (30). While the Broadbeach site is flat, the fragmented, fractured formation adopted for its block layout is very similar, notwithstanding the fact that Kooralbyn yields a more articulated result.

Like Seidler's Yarralumla Housing cluster of 1987 (31), the model for Kooralbyn is partly Scandinavian, even if the initial aim was to evoke something of the Aegean. Thus Kooralbyn, in the last analysis, seems to owe a lot to Denmark, above all to Arne Jacobsen's terrace housing built at Klampenberg in 1950 (32). The source for Seidler's preferred pattern for suburban settlement seems to have been Scandinavian organically planned housing, as one may judge from the cluster pattern employed in his Yarralumla development that bears a strong resemblance to the organisation of Alvar Aalto's Sunila housing cluster of 1939 (33).

Waverley Civic Centre, 1984

While the double achievement, within a decade, of both Australia Square and MLC Centre has meant that Seidler has been in constant demand as a high-rise architect ever since, the first half of the 1980s saw him receiving a fairly broad spectrum of commissions, ranging from the Waverley Civic Centre, realised near Melbourne in 1984, to the Navy Weapons Workshop built at the West Dock, Garden Island, Sydney, between 1984 and 1985.

In many ways Waverley Civic Centre is an elaboration of themes first broached in the Ringwood Culture Centre. Not only is it a civic institution built for a relatively small ex-urban community near Melbourne but it is also a bipolar scheme, offset by a third term that in Waverley happens to be the council chamber and its ancillaries (34). While bipolarity in Ringwood assumed the form of mirrored quadrants, asymmetrically displaced in respect of each other, the dyadic scheme at Waverley comprises two virtual squares, diagonally rotated. Where the Ringwood quadrants are linked by a rather arbitrary bridgeform, the twin squares at Waverley are connected by an arc, struck between their leading outer edges (35, 36). Where Ringwood verges on the formalistic with its accommodation of different institutional programs within very similar quadrant forms, Waverley employs strict geometrical differences to discriminate between programmatically distinct parts of the same institution. Moreover where the connections at Ringwood are sculptural, yet geometrically arbitrary, the integration and differentiation at Waverley is achieved through the interpenetration of two identical quadrants, intersecting about an axis that is normal to their cross-axes.

The formal sophistication of Waverley does not end here however, for three very ingenuous operations serve to enrich the geometrical order and to bestow a higher degree of spatial complexity on the resultant form. The first of these turns on the asymmetrical placement of the council chamber itself that symmetrically interpenetrates one side of the central quadrant plan. This last confronts on axis the bipolar form of the twin squares. The second operation is the introduction of a smaller radiused counter arc that by intersecting the main outer arc establishes a 45-degree counter mass at grade.

This convex mass-form, reminiscent of the undercroft of the Villa Savoye, balances out the opposite diagonal axis assumed by the council chamber on the first floor. At the same time the initial counter-arc at grade cuts into the volume of the central three-storey atrium. Taking the form of a ramped staircase that ascends to the ground floor of the atrium, this same counter-arc also engenders the form of the main portico.

The chamber itself is articulated by a series of microdevices that while equally sophisticated in geometric terms are also significant at a symbolic level. Indeed the symbolic centre of the entire complex is not the central atrium but the single semicylindrical column that stands at the apex of the council chamber and supports its cantilevering form. This *axis mundi* is intimately related to three other elements that mutually reinforce the institutional status of the work. The first of these are the two adjacent piers set on either side of the council chamber that not only complete a tectonic trinity with the cylindrical column but also reiterate at a microcosmic level the *parti* of the single council quadrant form opposing the two squares. The second device is the central column that rises up through the back wall of the council chamber to issue forth as a continuous semi-circular concrete vault above. This vault allows daylight to enter the windowless chamber, as though this light represented the essence of enlightened governance. Finally, there is the circular reflecting pool that lies to one side of the single cylindrical column. This semantic *tour de force* is consummated by the reverse quadrants (34, 37) that set back to back are reminiscent of the Veronese castellated form and hence evocative of the original Italian 'city-state' (38).

The spatio-symbolic complexity of Waverley is hardly exhausted, even by an analysis as protracted as this for we have yet to mention the first floor *passerelle* that spans across the public atrium to link the council suite to the executive offices or to remark on the fact that the *porte-cochère* for visiting dignitaries is formed by the suspended council chamber.

Garden Island Dockyard Workshop, 1985
It would be hard to imagine something more removed from Waverley than the Garden Island Dockyard Workshop in terms of type, scale and the expressive character. If Waverley is a geospatial symbolic *tour de force*, the new West Dock Workshop is a paradigmatic industrial structure. Erected as the first stage of a phased replacement of the colonial naval facilities at Woolloomooloo (39), this initial increment is essentially an industrial adaptation of the system that Seidler and Nervi had previously evolved for the offices in Canberra. Seidler's description of the structural system employed affords a clear

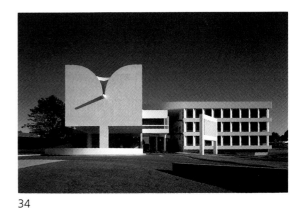

34

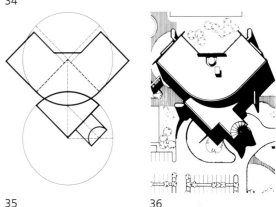

35   36

37

38

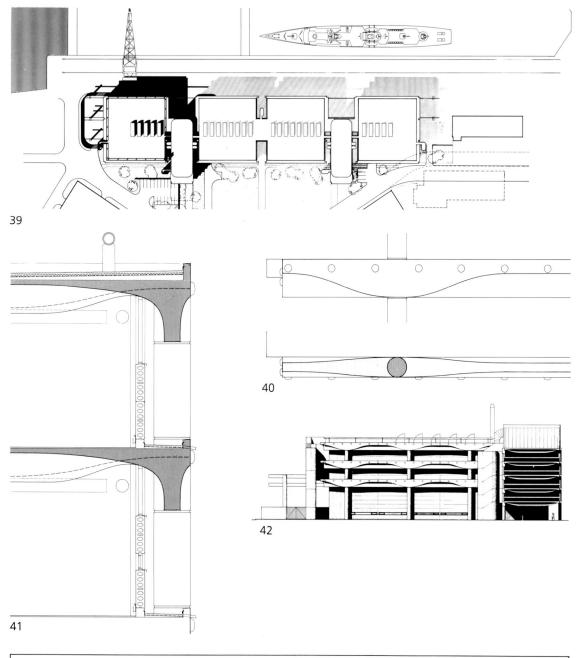

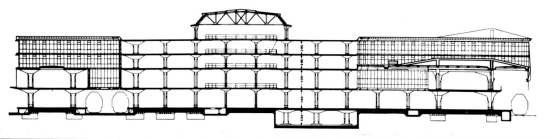

idea of the subtle way in which the Canberra format was adapted in terms of both constructional method and resultant structure:

All of the structure was exposed inside and out, to help create the overall architectural impact. The form of the individual structural elements was designed to respond to the needs of statics. The shapes developed reflected not only the structural demands but also the need to provide for services to pass integrally within the floor structure. As a result, the form of the structural elements used were organic in character; they were gradually changed in section along their spans to give visual evidence of the forces they resist. The solid rectangular cross-section (to resist shear) over the supports of the continuous primary beam was hollowed out progressively following a parabolic curve towards mid-span (and the end of the cantilevers) to take on a T-shaped profile in order to resist bending. This created natural passages for service runs to be accommodated within the depth of the structure in both directions. Main air supply ducts were run alongside primary beams, and distributing ducts then run out between the cross T-beams . . .

Conventional concrete formwork could not achieve the organically moulded forms required for this structure, so instead segmental fibreglass moulds were assembled, mass produced in manageable lengths and reused throughout construction. Whilst the initial cost of this formwork was higher, reduced labour costs and the reusable nature of the formwork meant overall costs were less than traditional formwork construction, and the builder found that this phase of the construction was completed in a much shorter time than first expected . . .

Anchorages of prestressing cables were sealed in epoxy and covered with dome-shaped stainless steel caps, which form an important part of the structurally expressive facades.[7]

Despite the unduly decorative effect of the repetitive caps, particularly at the beam ends, the overall expressivity of this framed structure reminds one of the masterly pharmaceutical plant, built for Boots at Beetson in 1932 to the design of Owen Williams (43).

Four other refinements are worthy of comment with regard to the detailing of this work: first, the plastically effective use of cylindrical columns to support the organic profile of the main spans (40); second, the alternating use of cylindrical air-conditioning ducts and lighting battens between every other T-section floor unit; third, the use of prestressed, hollow concrete planks with exposed aggregate finish, as nonload-bearing spandrel panels (41); and last, the subtle but nonetheless evident differentiation between the structure of the offices and the structure of the workshops, since each one was designed to meet different floor heights, loads and spans (42).

Hong Kong Club Tower, Hong Kong, 1984
All these developments converge in the realisation of Seidler's Hong Kong Club, located axially on Cenotaph Square in the central business district of the city (44). While remaining classically symmetrical about its major and minor axes, with the exception of the service 'bustle' attached to the rear of the 16-storey slab, the Hong Kong Club is a pyrotechnic display of plastic exuberance and if any recent work should merit the designation 'Baroque', this surely is it. Compositionally this building is a remarkable synthesis of the two primary types to be found in Seidler's later practice: the horizontally differentiated public institution and the vertically repetitive commercial high-rise. Both types are equally present here in the superimposition of a four-square, medium-rise, 16-floor office tower over a four-storey public podium. No-one has written more lucidly of the various factors that led to this unusual juxtaposition than the architect himself:

With mushrooming new development all around it, in recent years, the site has become immensely valuable. This prompted the developer's offer to build a new building for the club if he were given the right to construct new rental offices above it to fully utilise the site's potential. The two uses were to be kept strictly separate, the club maintaining its private entry in the old axial location facing the Cenotaph and the offices entering from the wide street. The club occupies the podium of the building to a four-storey height up to which regulations allow almost total site cover, and the offices above, the permissible two-thirds of the area.[8]

The common modern paradigm of a high-rise block over a low-rise podium, that has so often proven resistant to a convincing resolution (cf. Gordon Bunshaft's House of 1956) is here, for once, integrated in a felicitous way. This synthesis is largely the result of certain formal reciprocities: first, the implantation of the tower immediately above the podium; and second, an orchestrated rhythmic syncopation, in which plastically oscillating planes within the podium find their muted counterpart in the inflected spandrel beams running the width of the tower, as well as in the organically shaped piers that establish the four corners of the high-rise (45).

From a structural and conceptual standpoint, the extremely long spandrels (stretching 34 m across the long facade of the 'pagoda' tower) transform the received high-rise topology into a form of bridge construction wherein the column-free, clear spans liberate the public space of the club beneath (46). Nothing could be further, however, from Le Corbusier's *plan libre* of 1926, for here the free plan does not arise out of the interarticulation of free-standing planes and columns. Instead, the freedom in question is largely a matter of large-scale volumetric displacement, reminiscent say, in its overall elaboration, of Frank Lloyd Wright's Guggenheim Museum of 1956 (47).

With the street level largely given over to retail and services the main unifying volume of the club is a circular void cut out of the fourth floor mezzanine level. While accommodating ancillary lounges, this level looks down onto the main dining floor situated beneath (46). This floor in turn is connected to the main, multi-purpose hall situated at the first floor. The whole spatial sequence is animated vertically by a bipartite, semi-cylindrical elevator

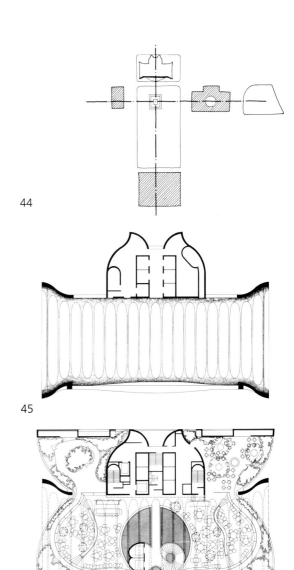

44

45

46

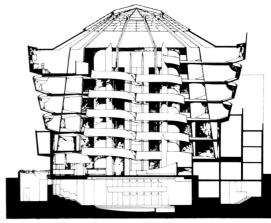

47

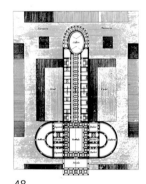

48

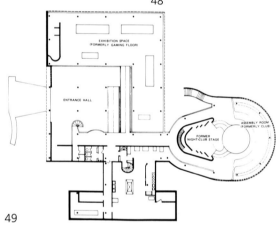

49

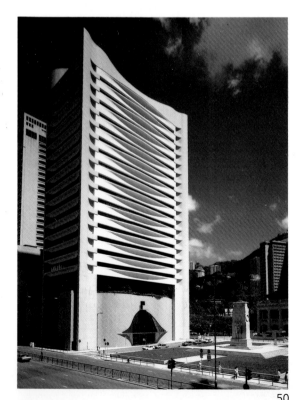

50

shaft and an open, helicoidal stair. This composite form runs up through the continuous volume to link, via intermediate floors, the foyer at grade to the bar/buffet and garden on the podium roof. It says something for the neoclassical aspects of Seidler's isostatic practice, that the bridge-link at this level should inscribe the outline of an erect penis into the fourth floor plan (46). Volumetrically imperceptible, this allusion to Ledoux's Oikema (48) certainly appears in the published plans of both works, the Oikema being a fictitious Utopian institution wherein the erotic drives of youth were to be satiated through excess. In more ways than one, we returned here to the hedonistic ethos of Niemeyer's Casino, erected in Pampulha, Brazil, in 1942 (49).

We cannot conclude this analysis of the Hong Kong Club without discussing the structure, for once again Seidler was to modify his production methods in the light of the local economic conditions. Of these he wrote:

In industrialised high labour cost countries, the structural form was used as a precast element lifted into place by crane. . . . To force this notion, however logical, into the Hong Kong labour scene would be unreasonable. Here ample labour was available at costs far lower than in Europe, Australia or the USA. It is therefore more 'in tune' economically to form these floor elements conventionally and pour concrete on site, a procedure which readily allows for the varying length and radiating pattern of the beams.[9]

Finally one needs to comment on the curiously oriental inflections that appear in the work, such as the horizontal slots of the tower windows that seem to cut across its vertical mass like the eaves of a pagoda or the glass canopy over the main entrance that recalls the manifold curves of a traditional Chinese roof (50).

Malaysian Interlude, 1980
Seidler returned to high-rise construction in 1980, when he began a series of commissions for downtown developments in Malaysia, first in Kuala Lumpur and then in Singapore. With these works he developed the basic prototypes for a new generation of medium to high-rise commercial structures technically and aesthetically derived from the plastic potential of clearspan T-sectioned planks, arrayed like the spines of a snake's skeleton. These planks enabled the Kuala Lumpur blocks to assume a curvilinear shape in plan. In this instance the T-sectioned beams spanned 12.2 m clear on either side of an irregularly shaped core (51). This format would eventually become the *parti* for two subsequent high-rise proposals: Grosvenor Place, first projected in 1982, and Shell House, initially designed in 1985.

The Kuala Lumpur proposal is a canonical work from another point of view, for it is the first occasion on which Seidler projects freely subdivided office space (53). Equally audacious are the split-level parking floors, wherein car ramps encircle the service core (52). The so-called New World development for Singapore is by no means as ingenious but it is equally seminal from an urbanistic standpoint. It is a project that will have a decisive influence on subsequent projects of similar scale and scope.

Grosvenor Place, Sydney, 1982–87
Comprised of two opposing quadrants the 46-storey Grosvenor Place is a masterwork. Its status as a new paradigm for the high-rise office tower puts it on a par with Seidler's 39-storey Riverside Tower completed in Brisbane in 1986 or his 40-storey QV1 tower projected for Perth in 1987. Common to all three is the landmark *Gestalt* of the tower-form that in each instance is derived from a paradigmatic plan; ellipsoid in the case of Grosvenor Place (54) and triangular and diamond shape respectively in the case of Riverside and QV1 (55).

Grosvenor Place represents a technical break in the progressive evolution of Seidler's isostatic architecture inasmuch as it is structured entirely about a steel frame (57), thereby dispensing, by definition, with the characteristic T-sectioned floor. This tectonic change, enforced by economy, led inevitably to the provision of suspended ceilings. Of this expediency Seidler has written:

The use of steel saved construction time and resulted in economics in height. The mass-produced floor beams are only 600 mm deep and are perforated for the passage of longitudinal services. Steel decking between the beams acts as permanent formwork for the concrete floors.[10]

It can be claimed, with Grosvenor Place as an example, that Seidler is constantly engaged in three interrelated operations: first, in an effort to render the tall office building as an integrated urban landmark; second, in a parallel endeavour to treat the landscape at grade in such a way as to create a civic arena, frequently under difficult circumstances and more often than not without those public institutions that are essential to the public realm; and finally, Seidler continually tries to create enclaves within the chaos of the modern city and to augment these enclaves where possible with subsequent developments as in the addition of the Phoenix Tower to Australia Square (56) or in the recent extension of the Riverside development in Brisbane.

Grosvenor Place is noteworthy for the harmonic volumetric rhythms that Seidler has been able to conjure out of what would otherwise be standard office subdivisions. Seidler's organisation of the available floor space as variety of freely flowing corridors, waiting spaces, foyers, conference rooms and lounges, etc., is still exceptional in today's practice and his approach is comparable to that of Herman Hertzberger's, when it comes to the provision of adaptable office space. Indeed a case can be made that Grosvenor Place posits a totally new approach to office planning in that it combines the advantages of open office floors with standard individual offices.

One further device sets Grosvenor Place apart from all previous Seidler high-rises, namely the use of deep landscaped terraces randomly disposed within the facade so as to introduce light and air into the interior and to impose a unique elevational figure on the overall form of the building (58, 59). This syncopated pattern is comparable to the plastic approach taken by

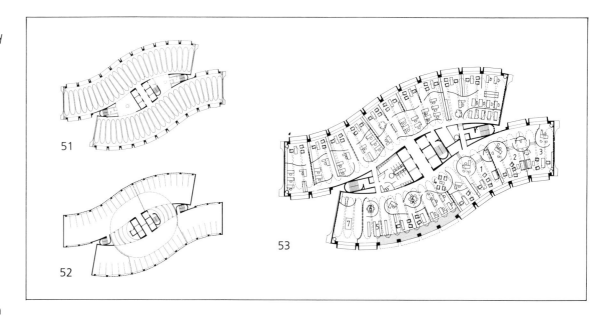

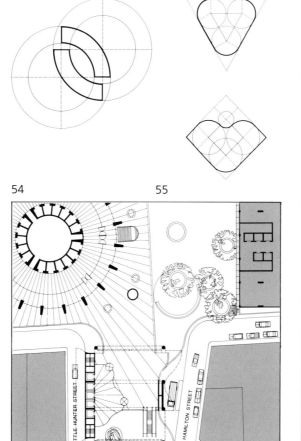

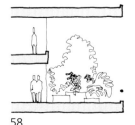

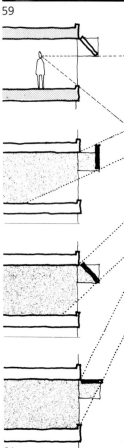

Walter Gropius and Adolf Meyer in their *Chicago Tribune* competition entry of 1922 and indeed suffers from a similar arbitrariness (60).

The plastic character of Grosvenor Place is also affected by the shifting angle of its *brise soleil* that, while set vertical on the eastern and western facades against low-angle sun, inclines to horizontal on the north where the sun is high (61). This progressive shift imparts a changing rhythm to the curvilinear mass-form according to the orientation; an ecologically responsive inflection that is complemented by a number of energy-conscious provisions, ranging from solar collectors, to off-peak thermal storage and variable volume air-conditioning.

Shell House, Melbourne, 1989

Shell House, opened in Melbourne in April 1989, once again demonstrates the architect's ability for dealing with idiosyncratic sites. Seidler's effort to provide an optimum output for both the developer and the society is evident from the diagrammatic evolution of the scheme. Thus we pass from a rectangular slab with a central core on a corner site (62), to a recognition of a restricted outlook to the north and an undesirable orientation to the west. This recognition shifts the core asymmetrically towards the north (63). From these initial stages, we pass to stage three where the architect reduces western exposure to a minimum thereby yielding a column-free office space of no more than 15 m in depth (64). Finally, stage four (65), the schematic clipped L-plan is given a curvilinear inflection in order to maximise its length as a continuously undulating east/south elevation, 91 m in length. This organically extended face permits the greatest number of offices to take advantage of the favourable orientation and of the views over both Port Phillip Bay to the south and the immediate park space, together with a distant mountain prospect to the east. The ingenuity displayed at the level of plan-form is fully complemented by an equally imaginative approach in section on an eccentric corner site that falls some two storeys, from Flinders Lane on the north to Flinders Street on the south. This dramatic change in level is further complicated by the fact that the southern frontage also slopes from east to west. Since an existing public right of way runs through the site linking the two Flinders passages, Seidler was to devise a highly ingenious form of sectional interpenetration in order to receive the various pedestrian routes into the site and at the same time to focus them about a central control point (66).

There is surely no other Seidler building in which the service and semi-public uses are so brilliantly integrated into the podium and its undercroft. This is evident from the split-level entry concourse and from the provision of a two-storey cylindrical light-court within the upper podium, the so-called levels 1 and 2. Banked escalators crank through these levels to permit continuous pedestrian movement from the highest to the lowest public floors. Seidler exploits this continuity as a way of accessing a series of public uses including a 200-seat theatre, a series of radial conference rooms and a staff cafeteria, this last being lit by the cylindrical court (67). The stacking of five floors of parking and other services such as the cafeteria kitchen beneath the 'bustle', at the top podium, testifies to Seidler's consummate skill as a planner, as do the stepped executive offices and adjoining landscaped terraces on the 27th and 28th floors (68).

Grosvenor Place was obviously the tectonic and technical model for Shell House. This largely explains the all but identical application of similar elements in both works, ranging from the radial structure to the inflected sun-screens and to the general adoption of a similar syntax.

Seidler's description of the *brise soleil* at Shell House could just as well have been written about those of Grosvenor Place:

Unprotected glass curtain walls are inappropriate in our climate with its prolonged hours of sunshine. Glass walls allow enormously high levels of radiant energy to enter and heat interior spaces which must then be cooled and the heat removed by mechanical means. External sun-control and anti-glare blades have been designed at Shell House to exclude excessive solar penetration without compromising the outlook ... The lower edge of the blade is 1900 mm above the floor level. To maximise the downward outlook, the window sill height is 400 mm above the floor with the glass extending in height to the false ceiling at 2700 mm. All windows are glazed in sealed double-pane units for both thermal and noise transmission efficiency. The outer pane consists of tinted non-reflective glass. Garden terraces are dispersed through a variety of levels in the tower. These offer a welcome relief from a totally sealed air-conditioned environment.[11]

For all these similarities Shell House presents an entirely different order from Grosvenor Place for where Grosvenor is an urban landmark visible from all sides, Shell is a *bâtiment d'angle*, a prow-like building that establishes the end of the city grid, as the land falls south and east towards the rail yards and the river in one direction and towards the Treasury and Fitzroy Gardens in the other.

Capita Building, Sydney, 1984–89

An equally empirical work, having a quite different typological base, is the 31-storey Capita Building, first projected in 1984 and finally realised in 1989. A 'shoe-horn' exercise on a ridiculously small site, Capita could hardly have been realised without the use of trussed steel mega-construction. Once again one can hardly improve on the architect's own account of the effort to find a feasible solution for a very restricted site.

Surrounded on three sides by buildings 20 and 25 floors high, left only the narrow street facade for windows and outlook, it became necessary to create an internal outlook for the 12 m-deep offices, by only covering two-thirds of the site with building and leaving the balance as urban space.

To create something more than a mere light well, the building is hollowed out for its full height by an open atrium. Changing its position from the south side to the centre and stepping up to the north, ledges are created and planted with trees and shrubs, with northern sun penetrating down the full height of the building's hollow centre.

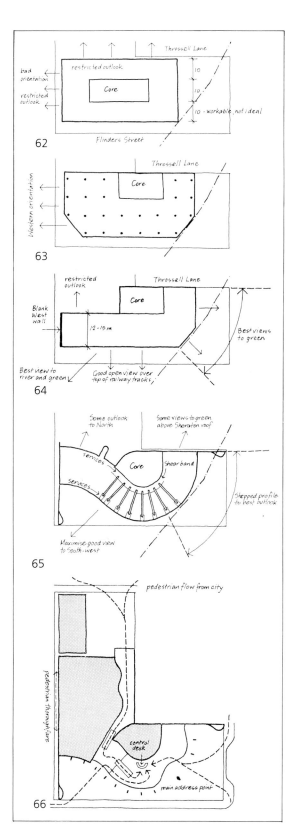

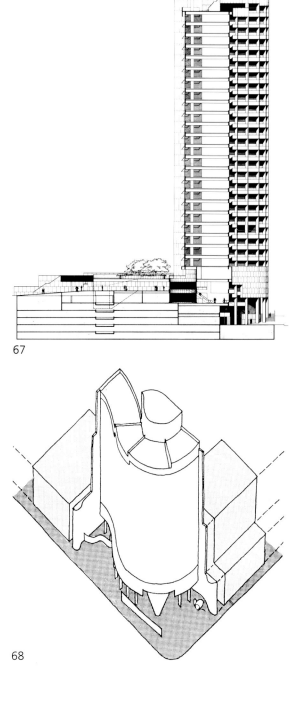

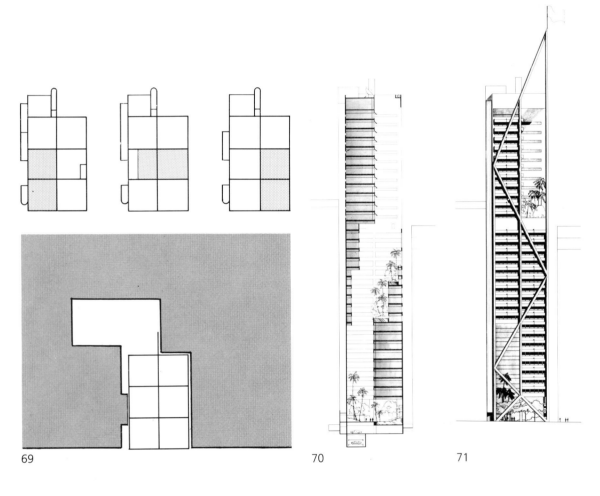

The ground level is left entirely open, becoming a landscaped pedestrian thoroughfare between streets with high palm trees, a waterfall fountain and glass-roofed public galleria space.[12]

The planning of Capita turned on resolving a geometric, light puzzle in which the six 12 m by 13 m 'squares' of a subdivided, buildable area were manipulated in section so as to shift the position of the available atria throughout the full height of building (69). The lowest atrium, treated as a high entrance against the southern boundary, shifts at mid-rise to a central square position facing north. This hollow space then steps progressively outwards towards the northern boundary, from which sun and daylight penetrate into the base of the structure. Planned on a 12 m module, each office overlooks one of the atria, all of which are landscaped with large trees (70).

Capita's megastructural frame in tubular steel was based on a more generic formulation of the same idea, as this had appeared in the 50-storey Landmark Tower projected for Brisbane at virtually the same time (72). The necessity of using steel in the development of Grosvenor Place clearly compelled Seidler to rethink his predilection for isostatic concrete construction and thus to develop a new expression based on the use of tubular steel exoskeletons of megaproportions, not unlike the suspended tubular system adopted by Norman Foster in the Hong Kong and Shanghai Bank, although clearly Seidler's bracing of a multistorey high-rise by an external megastructure clearly has other precedents. It is important to note that even this structure has an isostatic aspect to it in that the outer cage acts as a lateral space-frame, in conjunction with the secondary framing of the floors within (73).

The most important innovation of the Landmark Tower is clearly the provision of two-storey transfer trusses, every 14 floors. These trusses spanning clear over the longer mid-span in each side of the square tower serve to distribute the transfer load over the full height of the building. This distribution lessens the number of columns on the ground

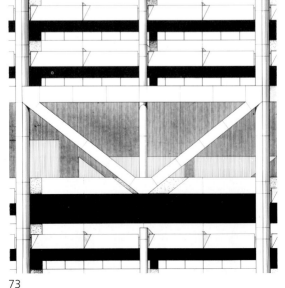

floor, thereby permitting a freer approach to the planning at grade. A similar principle makes itself manifest in the Capita Building, where a diagonally trussed exoskeleton of tubular steel runs up for the full 30 floors (71).

Phoenix Tower, Sydney, 1987
Seidler's reputation for being able to build marginal high-rise developments on extremely restricted sites led directly to the 26-storey Phoenix Tower, designed for a small site adjacent to Australia Square (74). As in the Capita Building the service core for the Phoenix Tower is located on the disadvantageous western boundary thereby allowing the rental space to address more favourable aspects on the other three sides. At the same time, Phoenix is, in many respects, a realisation of a fragment taken from the Landmark Tower. It is, in effect, the wide, mid-span bay of the Brisbane project, with transfer trusses sustaining the 22-floor office building, some 20 m above the street level. This exceptionally high portico, allowing full penetration of light at grade, and recalling the foyer of the Capita Building, is divided in sections into an upper and lower plaza level, the former linking to the elevated podium of the Australia Square development.

The synthetic typological aspect of Phoenix does not end here however, for the semi-opaque, angled eastern facade of an otherwise curtain-walled shaft is reminiscent in its undulations of the facade of the Hong Kong Club. In fact, Phoenix unites the two tectonic modes of Seidler's later career for, as the architect puts it, Phoenix combines 'stunning structural expression with curvilinear sculptural, geometric form'. This last serves to animate the volume of the atypical semipublic floors, first at the level of the second truss (level 9) where there is a restaurant (76) and then at the top of the shaft (level 18) where one finds the executive suite (75). However, the intermediate office floors are just as freely planned. All in all Phoenix is a remarkably lyrical work and far more integrated as a civic institution than the Capita Tower.

Riverside Centre, Brisbane, 1986
Under construction in downtown Brisbane from

74

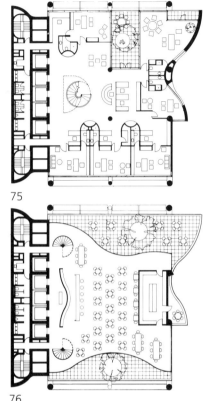
75

76

77

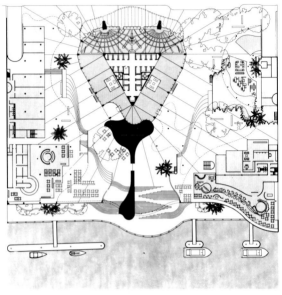

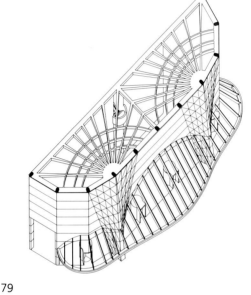

78
79

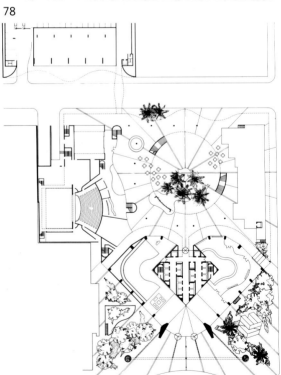

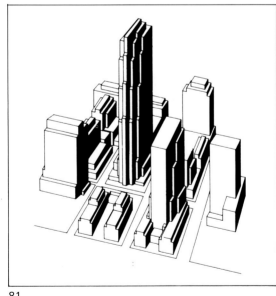

80
81

1983 to 1986, the 40-storey Riverside Centre is in some ways a synthesis of everything that Seidler has realised over the past two decades (77). Riverside is a further consummation of Seidler's capacity to handle free forms at grade and to integrate their articulation about a single shaft. Situated at a bend in the Brisbane River, Riverside Centre attempts to reorganise a large extent of the existing waterfront. Indeed Seidler tries to stretch the lateral impact of the tower to its maximum. At the same time it is the first landscaped civic complex of the last 20 years to pick up where Niemeyer and Burle Marx left off, at the apogee of their careers in the mid-1950s.

Seidler's ability to extend the plastic energy of isostatic form beyond the confines of the building itself, his capacity to activate the entire domain, takes Riverside beyond the pyrotechnic plasticity of the Hong Kong Club. Here a remarkable synthesis is established between the various dialogical vectors that determine the work. In the first place, the opposition between the tower as an urban landmark (inherently weak in Capita and Phoenix) and the horizontal extension of the site itself. In the second, the contrast between the tectonic logic of the skeleton structure and its plastic amplification as an isostatic form. Finally, there is a play between symmetry and asymmetry that activates the entire development.

Equilaterally triangular in plan, Riverside divides into an up-stream and down-stream aspect, in relation to a bisecting southwest/northeast axis (78). While this biaxial symmetry helps to establish Riverside as the symbolic centre of the downtown, the asymmetrical architecture of the waterfront opens the site to a panorama of the river as it moves away from the bridge towards the confluence of waterways bounding the city. This relation between tower and river is comprised of two movements: on the one hand, the centripetal compression of the tower, which seems to draw everything into its vortex; on the other, the centrifugal motion that radiates its energy out from the tower so as to animate the carefully contoured layers of the site. Riverside comprises a dialogue between the symmetrical, crystalline form of the tower and the asymmetrical, organic form of the site. Appropriately enough these 'countertheses' attain their synthesis in the monumental glazed canopy that announces the principal entrance. The dyadic principle does not end here however, for the canopy itself assumes a bipolar character, in its suspension from the two hyperbolic pilotis that flank the main entrance. Isostatic rib-lines radiate out from the centroids of these pilotis to support the ceiling of the foyer and celebrate its monumental character (79).

QV1, Perth, 1987–91

Planned around a diamond-shaped core the 40-storey QV1 Tower, projected in 1987, is in many respects a variation of Riverside (80). By modifying the equilateral, triangular plan to a 90-degree apex facing south, Seidler was able to increase the amount of office space having a prime outlook without unduly exposing the mass to low angle sun. It was, nonetheless, still necessary to add large side-baffles to Seidler's standard *brise soleil* in order to exclude western and eastern sun. The transverse office section of QV1 is otherwise identical to that adopted for Grosvenor Place and Shell House.

As expansive at grade as Riverside and far more ambitious than the circumstantially restricted plazas of Australia Square and MLC, the organisation of the QV1 site comes closest to the Rockefeller Centre paradigm (81). This exceptional civic potential largely derives from the amplitude of the site itself and from the presence of an extensive commercial frontage in conjunction with two major public institutions: a 700-seat proscenium stage and a 250-seat experimental theatre. As in Seidler's previous high-rise developments, the plaza space at grade is organised on more than one level and while focused about a central fountain court, affords many alternative routes and vistas.

Urban Fragments: Darling Harbour, Sydney 1986–89

Despite his intense concern for the public realm Seidler has received few opportunities to develop his civic vision at a truly urban scale. Aside from low-rise housing schemes, there have been only two instances of recent date when Seidler has had an opportunity to design an extensive urban fragment. The first of these came with the New World Development of 1982 when, in collaboration with Van Sitteren & Partners, Seidler was asked to design a city-in-miniature for Singapore, comprising a 40-storey cylinder, accommodating an hotel with offices above and three 20-storey residential curved slabs (82). These last were organised as three circumferential slabs pin-wheeling about an open centre; a kind of minimalist variation on the *bloc a redent* employed by Le Corbusier in his famous Obus plan for Algiers. In this particular instance, the lower two floors of Seidler's arabesque were occupied by public uses of various kinds, foyers, retail space, cinemas, etc., with their freely planned lobbies opening out to flowing organic landscape on either side. While the same dense landscape treatment is a hallmark of Seidler's work, only in this instance do we find it extended over two large city blocks.

Thus the New World Development anticipates the basic strategy that would have been employed in Seidler's second extensive urban work, the Hotel–Casino complex designed in 1986 for the American entrepreneur Donald Trump, as part of the Darling Harbour development in Sydney (83). It is regrettable that this proposal will not be executed since the density and ingenuity displayed in its organisation makes it an exemplary work. The reparatory aim of this urban microcosm was to bridge over the expressway currently separating the city from the harbour, thereby allowing pedestrians to gain easy access to the water's edge. The primary urban design goals are explicitly stated in Seidler's design criteria.

The building mass should generally rise from the waterfront to the city edge. Both hotel and casino entrances should address the city and have prominent and separate access from Sussex Street. The Darling Harbour waterfront is to be an active pedestrian promenade, lined with people-related facilities. Pyrmont Bridge is to be part of an upper level of the pedestrian promenade and must be connected to the waterfront.[13]

82

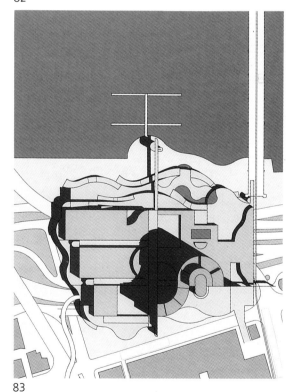
83

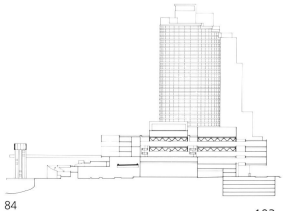
84

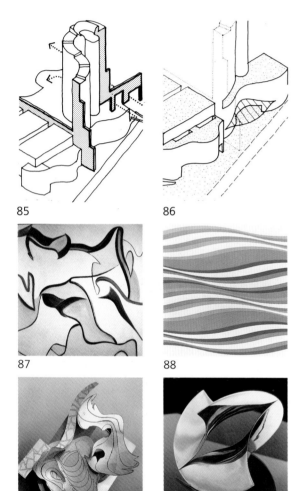

The overall morphology and distribution of the scheme patently derives from these goals and from Seidler's sensitive attitude towards the maximisation of desirable views. This last was of such importance as to lead him to design a single loaded corridor scheme for the hotel tower, thereby giving an optimum prospect to every room. At the same time, the huge windowless bulk of the casino was ingeniously broken up into three hangar-like masses, with the clear span of each module bridging the expressway beneath (84).

The natural opposition between these two forms and uses, the glazed sinuous tower versus the blank orthogonal hangar, initiated the dyadic theme of the whole complex, geometrically echoing the range of different morphologies employed on the opposite side of the harbour. This dyadic composition was reinforced by two gigantic 'blade' walls, set at right angles to each other, the one running east/west, paralleling the line of the Pyrmont Bridge, the other responding in a north/south direction so as to afford a terminating gateway to Pyrmont Bridge (85). Where the first wall served to differentiate between the hotel and the casino, the second established a more fundamental boundary between the city and the harbour, thereby converting the entire complex into a kind of extended bridgehead.

The other oppositional device was the transverse section with the masses stepping up from the water's edge on the west, to attain their highest point along Sussex Street thereby reinforcing the eastern limit of the site. This boundary was also doubly articulated so as to announce the respective approaches to the hotel and the casino; the hotel proclaiming its presence through a glazed canopy over the street while the casino cantilevered out to form a solid *porte-cochère* (86).

The morphology of the multiple landscaped terraces, stepping down to the water's edge were to have their independent genesis, as Seidler readily conceded, in the hard edge linearity running through the last 30 years of modern art, as is evident say in the work of such artists as Willem de Kooning (87), Frank Stella (89), Sol Lewitt (91) and Bridget Riley (88). Thus while the ultimate source of this free form is still Brazilian, the specific geometries employed, the cadences and exfoliation of the fugal elements all find their method, if not their deepest inspiration, in recent examples of Minimalist or Concrete Art. For Seidler this last covers a wide range extending from the ex-Bauhausler Josef Albers on the one hand to the American Minimalist Charles Perry (90) on the other. Perhaps one of the most remarkable aspects of Seidler's Darling Harbour proposal resides in the way in which its overall morphology is integrated with the organic trajectories of the expressways running beneath the podium and interwoven with the access ramps feeding cars, taxis and buses in and out of the undercroft. That this whole amounted to a wilful overcoming of a man-made barrier is borne out by Seidler's account of the way in which he maximised pedestrian access across and through the site (92).

Public open space should be regarded as a major unifying device for the whole development and the element which ties the Waterfront Promenade to the city street fabric. Pedestrians will be using the complex for many reasons and in differing ways. The provision of various 'pathways' to and through the site is considered to be of paramount importance to the ultimate success of the development.

The major problem to be addressed is that of bridging the expressways and the inherent corollary of moving large numbers of people vertically through the equivalent of four storeys in height . . . (datum has been carefully fixed to give minimum expressway clearance and to keep the scale of vertical circulation to an absolute minimum) . . . The Main Plaza stretches east to west across the site and functions as the primary public link between the city on one side, the Waterfront Promenade on the other and the hotel and casino between . . . The edges of the plaza are defined continuously by varied retail outlets, an entry to the hotel, the monorail station and landscaping. Curvilinear shopfronts and parapets provide a changing, tightly framed vista across to Pyrmont and assist in drawing the public toward the water.

Upon arrival at an elevated viewing promontory over Darling Harbour pedestrians then have a variety of choices, to descend directly to Pyrmont Bridge and/or the Waterfront Promenade via a series of cascading ramps, stairs and lifts. Retail facilities are interspersed at various terraces with fountains and landscaping thus providing a gradual, relaxed and interesting transition to the Promenade.[14]

What Seidler neglects to mention here is that this progression would have entailed an escalator rise through two full floors in order to attain the principal entry foyer of the hotel and the casino (93). Seidler's brilliance at this juncture is displayed in the cross-views and overlooks that serve to unify the volume of this double height space, while providing lounges that overlook the casino and the hotel ballroom. Suspended above the main plaza level was a mezzanine accommodating specialist restaurants on the hotel side and gaming levels on the casino side.

Two received 'types' were to prove essential to the design of this complex and their presence merits some comment. The first of these is the provision of interstitial service floors between the stacked gaming levels of the casino, a fairly extravagant sectional provision that has its origin in Louis Kahn's Salk Laboratory in 1959 (94). Such a provision is justified here on two grounds, first because a certain structural depth was required to bridge the expressways and second, the need for full height interstitial space in order to service and survey the activity on the gaming floors below (95). The second generic type is the atrium hotel as pioneered by John Portman in the Peachtree Centre Hotel Atlanta in 1961 (96); evident here in the projected 27-storey semi-cylindrical hotel atrium.

Seidler's vaulted light-scoop, first devised for Waverley Civic Centre, reappears here as an honorific element, indicating the main entrances of both the casino and the hotel. Similarly the floor section and sunscreening are modelled after the devices employed for Grosvenor Place and Shell House (97), only here the *brise soleil* extends for the full floor, while horizontal screening is effected by a perforated grille (98).

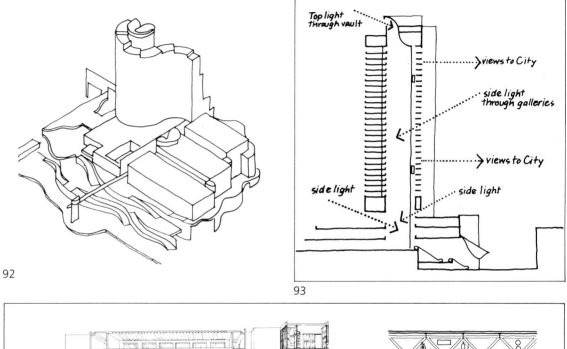

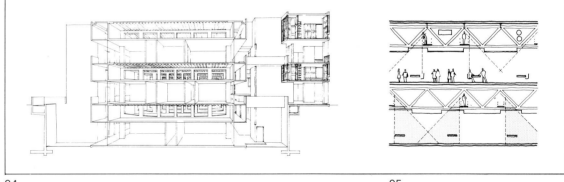

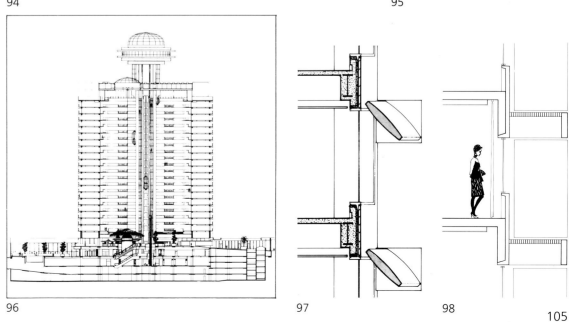

99

100

Late Domesticity

While it is obviously premature to assess the total achievement of an architect who is still practising, a comprehensive overview nonetheless demands that an attempt be made to situate the work within a larger perspective. At 68, Seidler patently belongs to the first generation of the American Bauhaus, and his indebtedness to Walter Gropius, Josef Albers and Marcel Breuer in this regard is inescapable. Unlike Breuer, Seidler has had the good fortune to mature in a more consistent way as a public architect, so much so that a decisive break seems now to separate the lightly cast domesticity of his early career from the bold, audacious, and decidedly sculptural character of his later houses. This difference is evident from the character of his most recent residences, such as the Hannes (99), Mitchell and Hamilton houses, that unlike his early domestic work, display a bold and massive plasticity. In each instance the organic masses seem to fuse naturally with the topography of the surroundings. Nevertheless these later houses are removed from both the tectonic order of Breuer's New England houses and the ineffable cubistic form of Le Corbusier's Purist Villas. We are moreover equally removed from the Wrightian heritage that runs through the works of Richard Neutra and Rudolf Schindler and reappears in the later domestic culture of Southern California, to culminate in the Case Study Houses of Charles Eames, Craig Ellwood and Pierre Koenig.

Seidler's recent houses are closely linked to his larger public work, with the result that they often appear overscaled and rhetorical (99). More often than not they seem to be extracts from a larger sequence so that they are more convincing when the unit in question is part of a larger whole as in the stacked beach apartments known as La Plage; 1988 (100). In this instance, as opposed to the individual houses, the sinusoidal balconies combine together to form a convincing overall form.

Part 2
Assessment: History, Art and Modernity

Seidler has been explicit about his debt to history, citing for example the geometrical schema of Borromini's San Carlo alle Quatro Fontane in Rome (101, 102, 103). However, his affinity for this work goes well beyond the dyadic planimetric scheme that is reinterpreted in so many of his later buildings. Thus the undulating facade of Borromini's masterwork finds itself discretely reinterpreted in the elevation of Seidler's Hong Kong Club (to mention only one instance) while the coffered ellipsoid dome of this same church is translated, via Nervi, into the isostatic ceilings of Seidler's public spaces. This double Roman debt, to Borromini and Nervi, is very evident in the foyer and *porte-cochère* of the Riverside Tower.

The Baroque in general has patently served as an inspiration for Seidler's later career, just as the Portuguese, Brazilian Baroque of Antonio Francisco Lisboa, the so-called Estilo Aleijadinho in Minas Gerais was to serve as a latent influence on Niemeyer's architecture some 40 years ago. Borromini and Guarini are jointly detectable in Seidler's later work as is Balthazar Neumann's Vierzehnheiligen Church of 1753. At the same time, Seidler's constant recourse to ribbed ceilings owes something to the late Gothic interior drawn from a wide range of examples extending from Prague to Segovia. At an urbanistic level Seidler's references are understandably more general, ranging from the urban *scena* of the Baroque display city to the Mediterranean hill town.

As far as the modern era is concerned Seidler's debt to Breuer and Niemeyer is by now obvious. More ambiguous however is his relationship to Le Corbusier, for aside from his extensive use of *brise soleil* and his penchant for *pilotis*, it is to be doubted whether the Purist master has ever served as a model for Seidler. This much is suggested by his seeming indifference to the intercolumnar/planar play of the Corbusian *plan libre*. Where Seidler's plans are free, they are liberated in a much more volatile and volumetric sense than that which is apparent in Le Corbusier's canonical works of the 1920s. Moreover, the frontal layering of French Classicism is always latent in Le Corbusier and this sensibility is largely absent from Seidler's architecture. Nevertheless Seidler does seem to be indebted to the Structurally–Rationalist line extending from Viollet-le-Duc to Auguste Perret. The common denominator here is of course the tectonic use of concrete and not the axial order to be found in Perret's work. The other late Modernist to whom Seidler is obviously indebted is Louis Kahn, particularly for the separation of servant and served services, as evidenced in the Canberra offices and elsewhere.

It says something for Seidler's roots in the New Bauhaus that his relationship to Modern art is of a dense and complex nature. Profoundly influenced by Albers' colour and design courses, given in Black Mountain College, when Seidler was a student there in the summer of 1946, Seidler has often developed the plastic form of his later work about interlocking matrices, the roots of which may be found in Albers' play with geometrical progressions and inverted symmetries, as evident say in such works as *Vice Versa* (1943) or *Despite Straight Lines* (104). As far as the organic compositions of Seidler's later landscapes are concerned, the architect, as we have already seen, was as much influenced by Kandinsky, Miro and Calder as by the Minimalist artists we have already mentioned.

There are few contemporary architects of Seidler's stature who are so overtly involved with contemporary art and when one looks for a comparable figure, one is compelled to return to the 1950s and to the career of the Venezuelan architect Carlos Raoul Villaneuva. What the two men have in common goes well beyond the role art plays in their work, for the art they favour covers a similar range of expression, running from 'concrete art' to more freely expressive forms of abstraction as manifest for example in the work of Alexander Calder, who was a seminal artist for both. The parallels do not end here however, for where Villaneuva employed Venezuelan or Latin American representatives of the Concrete Art Movement, such as Mateo Manaure and Pascual Navarro, Seidler has consistently gravitated towards American artists whose work is a continuation of a similar cultural spectrum. To this end he regularly employs late 'concrete' sculptors such as Norman Carlberg and Charles Perry. At the same time the American Frank Stella has come to assume Calder's role, in that he has been the author of most of the iconic centrepieces hung in Seidler's later work. It is hardly a surprise to find that Stella and Carlberg come from the same Albers school, namely, the department of Fine Art at Yale.

It is difficult to situate Seidler within the pluralist spectrum of current production, for to think of him as nothing more than a latterday Modernist is to fail to do justice to either the fertility of his work or to the critical ethos of his stand against the 'degeneracy' of Post-Modernism. Australia has been a fortunate redoubt for Seidler in this regard, for while it has never afforded him a congenial milieu, it has nonetheless given him an opportunity to establish his own mode of expression. Above all it has guaranteed him a space apart in the antipodes; a space that has nurtured his creative psyche in such a way as to allow him to operate both within and without his own moment in history.

Australia's relative remoteness has afforded Seidler a certain isolation from the oppressive conditioning of international media and this has guaranteed him a kind of freedom, even if the price at times has been to have to deal with all but impermeable levels of local indifference. Much of this indifference may have had its origin, as Philip Drew has pointed out, in the fact that Seidler was not to concern himself with creating a recognisably 'Australian' idiom. As Drew writes:

The self-consciously 'Australian' architects were just as international as Seidler. Where they differed was on sources and here Seidler was at a distinct advantage, because his devotion to Modern architecture was based on a heritage won by personal experience, rather than a tasteful eclecticism.

101

102

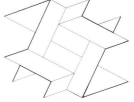

104

Seidler was not alone in bringing Modern architecture and Bauhaus values to Australia, but he must be considered its leading exponent. If he wrote less than Robin Boyd, he surely surpassed him in the quantity and quality of his architecture. It was not until the mid-1960s that Seidler's ascendancy began to be challenged by a rising generation of young Australian architects. His reputation, and indeed, importance, rests on his relationship to post-war Modern architecture, his achievement is that of a gifted disciplinarian whose work in Australia served as a model of the new architecture, but in its forms, and in its representation of the ethical basis of Modernism.[15]

Seidler is surely justified in insisting on the necessity for continuing with the creative evolution of modern culture, as opposed to the superficial eclectic historicising of a great deal of so-called Post-Modern theory and practice. And while it is possible to detect a certain *naïveté* in his implicit advocacy of the 'open city' he surely has sufficient reason to challenge the reactionary arguments that have overtaken much of the current debate on the contemporary city. We can do no better than cite his own words in this regard, for they go right to the heart of the present controversy, in attacking the Neo-Biedermeier ideology that aspires to overcome the urban aporias of our time through a mandatory return to continuous street frontages.

To demonstrate the speed and effectiveness with which the media today disseminate these dissenting notions, one can cite the evidence offered by authorities in Melbourne, Australia, in their objectives to a large city building. They quote, verbatim, the recently proposed San Francisco plan and insist that this reactionary set of new rules imported from the USA be adopted, such as: prohibiting buildings with flat roofs, any blank walls and calling for 'a generous use of decorative embellishments'. To demonstrate what benefits are offered in return, these decorations are even allowed to protrude outside the zoning envelope. The San Francisco plan requires buildings to be 'shaped to appear delicate and of complex visual imagery'. Worst of all there is a dictate to 'return to the street wall', i.e. the constructing of 'street fronting bases' for tall buildings which are to have distinctive tops and tapering shafts. The rules in fact outlaw towers reaching the ground, with limited site cover.

To enforce such rules of this or any other persuasion is absurd and contrary to fundamental freedom of action, freedom for the advancement and development of architecture. To stifle creativeness by law is intolerable. We should want no part of a system in which bureaucrats become powerful arbiters of taste, imposing a dictatorship over the language of form.

The irrationality of insisting that urban development built to an index of 14 to 1, shall have 100 per cent site cover is obvious. To allow an increase in the population on a city block of that extent and then strangulate pedestrian circulation by restricting it to 3 m wide footpaths is inhuman and unworkable. And it is all apparently done for no other reason than a misplaced and misguided romanticism trying to re-create 18th- and 19th-century urban patterns with long-gone low-population densities, when buildings were rarely more than three or four storeys high . . .

It is socially irresponsible to build to high indices of 12 or 14 unless there is a limit on site cover of no more than 25 to 35 per cent. This should be so not only for the sake of the health and clarity of the inevitable huge structure that results, but also to generate breathing space for the additional thousands of people who work in such buildings; to create genuinely useful, new, open or sheltered urban spaces – places of repose and recreation – much-needed open public space on private land.[16]

This entire passage, including even the implicit contradiction of creating public space on private land, attempts to transcend the degenerate prospect of the scenographic city as the triumph of Disneyworld over everyday life. Indirectly Seidler implies a whole range of options lying between the superimposition of the tower/podium pattern and the free-standing high-rise planted in the midst of a semi-public enclave. In this critique he correctly opposes the kitsch streetfront that evokes the appearance of the traditional city without its substance to the *dystopic* modern city assembled out of a haphazard arrangement of free-standing towers. That these are polar extremes should go without saying for between these extremes other options exist.

Aside from his urban ambitions Seidler has graced the metropoli of Australia with some of the finest high-rises built anywhere; skyscrapers that may be readily compared to the best Neo-Miesian work of SOM in the 1950s and even to the canonical works put out by the Mies studio itself. Nonetheless, these works are still spot developments and as such they can hardly compensate for the lack of lateral continuity in the metropolitan fabric. Seidler, like Niemeyer before him, can only regret the general absence of an informed patronage that remains as before, the precondition for an urban civilisation. One can only look back with nostalgia at such figures as Jacob Fugger, Cardinal Richilieu and Baron Haussman, or to the patronage of James Wood in Bath or Thomas Cubitt in London, all of whom were speculators, but in a more urbane and cultivated climate in comparison to the general level of barbarism that surrounds us today. The restrictions imposed by current forms of abstract, multi-national investment tend to have a subtle impact at an almost intangible level, so that an architect of Seidler's capacity and experience remains only partially used by the promoters of contemporary development. Whether he admits to it or not, the severe conditions imposed by speculation set very severe limits on the socio-spatial and syntactical potential of architecture as a civic art.

Seidler's ability as a teacher as evidenced in the studios he has given at Harvard in 1977 (105) and at the University of New South Wales in 1980 (106), gives some indication of his still untapped capacity as a civic architect, as does the art centre that he has recently projected for Waverley. In each

Seidler's studio: jury presentation at the Graduate School of Design, 1977 (Jury members: Jerzy Soltan, Peter Blake, Edward Seckler, Werner Seligmann)

'Centre of Australian Studies' at Harvard project by G. Wiedemann

105

106

Seidler's studio at the University of NSW, 1980

'New School of Architecture' project by Mark Edwards Butler

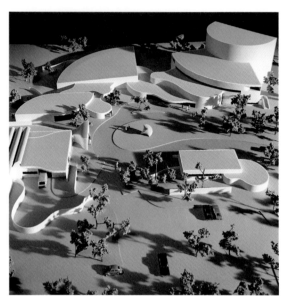

107

instance one observes the full semantic range of Seidler's maturity, the command over assertive geometries and dynamic structural forms, the full deployment of isostatic spans relieved by sculptural vaults and monitor roofs, the skilful balancing of rotund forms by undulating walls and, last but not least, the fusion of the rhythmic whole into the topography. The Waverley Art Centre (107) is Seidler at his best and one only wishes that Australia will have further occasion to use him now, while he is at the height of his power.

So much has been made, at times, of Seidler's supposed lack of originality that some strictures are in order about the nature of this tendentious term, for what, after all, do we intend by the value that we compulsively ascribe to the idea of origin. Indeed one might claim that in being so faithful to his origin Seidler has remained only too original, for while he has adhered to certain basic principles he has constantly elaborated them in unexpected ways. Like the Dutch architect Herman Hertzberger, he has taken a specific master as his point of departure and has laid over this base his own intrinsic patterns, so that the original is transcended rather than simply repeated or wilfully rejected. Thus where Hertzberger was to reinterpret Aldo Van Eyck through the filter of a specifically Dutch heritage, Seidler would enrich the Neo-Bauhaus paradigm that he received from Breuer, through the catalysts of Niemeyer and Nervi. What emerges from this hybrid transformation is not some arbitrary eclecticism, determined by picturesque values and stylistic simulation, but rather an entirely new work, methodically wrought for a totally other time.

If there is another Modern master whose work Seidler's architecture unconsciously recalls, then it is surely that of Erich Mendelsohn; for while there is nothing overtly expressionist about Seidler's architecture or, conversely, anything tectonic about Mendelsohn's form, the two share in common a mutual preoccupation with the 'city crown', that is to say, with the notion that every urban building must somehow assume the burden of the entire city; as though every commission is potentially a 'miniature city' standing in place of the absent or ruined metropolis that surrounds it. We could not be further here from the normative city of the Neue Sachlichkeit, or from the reciprocity that obtained in the traditional city between the one-off monument and the organic fabric, a difference that was consecrated, so to speak, by the institutional status of the former. In contrast to both these modes Seidler's urban high-rises tend to be singular statements derived from the empirical conditions of the site, just as Mendelsohn's Berlin buildings were uniquely tailored to their situations (108). For all the constancy of Seidler's principles and methods it is this empirical singularity that finally separates his later work from Neo-Miesianism and from his own earlier *Sachlich* tendencies.

If Seidler is, as Philip Drew has suggested, 'the last of the machine age architects', he has also remained consistently responsive to the impact of topography and light and in this sense Seidler's Modernism has always been regionally inflected. In this respect he remains close to the best of the International Style architects of the 1930s and 1940s; close, that is, to such figures as Niemeyer, Terragni and Sert. Thus unlike the Australian regionalists, whose output has varied in quality from romantic pastiche to sublime invention, Seidler's architecture has always maintained a tension between the universal paradigm and its local variation. This dialectic is always there, wherein the one can be read against the other and vice versa and this oscillation has helped to save him from lapsing into sentimentality. He has sought a modern building culture for Australia, that would as it were, come into being on its own. This precept is perhaps most evident in his Hillside Villas, realised in Queensland in 1982, for although this complex seeks to integrate itself with the landfall and the light, there is little that is folkish about its expression. This resistance stems in the end from a constructional ethic that in the last analysis, is the unvarying precept that informs all of Seidler's work. This ethic was forcibly reasserted in a paper that he delivered in Chicago in 1986.

108

Free rein must be given to the expression of the laws of nature – not what is imagined to be so by many structurally naive architects, but the unassailable physical truth of statics. Richness of expression can result from such a search, which will have that irreplaceable quality of longevity, of remaining valid, being born of the immutable and irrevocable truth of nature.

The approach to constructional systems has been far too simplistic, accepting any dull repetitiveness to be economically valid. Just as the revivalist architecture at the end of the last century was out of tune with the emerging industrial means, so I believe architects are not taking the lead in today's technological and manpower conditions with its new construction methodologies. This is why we are losing the grip on vital decision-making and are being replaced by hustling technicians. To design a tall building today which simply takes too long to build is a self-arresting, hollow victory which remains on paper.

It is our task to maximise systems of mechanisation appropriate and in tune with the particular task. Even though these must vary in different socio-economic and industrial climates, they must not stop at considerations of structure and covering only, as is so often the limit of prevalent thought, but also encompass simultaneously integral solutions to the problems posed by all services without the usual nightmarish afterthought complications of most modern buildings.

True modern architecture is not dead, as some will have us believe. We have hardly started to explore the potential of its methodology. The high principles and clear moral consequentiality of the pioneers needs to be constantly interpreted anew. They demanded basic integrity and an intrinsic honesty of approach. Only by making these part of our work will frontiers of development be pushed forward.[17]

This is Seidler at the end and also, paradoxically, at the beginning of the long march that dates back to the citation at the head of this essay and then runs forward, with ever quickening pace to carry in its wake Wagner, Perret, Mies, and Kahn, to culminate today, perhaps, on its leading edge, in the poetic traces one may detect in the finer works of so-called Hi-Tech architecture. This is the long haul of Modernism to which Seidler remains committed. It is a trajectory that as far as we can judge is by no means over, for although the traditional city is lost, the culture of building still remains.

Notes
1. Louis Sullivan, *The Tall Office Building Artistically Considered*, 1896.
2. Horwitz Publications, Sydney, 1963.
3. 'Collaboration with Nervi', *(RAIA) Architectural Bulletin*, January 1980.
4. *Engineering News Record (USA)*, June 1977.
5. Peter Blake, *Harry Seidler, Australian Embassy, Paris*, 1979, p. 55.
6. Philip Drew, *A + U (Architecture and Urbanism)*, Japan, November 1984, pp. 43–4.
7. *New South Wales Building*, Sydney, February 1987, p. 28.
8. *A + U (Architecture and Urbanism)*, Japan, September 1986, p. 79.
9. loc. cit.
10. Consultant's Report on the Rocks Gateway Project to Kern Konstruction Pty Ltd, June 1982.
11. Consultant's Report on the Rocks Gateway Project to Kern Konstruction Pty Ltd, June 1982.
12. Consultant's Report to Capita, May 1985.
13. Kern–Trump Casino Competition Report to the NSW Darling Harbour Authority, December 1986.
14. Kern–Trump Casino Competition Report to the NSW Darling Harbour Authority, December 1986.
15. Philip Drew, 'Ethic and Form: The Architecture of Harry Seidler, 1948–1980', *SD 81/02 (Space Design)*, pp. 89–90.
16. Theme address to The Third International Conference on Tall Buildings, Chicago, January 1986.
17. Lecture to the Royal Institute of British Architects, London, 1984 (published in *Transactions 5*, vol. 3, no. 1).

Australia Square
Sydney, 1961–67

'... The challenge is to elevate commercial building into significant architecture. It was my first chance to work with Nervi in Rome. He taught me how to build – construction took only four working days per floor including the exterior!

Harry Cobb in New York introduced me to the lighting genius, Richard Kelly, and through him to Edison Price, with whom we worked for many years on lighting our public spaces...'

This first of Sydney's tall office towers became reality due to the foresight and energetic enterprise of the Dutch immigrant developer, G.J. Dusseldorp, and his 'Lend Lease' corporation. It took some years to amalgamate a whole city block of over 30 different properties and absorb internal lanes so that a comprehensive development could be planned.

A 13-storey office building was built first along one edge of the property, while the rest of the site was being acquired.

The 50-storey circular tower was then planned, occupying only 25 per cent of the site with a total floor space of 12 times the site area. The remainder of the city block was given over to the public; newly gained usable outdoor space which is much needed in the otherwise congested centre of the city. This space between the two buildings on two levels is Australia Square, which since its completion has become the most popular urban space in Sydney.

It is an area of recreation where food is available and people can sit between trees and near a central fountain. Curved screen walls, being raised, separate the space visually and physically from traffic and parked cars in the surrounding streets. It is an area for people to linger and relax, attracting large lunchtime crowds. The square shows that the project fulfils an age-old need for people in a city to find areas of retreat and intimacy.

The upper square which surrounds the main entrance to the tower is a more formal area than the lower one. It is the public space housing the large artworks of the project and is visually part of the monumental lobby.

The circular form of the 50-storey office tower was arrived at by a process of elimination. Any rectangular building of such height and extent placed on this site would inevitably have created objectionable canyon-type spaces in conjunction with existing adjacent buildings which follow the rectangular street pattern. This would result in poor lighting and crowded appearance. By placing a square or rectangular building on the diagonal, much better open space results.

These considerations lead logically toward a circular building which creates more desirable space relationships toward adjacent properties and allows a maximum of light into surrounding streets. Wide, open spaces result outside the window areas of such a building which comes close to neighbouring structures at one tangential point only.

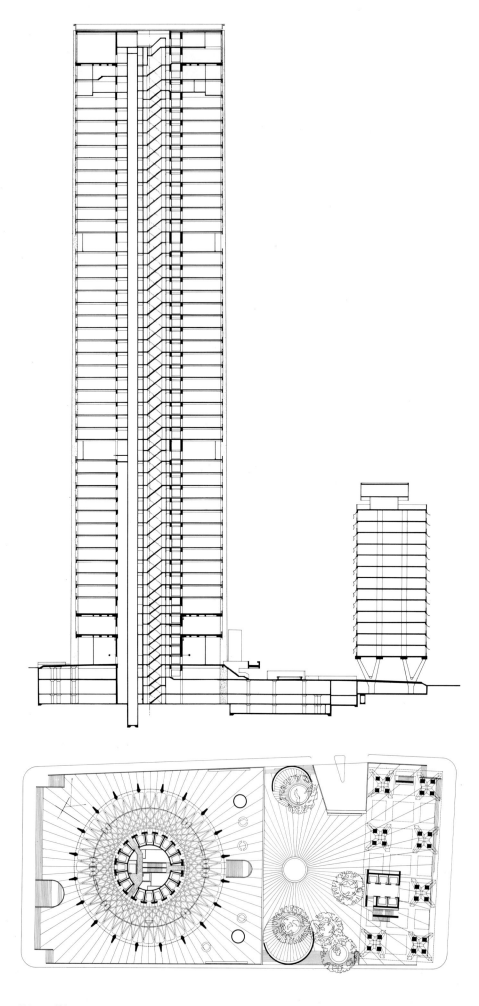

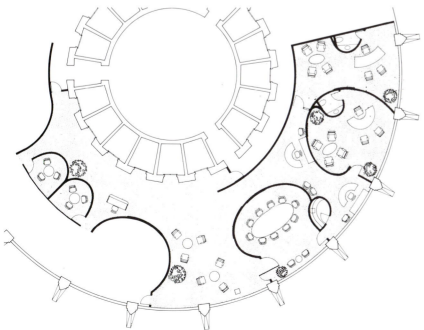

'... The ambitious client sent me around the world to find a suitable sculptor. We visited Henry Moore, Noguchi, Bertoia – but finally it was Calder – to me he is a great artist because of the joy of life that his forms express. He is the playful engineer, in his mobile constructions and his 'circus' – such fun! – and at the same time – such minimal statements. With just one piece of bent wire he can say so much and give so much pleasure and yet – with so little effort. I also love his big structural–monumental exterior works which have an immense tension about them, the way elements oppose each other and the way they interact with architecture ...'

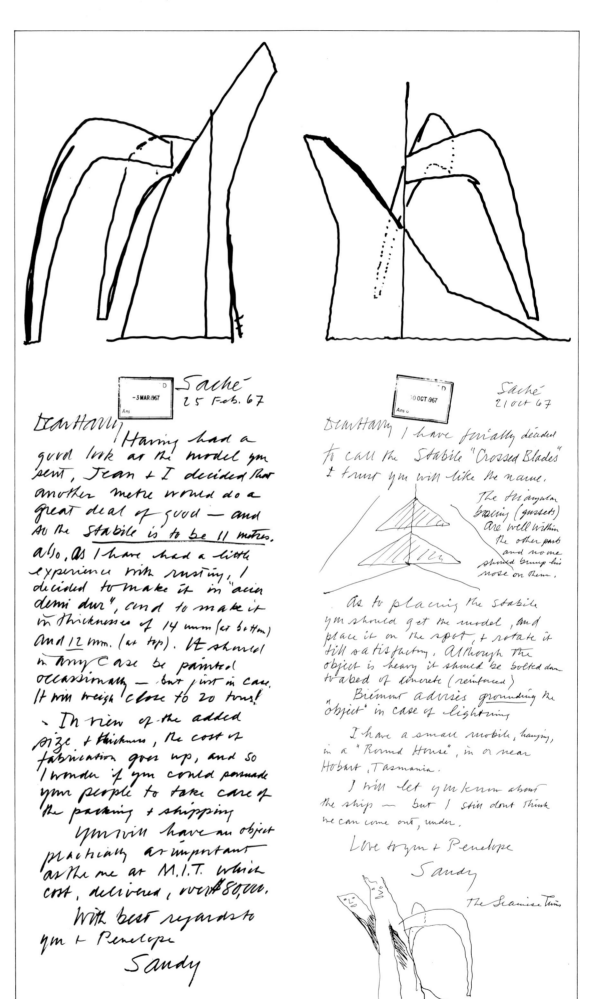

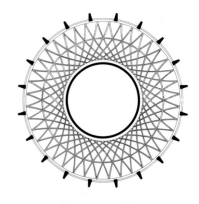

Structurally the circular form of the tower is most efficient in resisting horizontal wind loads. The lightweight concrete building is 42 m in diameter with a clear span of 11 m from core to perimeter. This configuration lends itself ideally to speedy, repetitive and mechanised component construction. Every elevator shaft, every radial beam and column is identical. The projecting columns diminish in size as the building rises. Precast permanent formwork for columns and spandrels has an exterior surface of white quartz chips.

The building has a usable floor space to service core ratio of 80:20. (This economical ratio was achieved in all subsequent office towers.)

The ceiling of the lobby is formed by the ribbed floor system employed for the first two floors of the tower.

The requirement for heavy load carrying capacity of the two special-uses floors above was solved by means of interlocking curved ribs. In curvature, taper, and variation in width, the ribs follow the stress conditions in the floors and also form a beautiful pattern on the ceilings. They were designed in collaboration with Pier Luigi Nervi, whose ferro-cement principle was employed in the construction of the ribbed floors.

Sequence of pre-casting ferro-cement pans
1. Rough brick mould
2. Brick mould rendered
3. Master mould poured
4. Master mould removed and turned upside-down
5. Ferro-cement pans mass produced on master mould

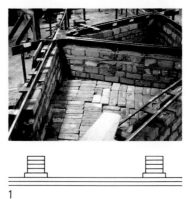

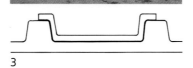
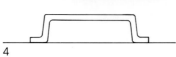

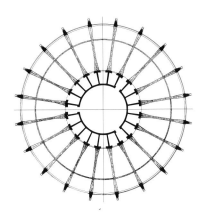

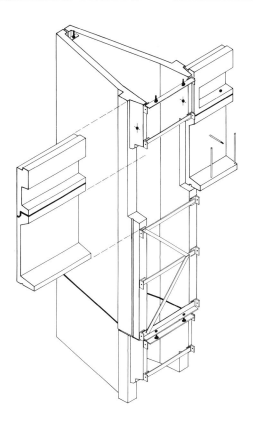
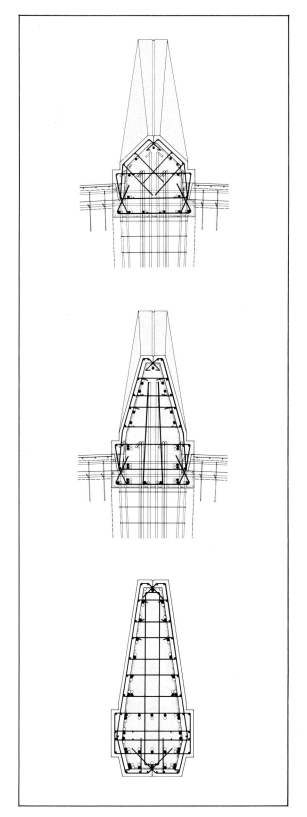

Exhibition Pavilion
Hyde Park, Sydney, 1970–72

This demountable pavilion, erected in a park to house an exhibition, covers a large area with a network of triangulated steel pipes, mechanically joined to each other by aluminium connectors.

The pavilion is 50 m long and of varying width and height up to 12 m. Its structure consists of a single layer of 50 mm-diameter pipes which take on a double curvature (hyperboloid) and is thereby made rigid due to this form's torsional resistance.

The geometry of the hyperboloid is such that its surface is generated by skewed straight lines drawn between points on opposing parallel circles. This property was exploited in the design so that the surface consisted of approximately 1500 straight tubes.

A luminous exhibition area results by covering the frame with a translucent, tough woven plastic material.

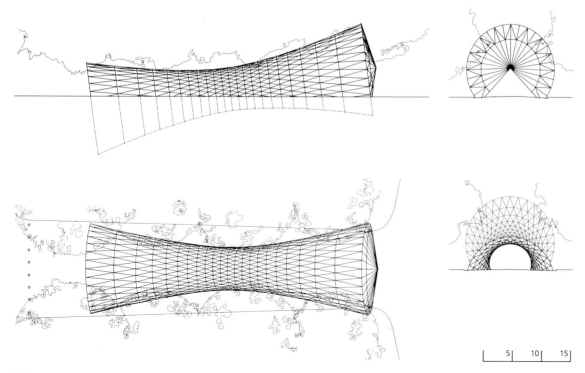

'... An almost instant building – it took only a week to put up and had a glowing interior ...'

Trade Group Offices
Canberra, 1970–74

Built along Kings Avenue which forms one side of Canberra's 'Parliamentary triangle', this complex of government offices is designed to house separate but related Federal Trade departments. It was built in two stages, accommodating a working population of 2000 people in the first stage and 1000 in the second.

The architectural aims were an expression of strength, simplicity and considering the location, an appropriate level of formality.

In addition to flexible, general office space, a computer centre, conference hall–theatrette and a cafeteria were to be planned. The different departments required separate entry–identities and some branches required easy communication between their offices.

The requirement for universally flexible office space suggested a systematised, prefabricated method of construction.

The solution uses a system of 16 m-wide connected five-storey wings joined by circular vertical access cores and creating two open courtyards between them. The ground floor with individual department lobbies is open under the building. Departments emanate from the cores in two directions using as much of any wing or floor as required and affording easy connection to adjacent departments.

Uses not readily accommodated in the column-free office wings are housed in the basement and in separate freestanding buildings placed in the landscaped courtyards.

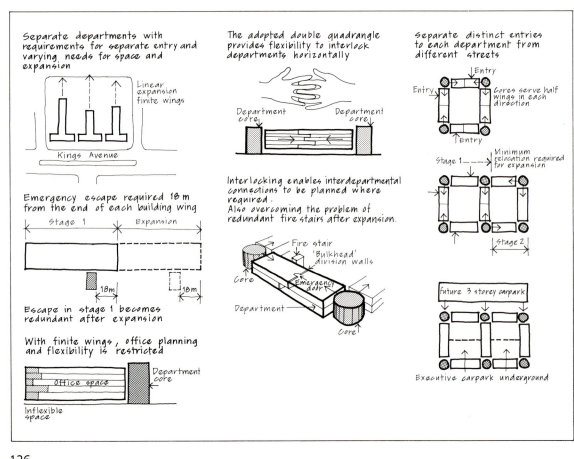

The building's elements other than the repetitive office space have been moulded in contrasting curved forms; the open ground floor accommodates quadrant-shaped glass entry lobbies for the three departments; the circular cores expressively turn the corners of the complex and deliberately hide the vertical services behind windowless walls; the quadrant-shaped, freestanding conference hall expresses its theatre seating and acoustic form; the cafeteria shows its long span thin segmental shell roof elements to all who look out of windows from above.

This theme of visual opposition and contrast between the rectilinear office wings and these curved elements has been further emphasised in the courtyard paving pattern, the fountain and in the two sculptures by Norman Calberg, one to each courtyard.

'... It has often been said that it evokes the image of a Carcassonne or Avila – I suppose it is a kind of bureaucratic citadel. Our client, Sir John Overall, head of the National Capital Development Commission, challenged me to produce the best "by world standards" in response to a very imprecise brief of usage – but the first stage had to be built quickly. The system building and long spans were developed further in later projects...'

A systematised repetitive structural–constructional scheme dominates the architectural concept; only three precast prestressed elements construct the office floors; a 26 m-long facade beam (with recessed continuous windows between them); a 16 m span 1.5 m-wide 'floor plank' and a 1.5 m-long column element.

The profiles of both the floor plank and the facade beams follow logically expressed structural outlines and allow for easy integration of horizontal service arteries.

All precast elements have a sandblasted finish and were erected by means of moving crane gantries. The prestressing anchorages are visible on the exterior by their stainless steel caps.

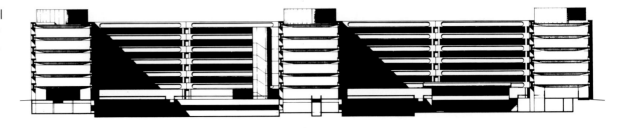

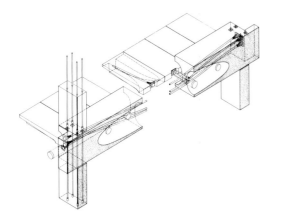

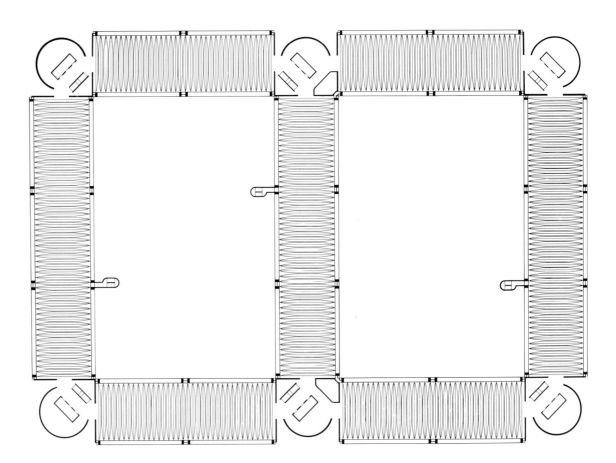

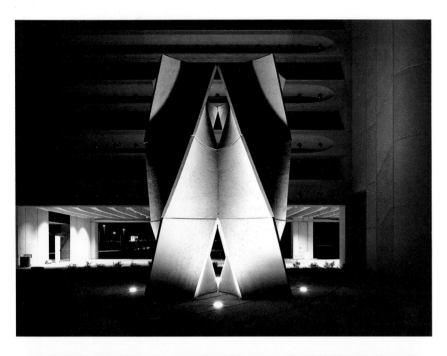

Tuggeranong Offices
Canberra, 1974–76

'... It was planned during a wave of optimism for the expansion of Canberra. We built on the experience gained with the Trade Group Offices and even planned to reuse the same erection gantries – the project was suddenly stopped in 1975. This was when I decided to accept an invitation to teach at Harvard. We only had the Embassy in Paris under way then...'

This complex of government offices is planned for a satellite township 20 km from Canberra. The brief called for universally flexible office space, built in stages to house up to eight government departments, with a total working population of 4000. A height limit of three storeys applied and carparking for 1500 vehicles was to be provided.

A column-free system of 20 m-wide wings allows freedom of space allocation for the various departments. Between them a central pedestrian concourse is created which offers enjoyable recreation space for walking, outdoor lunching and intimate areas for sitting at a waterpond with a large sculpture.

The area offers a variety of spatial experiences to the pedestrian, of opening-up, converging and channelling of vistas between the flowing lines of buildings, dramatically focusing and relating the distant hills into the complex.

Landscaped carparking is planned outside the wings related to the entrances of the various departments. Covered arcades reach the eight address points from public transport and together with the bridge connections provide weather-protected access.

Although most of the ground floor space is used for offices, some shops and the cafeteria open out onto the pedestrian concourse.

Ancillary structures house the uses not readily accommodated in the office wings, such as conference rooms, computer centre, telephone exchange and creche.

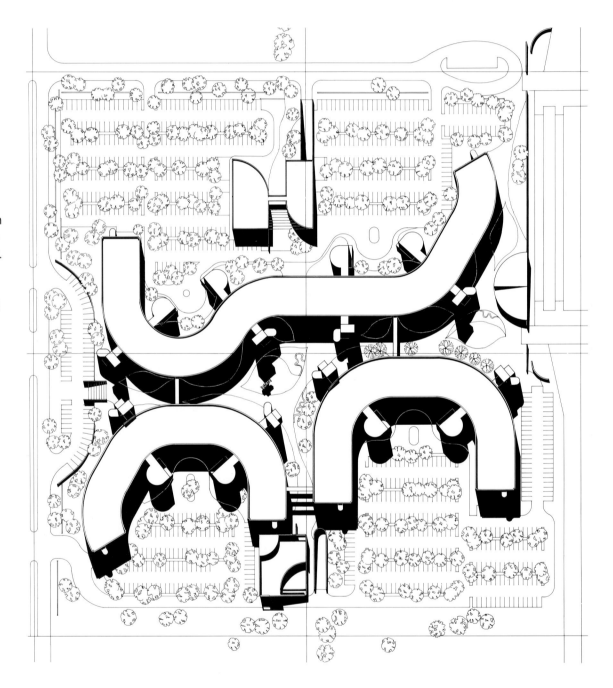

The essence of the design is longitudinal continuity of the office space, allowing flexible interlocking use of departments on different floors and unrestricted location of departmental boundaries.

The curvilinear plan building form is the result of accommodating the required length of three-storey structures. It is made constructionally possible by the use of precast prestressed parallel-sided and tapered floor elements. Straight, curved and countercurved assemblies result.

Considering the great number of floor elements required and the several moulds needed for their production, the introduction of a tapered element creates no disadvantages.

Supporting the prefabricated floor elements are straight storey-high precast concrete units which in assembly form slightly faceted facades. They express the decreasing load from ground to top floor by the reduction of area in the vertical elements.

So as not to impair the structural and constructional clarity of the continuous clear-span wings, all non-office uses are separated into external access and service cores containing stairs, elevators, toilets and vertical ducts, etc.

Mechanical services distribution is below and above windows. Air supply and return within the open office areas is by means of exposed circular metal ducts which contain indirect light sources above, illuminating the underside of the expressed clear span floor elements.

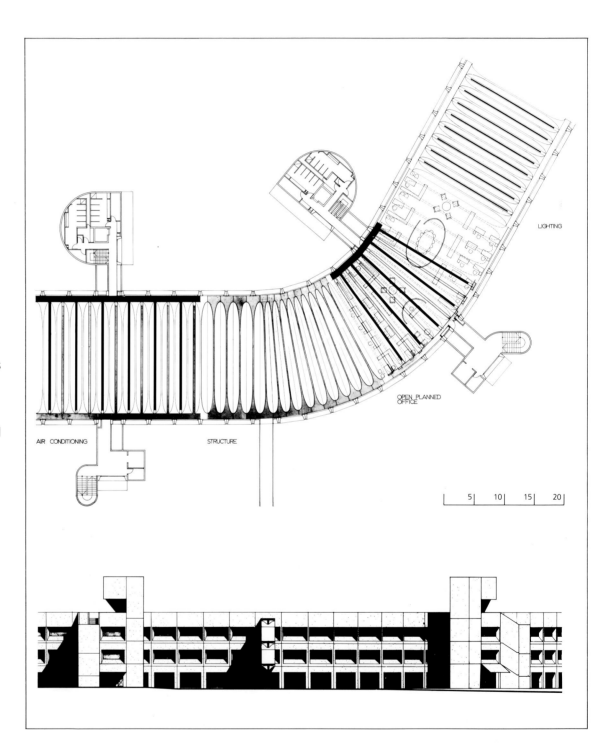

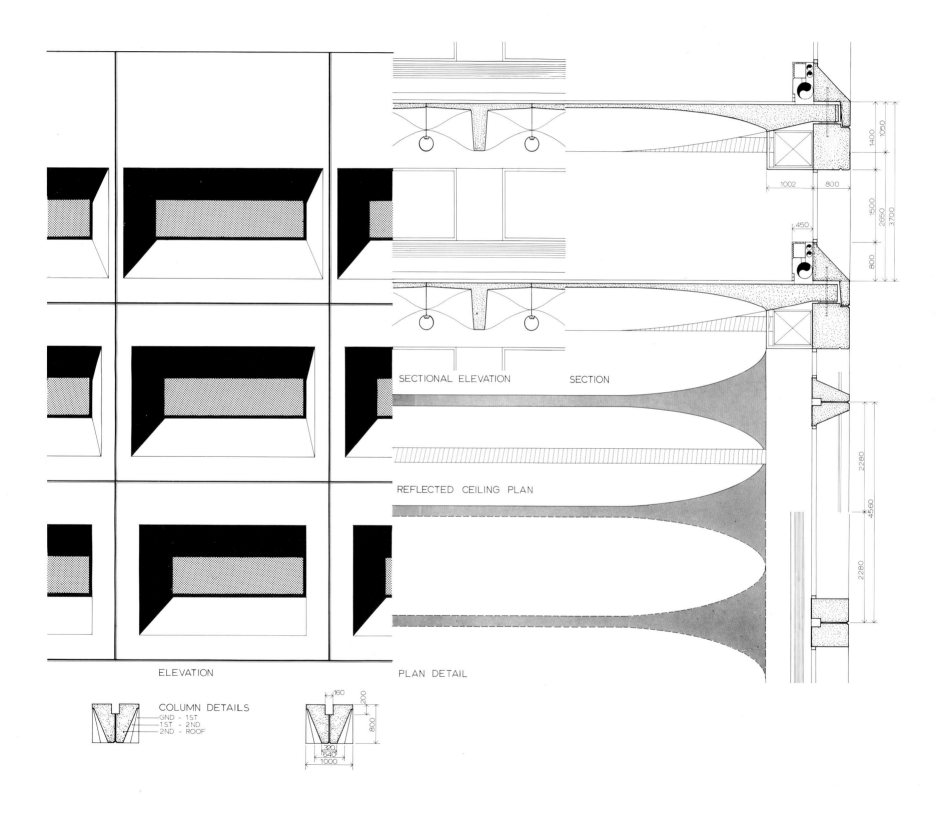

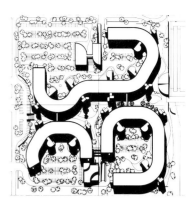

Possible future expansion

MLC Centre
Sydney, 1972–78

'... When I first discussed the idea of a 250 m-high concrete tower with Nervi, his advice was to limit the number of exterior columns and let them be heavily loaded. Just as a tree trunk, they should spread outward at their bases for greater stability ...'

Located in the centre of Sydney's business district, the site's 9130 m² area resulted from the amalgamation of 23 individual properties. The consolidation took place over a number of years and absorbed a narrow internal street (Rowe Street) in exchange for private land to extend another (Lee's Court). The resulting L-shaped site faces onto the pedestrian area of Martin Place and fronts Castlereagh and King streets.

The major constraint in planning was the existence of the Eastern Suburbs Railway tunnels running diagonally under the site. The tower columns had to be planned to avoid these.

Urban planning restrictions included an insistence on vehicle ramps parallel along the boundaries of King and Castlereagh streets and footpaths diverted around them so as to avoid any level crossings.

The final scheme containing a single office tower was determined by its economic viability and the condition of approval requiring replacement of the Theatre Royal which had stood on one of the amalgamated properties.

A number of existing retail stores and a private club had to be rehoused in their own new 'strata title' properties. The maximum site index of 12.5:1 was permitted.

Design studies were directed to enliven the street level spaces at the base of the inevitably tall office tower, which occupied only 20 per cent of the total site. To counter the results of the high development factor, the scheme aims to create open space in the congested centre of the city. The resulting privately owned land given over to permanent public use compensates for the intensification of land use. Useful and inviting open areas for the enjoyment of people have always been the essence of life in cities throughout the ages.

Being located in the retail core of the city, two levels of shopping arcades were required. A podium of plazas was planned on various levels, opening out

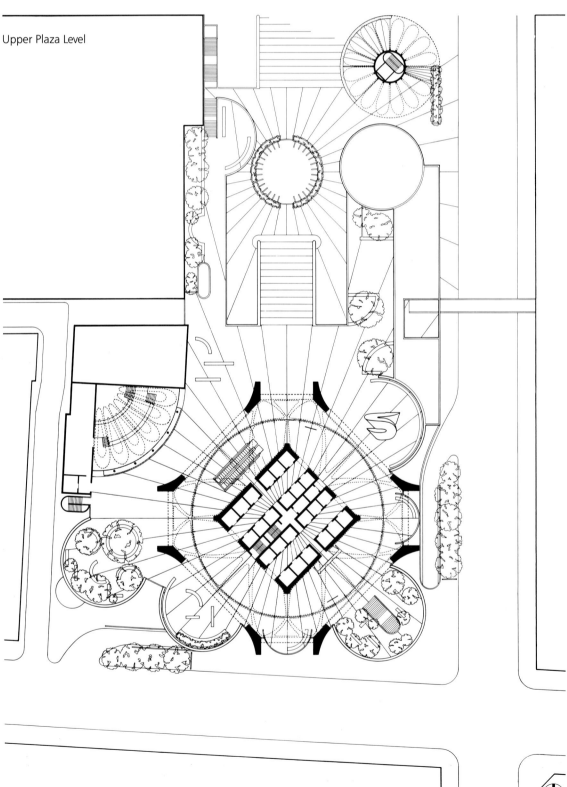

Upper Plaza Level

'... to finally proportion the plaza stepped ramps, I measured some of the age-old bridges in Venice...'

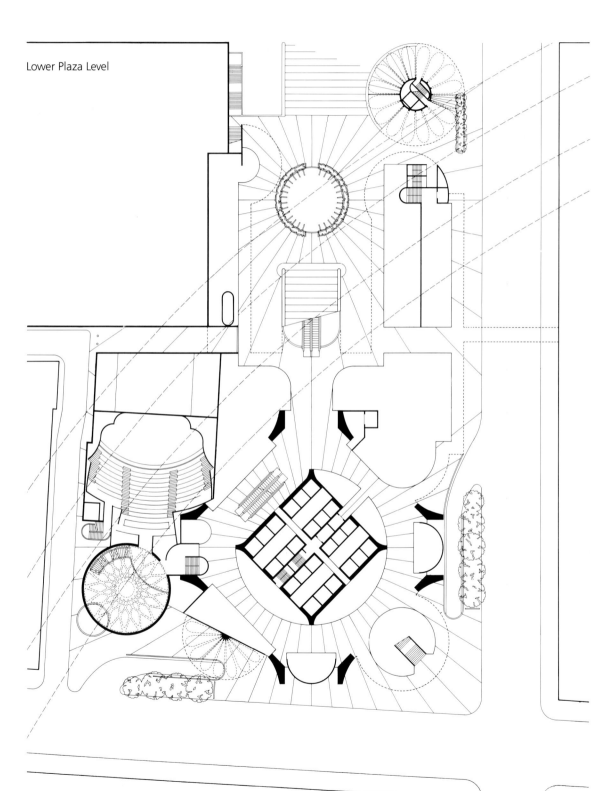

Lower Plaza Level

onto the surrounding streets. Along the boundaries, shops generally face outward, thereby continuing the adjoining existing development which extends into interior arcades. The central space of the site, however, is open and used for landscaped plazas, outdoor restaurants and a vertically connecting circular well containing a fountain. There is a cinema, a tavern, various coffee shops and restaurants which all open onto some part of the internal pedestrian area of the project.

The central space, open to the north, acts as the main axial formal approach to the office tower which is two storeys above the lowest street (Martin Place). To reach this without undue discomfort and also create usable open space, two sets of stepped ramps double as outdoor seating areas forming an amphitheatre for lunchtime group entertainment, public meetings and music making.

The space surrounding the tower lobby with its banks of elevators extends outward and is contained by circular projecting courtyards. These control the environment, containing a large sculpture, solid planting and outdoor seating.

The tower is square, angled diagonally to avoid the railway tunnels and has blunted corners, resulting in the irregular octagonal plan form.

It contains 1650 m² gross per floor with an average efficiency factor of 78 per cent. The building is 250 m high (making it the highest concrete office building in the world in 1980) and has 65 floors served by four banks of six elevators each.

The tower has a rigid load-bearing core of vertically poured cross-walled concrete. Its exterior is carried by eight heavily loaded massive columns which logically change in plan shape and area from bottom to top, as the loads in them decrease. For a structure of this height, there is great need for stiffness against lateral wind loads. This is achieved by turning the columns outward at the base and changing their hyperboloid form to become flush with the building facade at the top.

Together with the columns, the long spandrel beams (19 m and 11 m spans) constitute the entire facade, with the continuous windows between them recessed to the inner edge for effective sun protection.

The spandrel beams are I-shaped for bending resistance. The parabolic-shaped recesses in their profile change to a solid cross-section at their support to resist shear.

Pier Luigi Nervi collaborated on the design of the ribbed ceiling of the theatre lobby, the restaurant roof and the projecting mushroom-like structures to the club residential block and the overhanging plaza court over King Street.

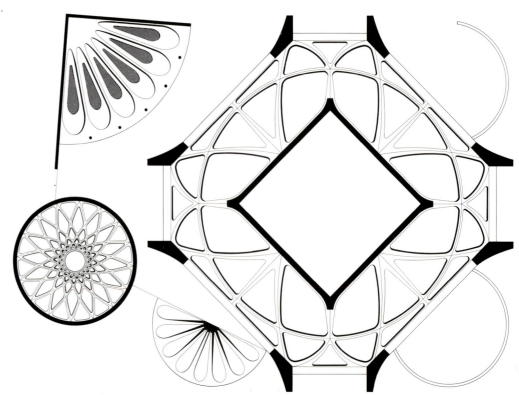

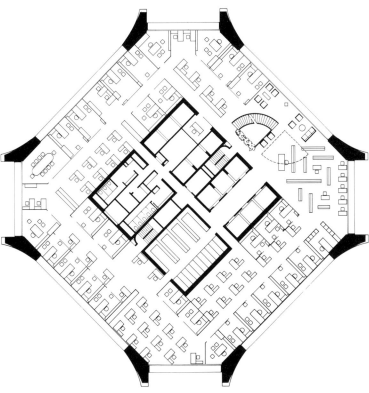

'... It took me a long time to get Albers working on the structural constellation "Wrestling". At 15 m, it was his biggest and last work before he died – his student at Yale, Charles Perry, did the sculpture on the plaza...'

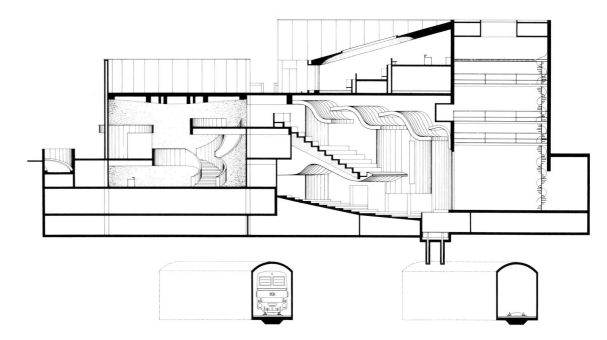

Replacing the old conventional proscenium-stage Theatre Royal, the requirements called for 1100 seats in stalls and a gallery. The form of the new theatre is fitted against the tower supports and is built over the railway tunnels. Rubber pads in the foundations assure sound isolation.

Entry is through a three-storey-high 18 m-diameter circular lobby at its intermediate level. The seating is reached by a wide central stair spiralling up and down.

The walls of the theatre are gold and the seating and carpeted floors, red. The proscenium curtain is royal purple. Curvilinear ribs forming the theatre ceiling conceal lighting bridges and air-conditioning ducts.

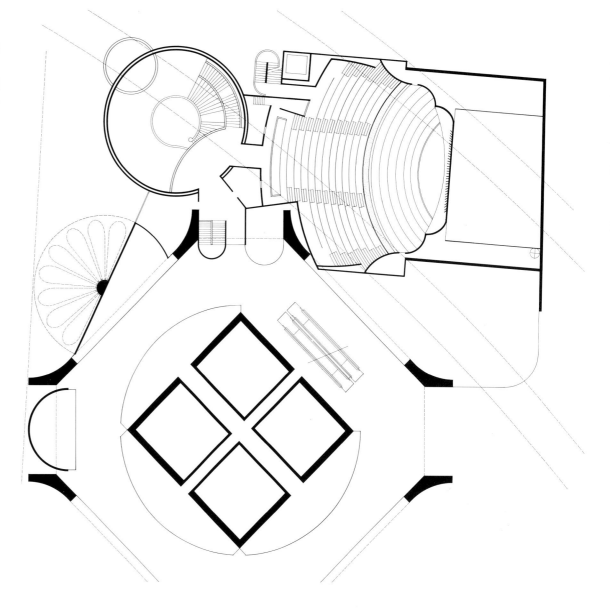

The interlocking ribs of the concrete theatre roof follow patterns of stress and were built with Nervi's well-known ferro-cement permanent pan-form system. Responding to stresses of bending and shear the ribs vary in depth and width, culminating in a central ring from which Charles Perry's hanging bronze sculpture is suspended.

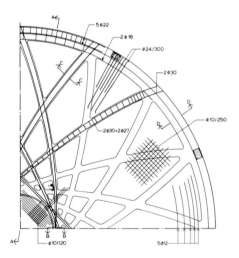

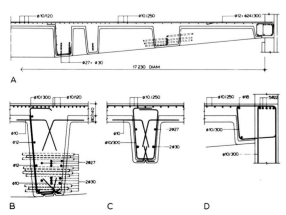

The exterior of the tower is made of precast, permanent form elements with a finish of crushed white quartz aggregate (for non-absorbency). The factory-produced elements are assembled and structural concrete is poured into them in a progressive sequence of columns, spandrel beams and ribbed floors.

The central core was built by means of a vertically rising formwork system, several levels ahead of the exterior and floors.

The 10 m clear span floors were built by a 'progressive strength' sequence which achieved a cycle of one completed floor (including its integrally finished facade) every four working days.

The system requires no conventional formwork or props by the use of reinforcing beam steel welded to form self-supporting trusses. Reusable plastic coffers are clipped onto these reinforcing trusses which are progressively concreted to complete primary beams, then secondary beams and slabs. This sequence proceeded on several floors simultaneously in vertical progressive stages which allowed a larger than usual workforce to operate and spread over a number of floors.

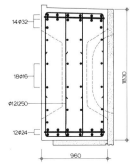
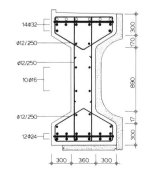

The Australian Embassy
Quai Branly, Paris 15, 1973–77

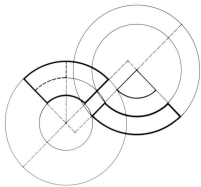

The Paris site acquired by the Australian Government is in a unique and dramatic location at the north-western end of the 15th district. Situated facing the River Seine on Quai Branly, the 6280 m² site enjoys magnificent views to the north, over a large landscaped public sportsground toward the Eiffel Tower (a mere 400 m away), the river palisades with its tree-lined parks, the Palais de Chaillot and the famous landmarks of central Paris visible in the distance.

The Australian Government's programme required the erection of two buildings on the site for different, but related purposes:
- The Chancellery, housing its diplomatic mission to France, the Australian missions to OECD, UNESCO, and an Ambassador's residence on the top floor, suitable for formal receptions.
- A residential apartment building containing 34 units of various sizes for some of the Australian diplomats and their families. The top floor accommodates a second ambassador's residence.

The two buildings have separate entries at opposite sides of the site, but are joined at ground floor level. Together they cover half the site and the remainder is extensively landscaped. A loading area, car-parking for about 170 cars, a swimming pool and squash court are provided in two basements.

Being located on the edge of, but within the historic central part of Paris, strict requirements were laid down by the various authorities. Aside from a height limit of 31 m and 50 per cent site cover, the authorities required that building design in the area 'respect' the nearby axis of the Champ de Mars and its right-angled cross axis.

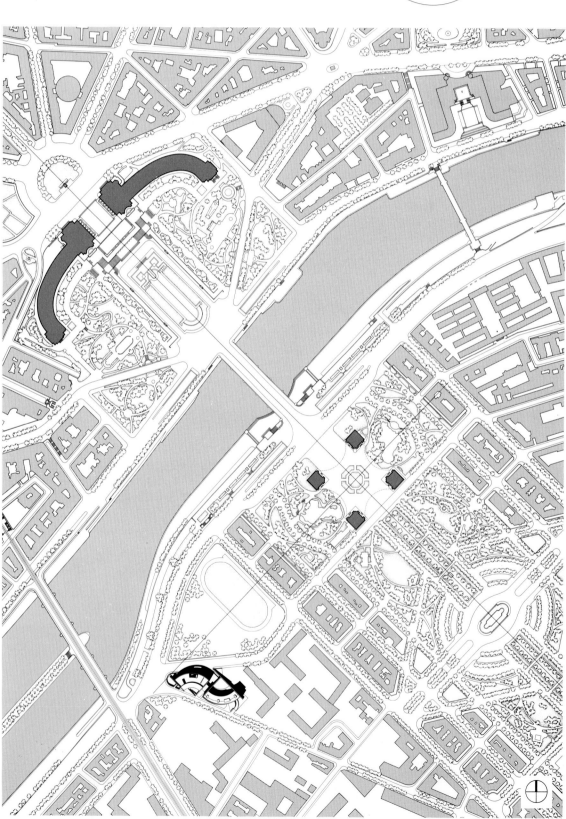

'... when commissioned to do a building in Paris, it was natural for me to ask Breuer's Paris office to be our "architecte d'operation" – it meant re-establishing a working relationship with him after many years. He loved our tapered T-beam design and helped develop the facade elements and sunshades. It was the first time I had the chance to build with granite...'

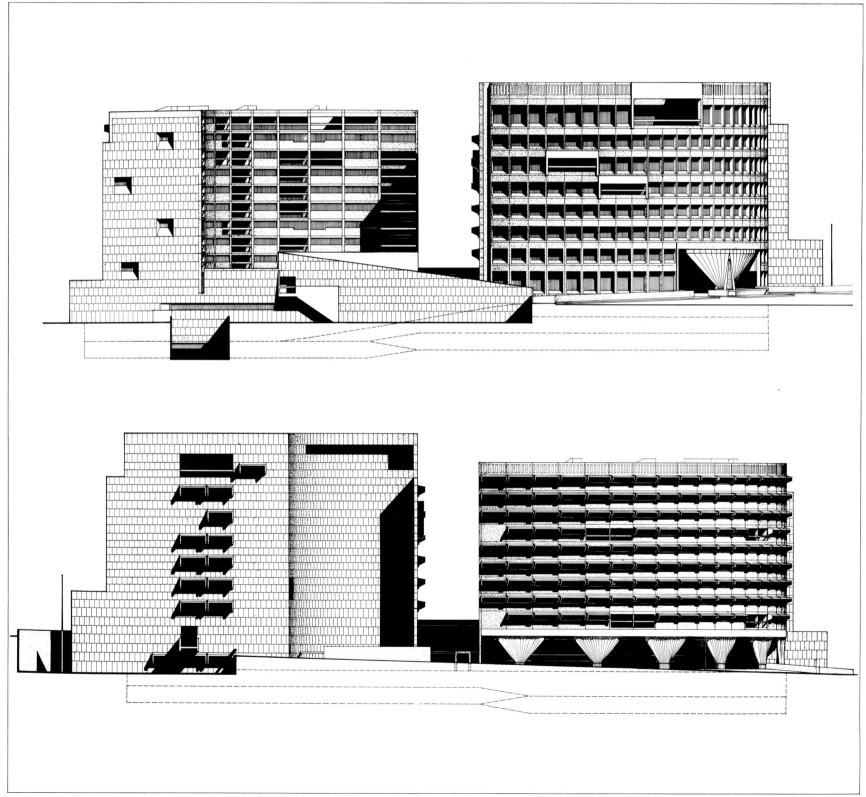

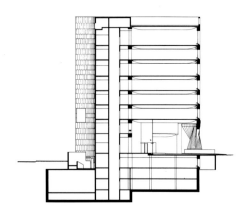

The design of the embassy responds to this planning edict (similarly to the Palais de Chaillot) by relating two, opposing quadrant-shaped buildings within the generating lines of the axes. The resulting concave and convex building facades are designed to take maximum advantage of the magnificent views and outlook to the north.

The main chancellery offices all face the view along the convex facade offering a maximum expanse of window area in relation to the floor space.

Every living room in the apartment building faces the same view and by curving the building away from the existing office structure to the east, it minimises the obstruction to outlook and maintains maximum possible privacy.

The relationship of the whole complex to the axis lines is emphasised by the projecting design of the end walls.

Entrance to the chancellery is by means of a curved drive under the building through a monumentally proportioned two-storey-high space. The focal point of the entrance is the large tree-like structure supporting the building's structural facade above the wide entry opening.

The main public areas are located on the entrance level: the reception, an exhibition area leading to a multipurpose space for functions, a theatrette seating 140 people, and a library–information centre.

First Level

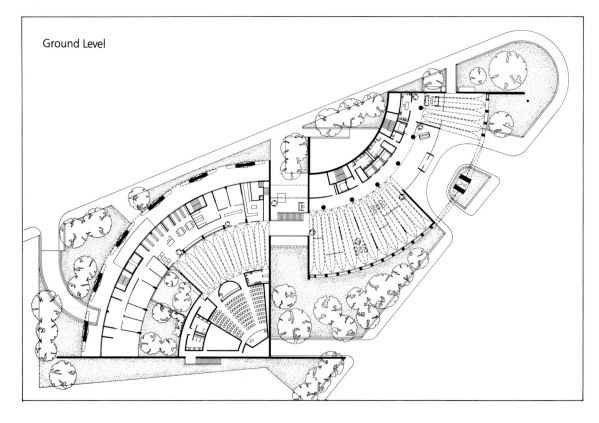

Ground Level

Fifth Level

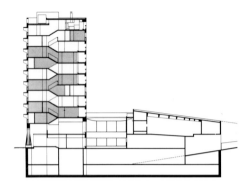

'... asked where he lived, "in Palais Seidler" was former Prime Minister Gough Whitlam's reply, when he was Ambassador to UNESCO.

In 1984 my family and I stayed with the Whitlams. The furniture had been totally rearranged by the previous Ambassador; I had to find the special vases, there were no tall candles, etc. I soon fixed it all up as designed and when Gough came in for dinner, he said to his wife Margaret: "Looks different – had the decorators in, I see".

They were a handsome tall couple to live there – in perfect scale with that huge salon...'

The entire top floor of the chancellery building is given over to the residence of the ambassador. It contains a centrally located large salon and dining room leading onto an open terrace from which access is provided to the roof garden. The salon and dining rooms are intended for entertaining large numbers of people. Huge pivoted doors give access during receptions. The focal point is a curved freestanding fireplace and an adjacent landscaped open court, separating the ambassador's private rooms.

The apartment building is planned on a 'split-level' system allowing the living areas of all 34 apartments to face the view, toward the Eiffel Tower and the river. The large number of required bedrooms are located on the opposite side, made possible by the long outside curvature of the building.

The apartments vary in size, containing from one to five bedrooms, with different sized living accommodation. There are only four internal access galleries in the nine-storey building, two and a half floors apart vertically, on either side of the mechanical core.

From these, the apartments are reached by half-flights of steps up or down. Within the apartments, a further half-flight connects the living and bedroom parts.

The smallest apartments open directly from the access gallery on the view side. Apartments on the first and top levels open out onto private landscaped roof terraces and all others have balconies which are recessed within the building's facade.

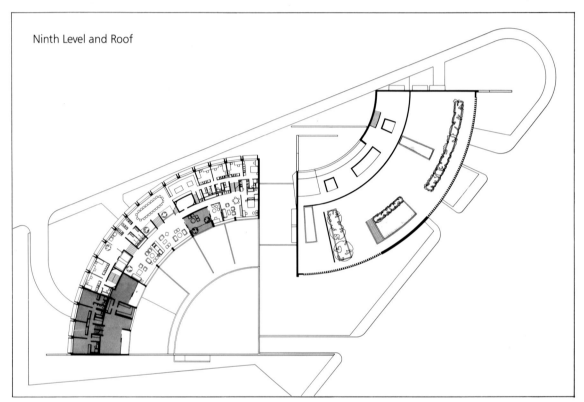

Ninth Level and Roof

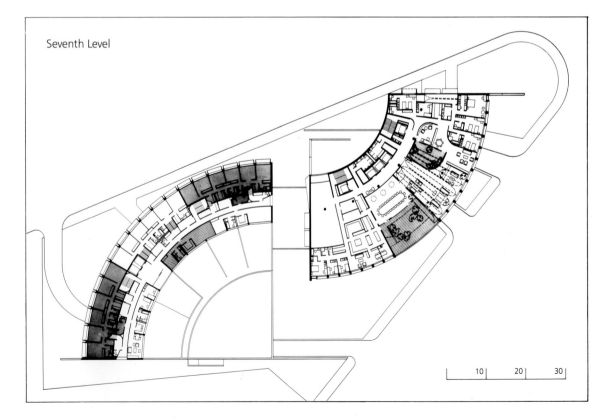

Seventh Level

'... We furnished all interiors totally, using Breuer's 1927 cantilevered armchairs which had just been reintroduced. It was the first time we worked with Claude Engle from Washington, DC who did some spectacular lighting...'

The exterior of both buildings is of supporting precast concrete elements made with white quartz aggregate which forms a tight-textured, non-absorbent surface. The end walls and those of the lower theatre structure are faced in exfoliated grey Limoge granite.

Between the chancellery's service core and the load-carrying glazed facade of precast elements these specially profiled, precast, prestressed concrete T-beams bridge the 16 m clear span. This allows maximum flexibility for internal office subdivision. (Their end form allows the passage of longitudinal service ducts.) The structurally expressive sweeping lines of the T-beams are exposed in public areas on the main entrance level and in the salon of the top floor ambassador's apartment.

The apartment building has load-bearing, precast concrete facades with exposed white quartz and flat-slab floors erected by the French *prédalle* system which uses on-site precast lower parts of all slabs as permanent formwork. The bottom 5–6 cm thickness of all flat slab concrete floors are cast on a steel platform at ground level, minimally reinforced. Their upper surface is left very rough and the concrete is steam cured overnight.

These panels, up to 50 m² in area, are then picked up by crane using a unique, equalising load multiple pulley suspension device which assures that the thin slabs do not crack. The slabs are deposited on minimal central formwork and supported by precast facade elements. *In-situ* top concrete completes the floors.

The precast carrying facades are interrupted where 'special' uses occur in the building, such as the two ambassadorial office suites which have wide balconies, the large terrace of the chancellery top-floor apartment and the main entrance. Here the large openings are spanned or supported by appropriate *in-situ* concrete forms. The main entrance support transmits the load of the curved building above down into wind-resisting rectangular supports at right angles to the facade. The transition is by means of straight lines of formboards producing hyperboloid surfaces.

Similarly, six tapered supports create an entrance arcade under the apartment building. These resolve the excentric loads created by the curved facade above into axially loaded circular piers.

Barranduda Town Centre
Albury-Wodonga, 1976–78

Urban expansion in most of the civilised world has resulted in deplorable chaos. The planning of comprehensive new satellite towns is of paramount importance.

With a present population of 45,000, the area was designated by the Federal Government to be a 'regional growth centre' with an ultimate 300,000 inhabitants.

The first stage is the design of the town centre, accommodating 2000 government and private work places. Integral to the plan is the provision of shopping, commercial, community and public facilities to serve the population in surrounding housing areas.

A series of interconnected pedestrian precincts, with changes in the scale of spaces, evoke a sense of urban well-being and invite pleasurable exploration. The varying, intimately narrow and expanding public spaces culminate in the civic square surrounded by public buildings and the town hall, focusing on a centrally placed sculpture and fountain. There is an awareness and enticing sense of the 'beyond' wherever one may be located.

Pedestrian and vehicular traffic are separated without sacrifice to the needs of either. 'Arbours' define the main pedestrian concourses. They are linear 'umbrella' structures, both solid and overgrown trellises, giving protection from sun and rain and also acting as visual tie elements incorporating lighting, directional and identifying signs.

The office buildings' plan forms are in reverse-symmetrical, three-storey structures connected by bridges. Vertical access cores are in separate towers and facilitate service through a common basement. The buildings are flexible to accommodate changing uses by having long-span column-free floors.

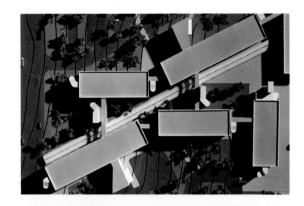

... Utopian Planning – commissioned by an ambitious but short-lived government. It was to lay the seed for population dispersion, to release pressure on the large cities. Sadly, ideas to build totally new environments have since been politically and artistically shunned ... But it gave me a chance to explore contra-spaces, experiences in reverse geometries which Albers had done in his "vice-versa" series ...'

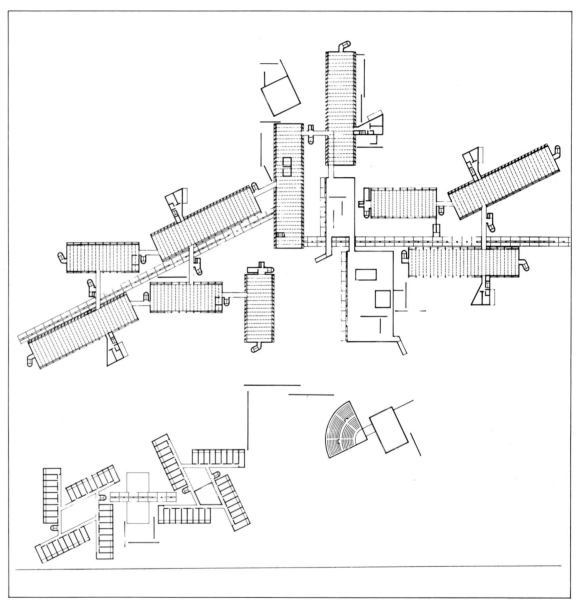

Ringwood Cultural Centre
Melbourne, 1978–80

This centre serves a large suburban community and is built on a sloping, beautifully wooded site with panoramic views to distant mountains.

A live stage theatre, seating 400, and a multi-purpose function centre for up to 800 people are accommodated in opposing quadrant-shaped structures. The form suits the theatre plan with the floor slope following the site's natural contours. The opposing roof slope rises to contain a limited stage fly-tower.

The function centre roof has an opposing roof slope. Its glass wall opens toward the view and the space can be subdivided into smaller sections, all served by a common kitchen. There is a minimum of public area connecting the two facilities.

Entry can be from the top or bottom of the site which accommodates carparking amongst trees, shielding it from view.

External cavity walls are of split concrete blocks supported on externally expressed concrete floors. The roof structure is of steel.

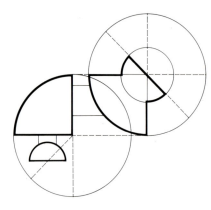

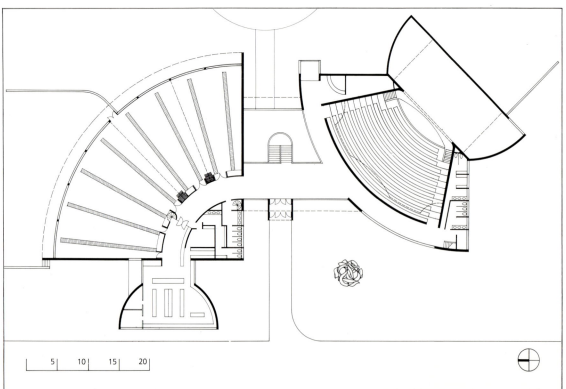

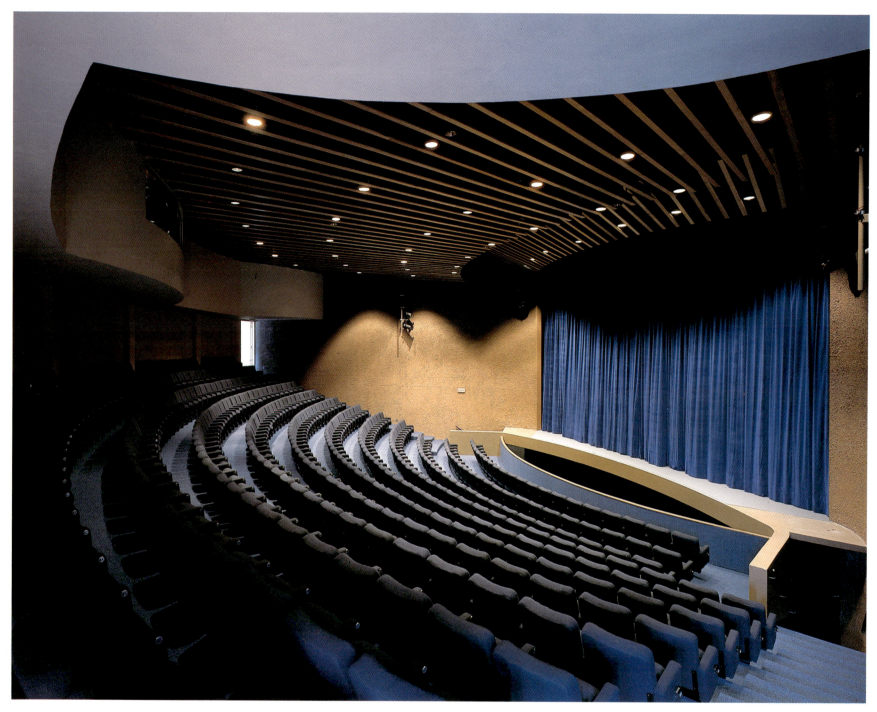

Hillside Housing
Kooralbyn, Qld, 1979–82

'... After experiencing the delights of ancient European hilltowns, this is a translation into our own times; there had to be more space between houses but the same limit on the use of materials produced unity and yet diversity ...'

This resort village is located in a beautiful valley with a number of lakes, about 100 km south-west of Brisbane.

The design of the grouped houses (they are to own or to rent) aims to avoid suburban solutions. The imagery, considering the rural location, the climate and topography, is more related to the ancient hill towns of Italy and Spain rather than modern suburbia.

Just as in many of these charming European examples, the site is sloping and offers fine views downhill to the golf course, the lakes and slopes on the opposite side of the valley. The housing units are in pairs and groups, varying and avoiding rigid regularity by changing the form, aspect and relationships into continuous soft curves following the irregular contours.

The houses are similar, using identical structural and manufactured elements (all are 93 m^2) and incorporate only minor variations of layout, with occasional opposing roof slopes. Due to the steep slope, the units are arranged on two levels. Approach is from the top, accommodating the bedrooms. These are planned to allow for the possible needs of separate holiday occupancy of each main bedroom. A stair leads down to the living areas. Vertical space results inside each unit with upper level bedrooms becoming open mezzanines in the high living rooms.

The roofs, made of Roman pantiles, are inclined parallel to the slope of the hill. Their distinctive texture combined with rough white-washed walls and the natural stone terraces increases even further the feeling of a Mediterranean hill-town. The focal point of this first group of 55 houses is a recreational 'village centre' with a swimming pool, terraces, barbecues and sheltered as well as trellised areas for relaxation.

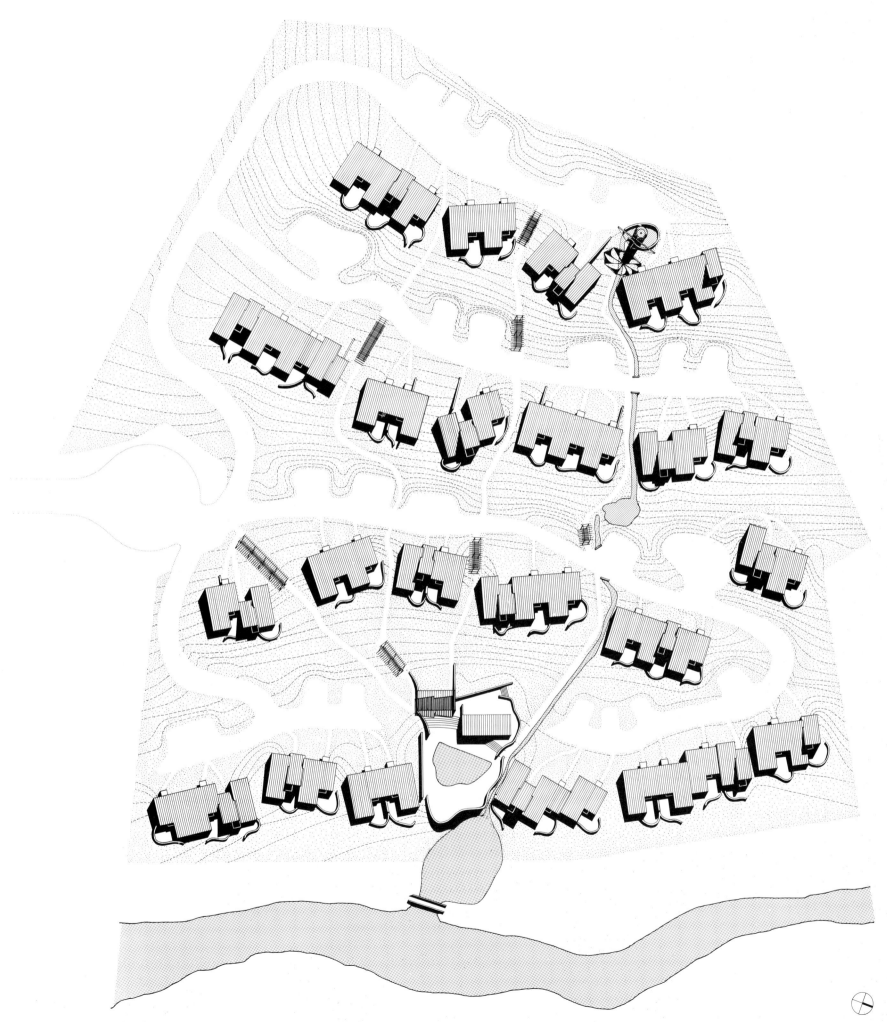

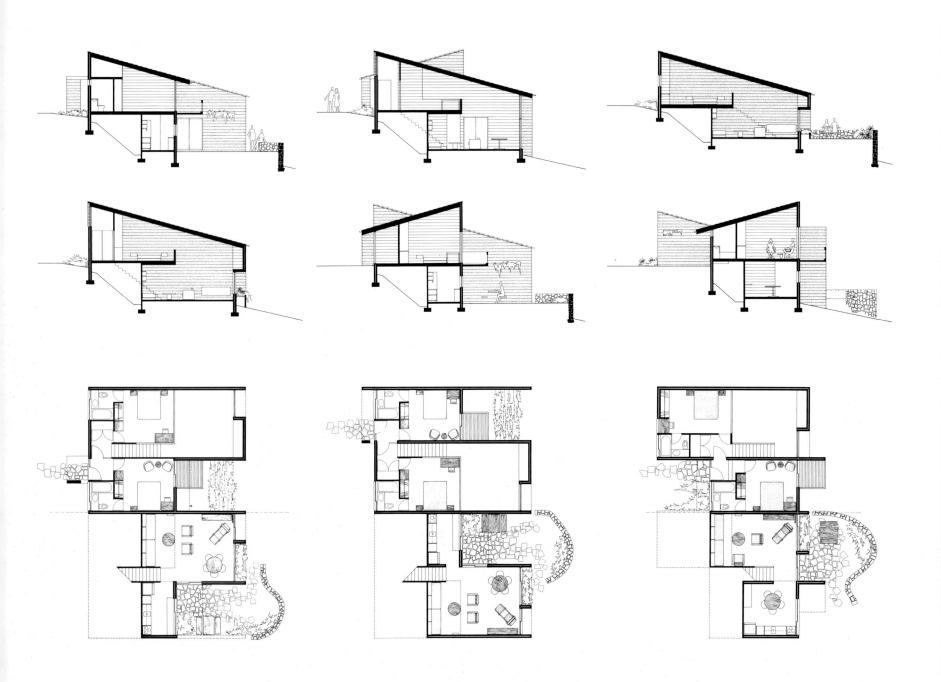

Yarralumla Group Houses
Canberra, 1982–84

'... Australia has a great heritage in its 19th-century terrace houses – the challenge was to produce sumptuous spaces not normally found in joined houses ...'

The site for these 11 townhouses overlooks Canberra's lake toward the north. It is in a 'front row' position and the design ensures that every house faces the view. The houses 'fan' out in their plan form toward the view, emanating from a central landscaped garden from which their individual, private entrance courts are reached. Garages are under this garden and daylight reaches the driveway below through large sculpturally formed openings which emerge in the planting areas above.

The plans of the 230 m^2 houses are the same and are arranged on three split-levels merging in a high clerestory-lit space above the central dining area. The introduction of wave-shaped plan forms finds its counterpart in the design of the entrance court and the communal swimming pool.

Construction is of solid masonry materials throughout. The supporting walls are of grey face brick cavity construction, floors are concrete and the steel-framed roofs support glazed tiles. Each house is individually air-conditioned.

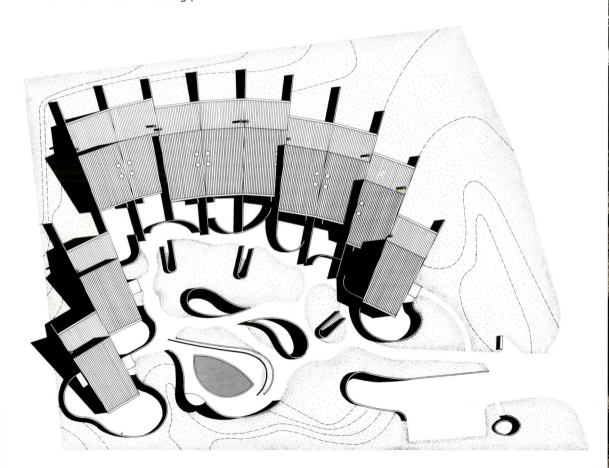

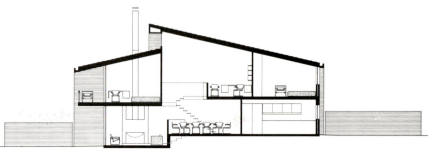

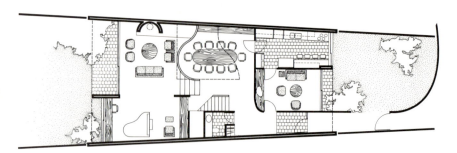

Australian Parliament House Competition
Canberra, 1979

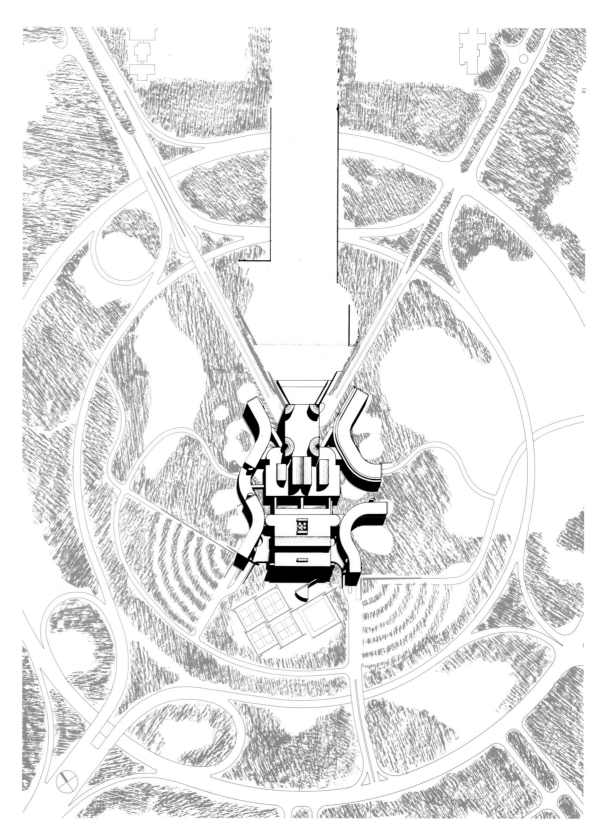

The importance of the new Parliament House and its setting on Capital Hill, focused on the main land axis of Burley Griffin's plan for Canberra, suggested that the building should be essentially symmetrical.

The centrally emphasised ceremonial entry and forecourt are placed at the convergence of three axes. The reception hall structure with its distinctive vaulted silhouette covers the entry, and the angled direction of the adjacent executive office wings further focalises the main entrance facade.

The two chambers, the House of Representatives and the Senate, are placed on either side of the Central Members Hall. They are symbolically recognisable by their overhead light-admitting, fan-shaped vaults. When seen from all sides they impart a 'citadel-on-the-hill' quality, rising out of the curvilinear office wings in the foreground.

There are panoramic views from Capital Hill in all directions toward a ring of distant mountains and the open spaces characteristic of the country. The underlying principle adopted by the design is to face every politician's office outward – so that they are constantly kept aware of and can enjoy the vastness of their country.

The shaping of the office wings allows for nodal connections to the central functional spaces. The wings can be longitudinally extended in the future should the number of representatives increase.

The method of construction envisages 15 m-long straight and tapered precast floor units and reconstructed stone facade elements.

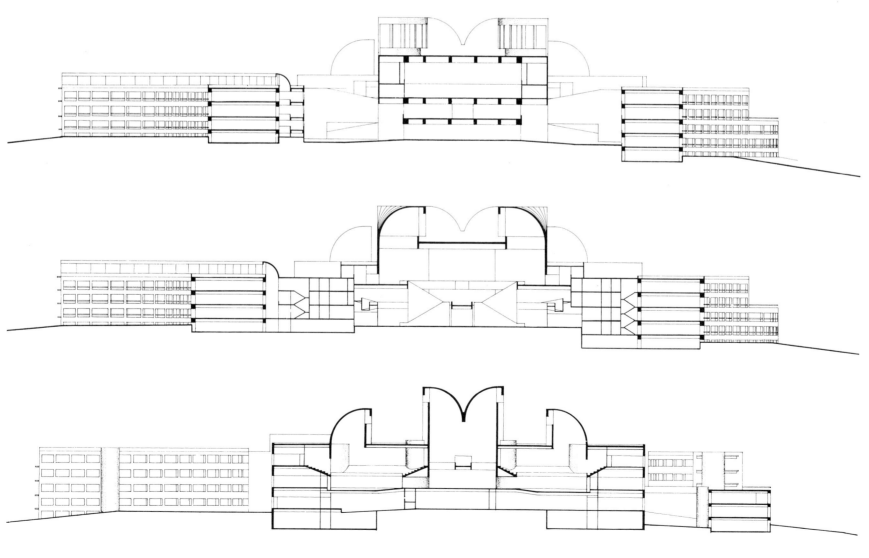

Navy Weapons Workshop
Garden Island, Sydney
1980–85

Built alongside the Navy's dry dock, this is the first stage of a segmental, long building to serve the maintenance needs of warships. The structure is positioned so that a 50-tonne dockside crane can lift heavy components off the ships and deposit these at either end of the building. High and medium-level cranes travel out from the workshop bays and bring the elements inside for dismantling, maintenance and repair. Electronic and other small equipment is taken to upper floors for service.

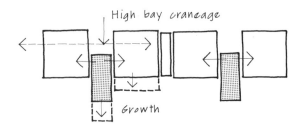

Between this first and the future workshop modules are the vertical core, administration office and amenities wings placed offset forward so as not to interfere with the continuous line of the high-level crane rails travelling longitudinally through and outside the building parallel to the dry dock.

The open gap separating the workshop building from the office wing is used for the vertical passage of air and other service ducts from and into the rooftop plantroom. With inevitable future changes in technology and the changing mechanical needs of the building, these services are readily replaced or added to without alteration to the structural fabric of the building.

The requirements for long-term freedom from maintenance in the corrosive salt-laden sea-air environment and for a three-hour, fire-rated structure, resulted in the use of post-tensioned reinforced concrete for the building's frame. Internal flexibility required large spans; 16 m for the continuous primary beams with 7 m cantilevered ends and 14.5 m for the T-beam cross spans, which are also used across the office–amenities wing.

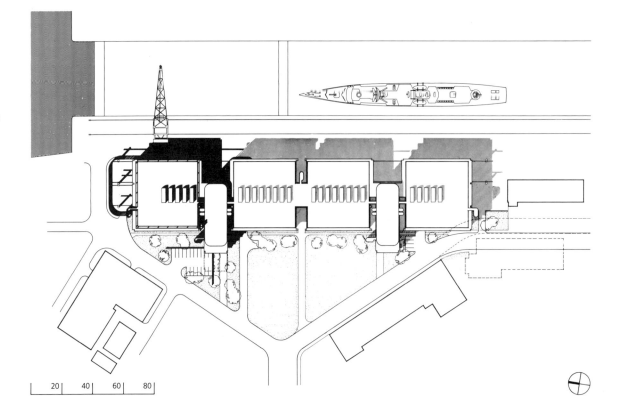

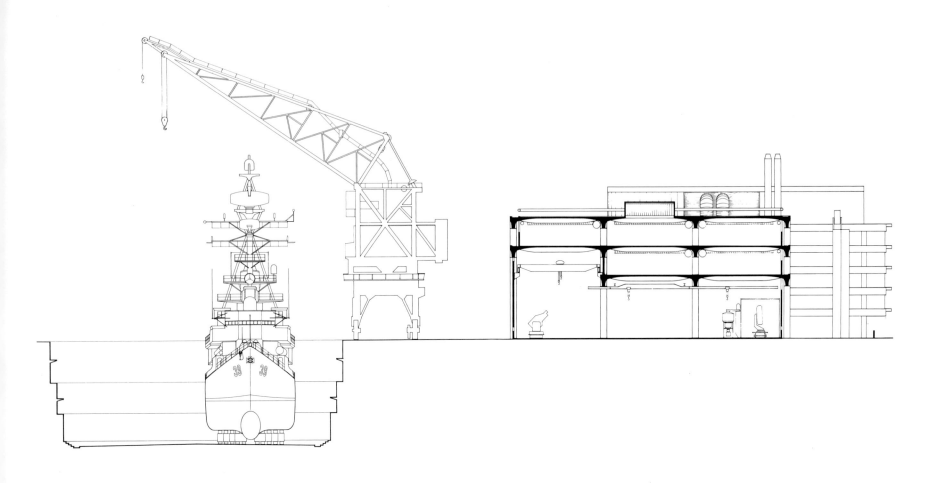

Elevations of Future Extension

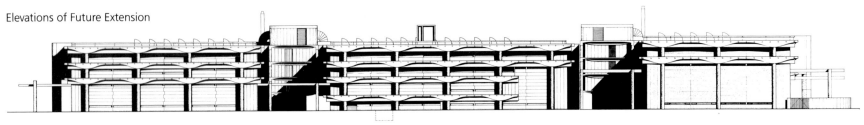

East

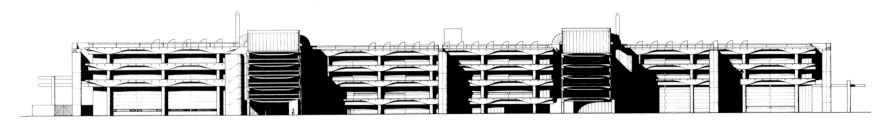

West

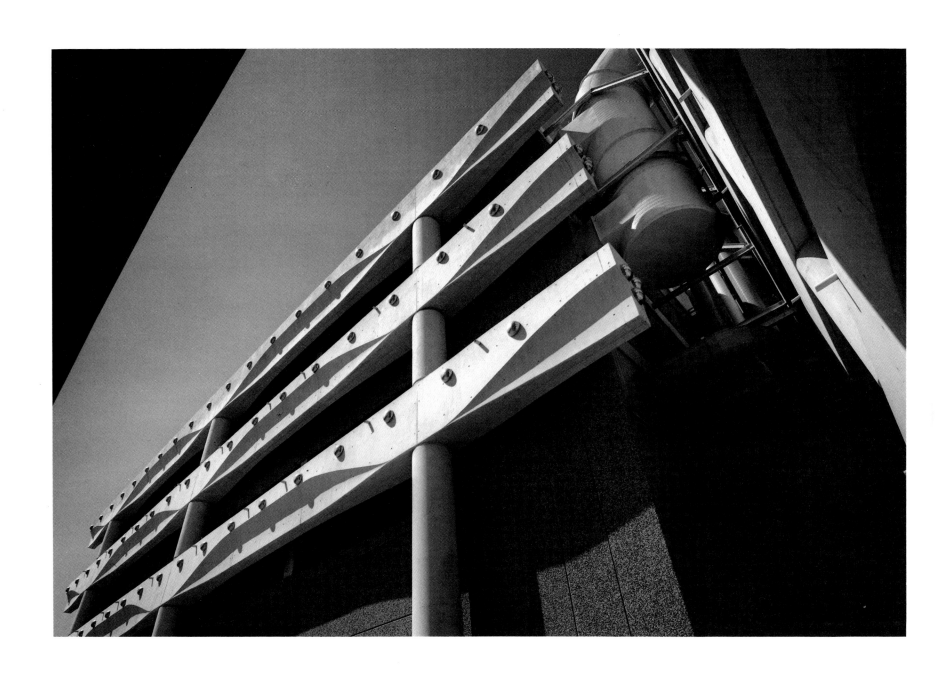

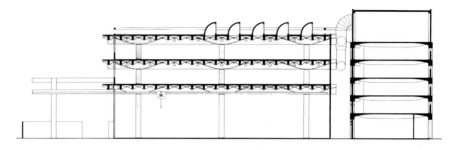

All of the structure is exposed in and outside. The design of individual elements reflects not only the structural demands on each, but also the need to provide for services to pass integrally within the floor structure.

The solid rectangular cross-section over the supports of the continuous primary beams is hollowed out progressively following a parabolic curve toward mid-span and the end of cantilevers to take on a T-shaped profile. In mid-span, the crossbeams are Ts to resist bending. They change to a rectangular section merging into the primary beams which results in needed shear-resisting support.

Main air supply ducts run alongside primary beams and distributing ducts use the spaces between the cross T-beams with indirect lighting or power supply trays above them.

Conventional concrete formwork could not achieve the organically moulded forms of this structure. Instead, segmental, mass-produced fibreglass moulds were assembled, and reused throughout the construction of the workshop and offices. Anchorages of prestressing cables are covered with dome-shaped stainless steel caps. Exterior walls are of prestressed hollow concrete planks with an exposed gravel aggregate surface.

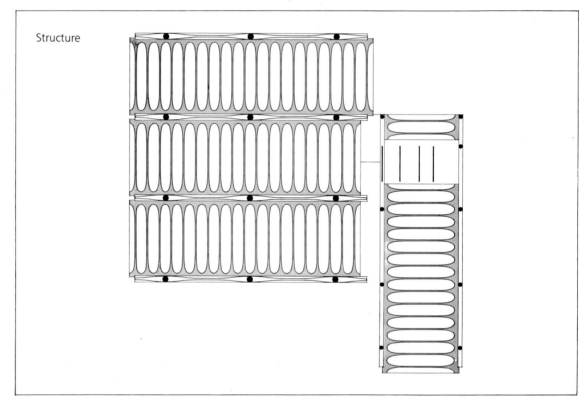

Structure

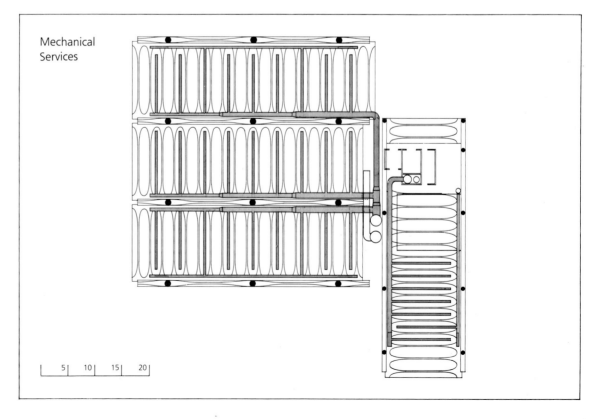

Mechanical Services

'... We gave the builder the choice to precast the structure. He chose to pour-in-place but used a mechanised system of plastic formwork which resulted in a continuous, organically more expressive structural form...'

Offices and Apartments
Kuala Lumpur, Malaysia, 1980

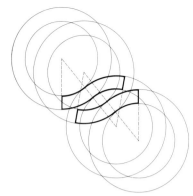

A bend in the tree-lined boulevard and the shape of the land suggested an undulating plan form for this company headquarters building which incorporates a ground floor bank and top floor lavish penthouses for executives, visitors' apartments and banqueting areas.

Groundwater conditions resulted in a five-storey, above-ground, continuously ramped, parking structure.

The reverse-symmetrical wings on both sides of the vertical service core consist of a single tapered T-beam floor element spanning 13 m. Reversing the assembly of the identical units' fibreglass forms achieves the desired curve and countercurved plan.

The exterior is of polished granite aggregate precast elements acting as permanent formwork for the columns and floors. Integral sunshades on north and south facades protect the glass walls from tropical heat.

The repetitive systematised structure is interrupted over the main entry, marked by a large opening, forming a covered portico. A specially formed hyperboloid, structurally expressive bridging facade beam is sympathetic to the architecture and creates a sculptured focal point for the building.

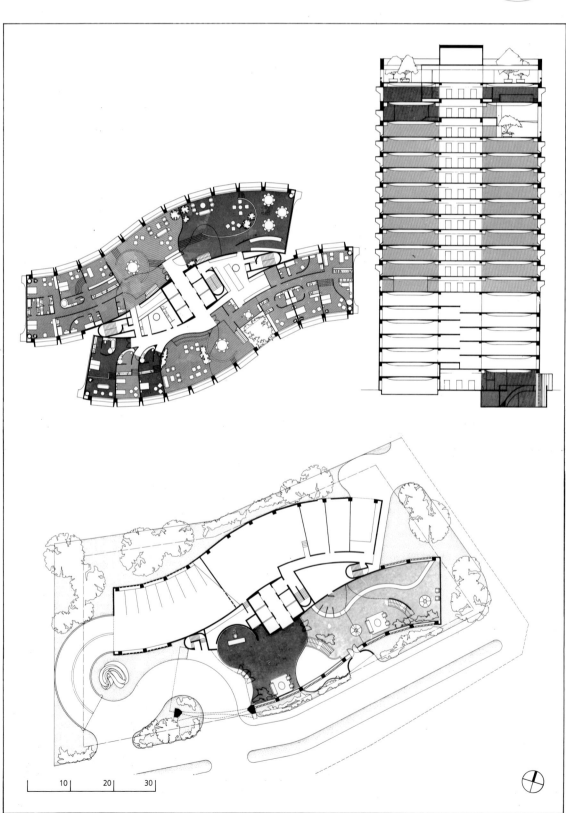

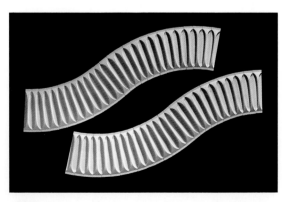

Hong Kong–Shanghai Bank
Hong Kong, 1979

The bank invited seven architects from around the world to compete for the design of its new headquarters, to replace the building on the same site it had occupied since the 1930s (the competition was won by N. Foster).

The Seidler submission proposed building in two stages; the first, a semi-circular, 12-storey structure at the rear of the site, maintaining partial occupancy in the existing building. The second stage, after relocation, consisted of a 40-storey tower facing the front onto Central (Cenotaph) Square.

On the ground floor is the main banking floor with a high atrium space above it between the two buildings. It is approached dramatically through a high space under the second stage tower, up escalators, which are flanked by the tower's only two central columns.

To keep the floor space and the facades unencumbered by columns, the tower's vertical loads and lateral typhoon stresses are resisted by four large corner piers. These change in shape from bottom to top as dictated by both structural and mechanical considerations. The expressive, changing section, 38 m long prestressed facade beams allow for unobstructed glass walls to open the interior to the dramatic views of the harbour.

Although Seidler did not win the competition, the bank's director in charge of the new building, Mr Roy Munden, was also the president of the Hong Kong Club and commissioned Seidler to design its new structure on an adjacent site, facing the same public square (see following pages).

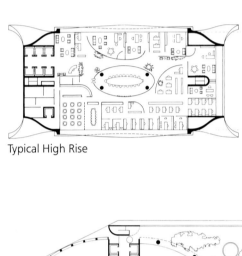
Typical High Rise

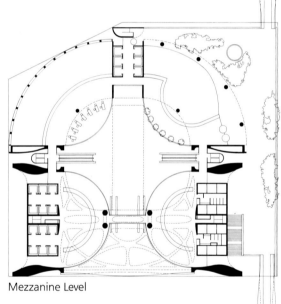
Mezzanine Level

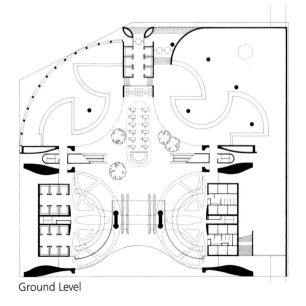
Ground Level

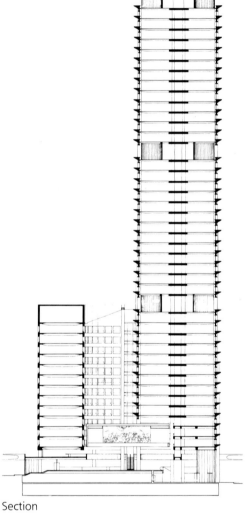
Section

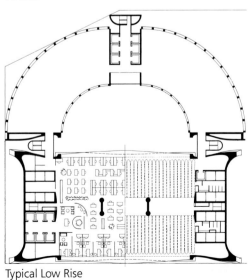
Typical Low Rise

Hong Kong Club and Office Building
Hong Kong, 1980–84

The club is the oldest and most exclusive in the ex-British colony since early in the last century and occupied a building which had long outlived its usefulness.

Located in the very heart of central Hong Kong, it faced the formal landscaped expanse of Cenotaph Square. New development all around it had made the site very valuable. A developer's offer to build a new building for the club was accepted, giving him the right to construct offices above it to fully utilise the site's potential.

The two uses were to be kept strictly separate, the club maintaining its private entry in the old axial location facing the cenotaph and the offices entering from the wide side street.

The club occupies the podium of the building to a four-storey height with almost total site cover, and the offices above, the permissible two-thirds of the area.

The spirit of the formal old club was reinterpreted in the new. It maintains the old symmetry and yet develops internally a controlled but joyous use of curved forms pulsating in and out between the independent huge supports of the superstructure.

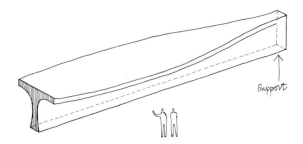

The office structure straddles the club podium and generates the most expressive image of the whole building: the unusually long (34 m) facade and internal spans (17 m). The absence of any interior columns created the required freedom for the club to plan internal spaces below.

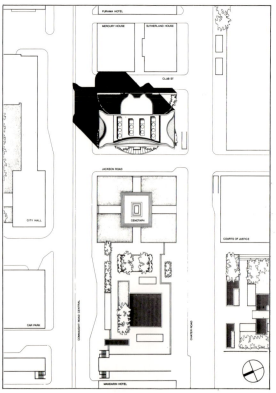

The club's facilities, function rooms, restaurants, bars and meeting rooms are grouped around a vertically open but changing rotunda space into which the various levels merge. This central void culminates in the high space of the garden lounge from which it receives its daylight. A 20 m-long Helen Frankenthaler tapestry forms a focus, and landscaped gardens and terraces surround the (typhoon-resisting) glass walls. Magnificent views exist here toward Hong Kong's harbour to the north and the island's mountain peak to the south.

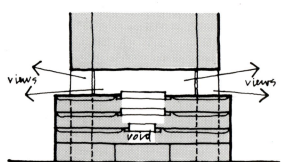

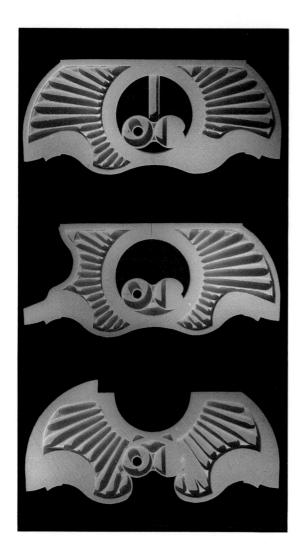

'... The colony's governor used to take the salute from the old club's balcony on Armistice Day – I provided a balcony over the entrance for the same purpose.

The conservative club members asked me whether I could keep something of the old club. I agreed to install the old granite entrance arches – not used structurally – but standing free against the main wall of the central hall ...'

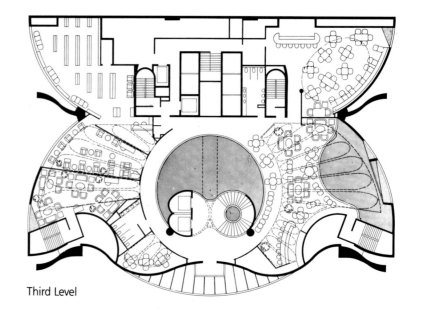

Third Level

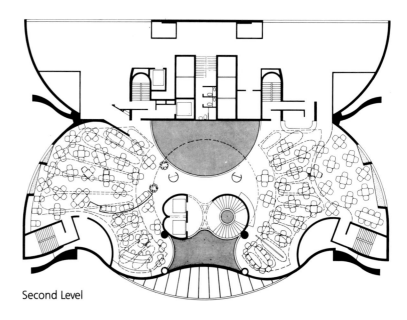

Second Level

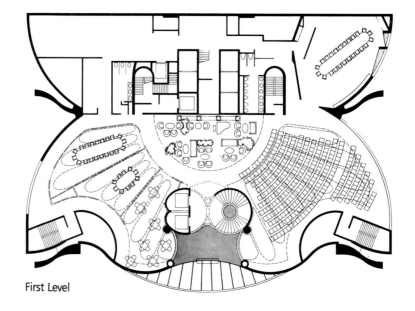

First Level

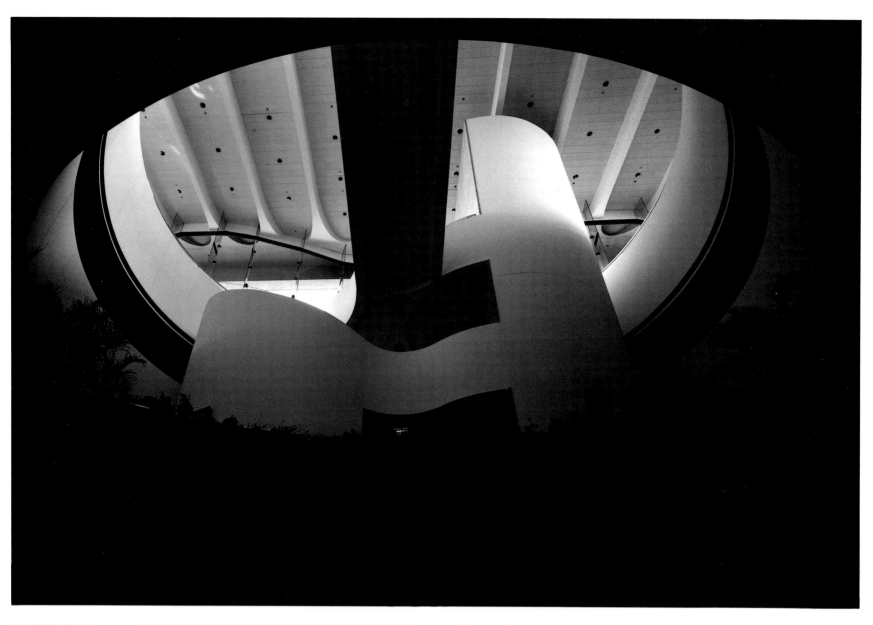

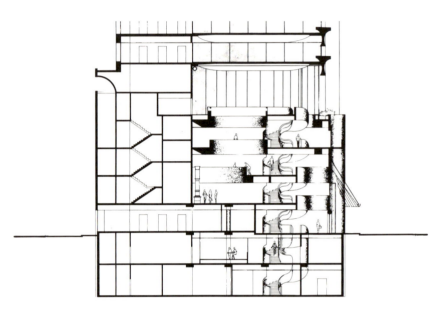

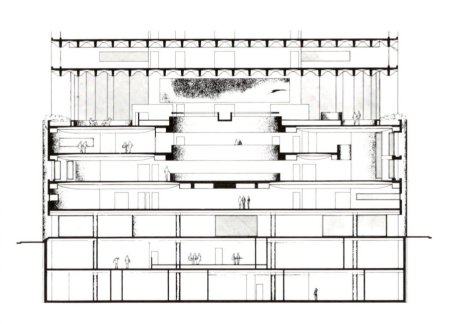

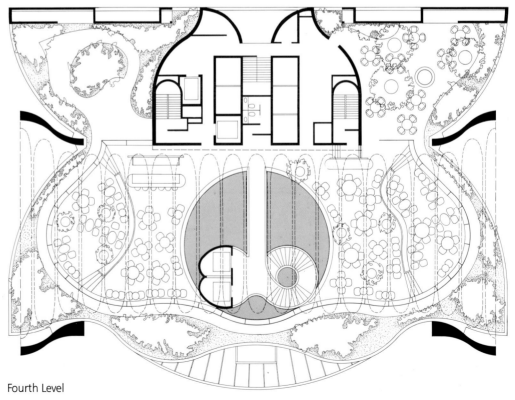
Fourth Level

'... On site I was fascinated to watch the Chinese formworkers – one man wearing a grey Mao-type jacket gave instructions to about 10 carpenters – and did they work! I have never seen such effective teamwork elsewhere ... I brought dozens of those jackets back for everyone in our office – to do likewise ...'

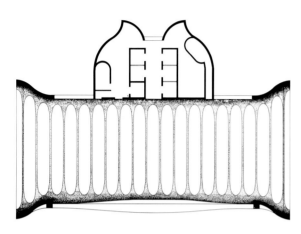

The independent superstructure's four huge corner columns are shaped to act as lateral wind braces, but also fan out to offer maximum views from the interior to the north and south.

The expressive form of the facade beams was originally evolved with Pier Luigi Nervi on a number of projects in the 1970s. They are pre-stressed and shaped to create an increasingly wide top compression flange. As stresses alter to shear toward the support, the beam profile becomes a vertical rectangle. Internal spans are formed by changing-section Ts.

In industrialised countries with high labour costs, these structural forms were used as precast elements lifted into place by crane. To force this notion, however logical, into the Hong Kong labour scene would be unreasonable. Here ample labour was available at costs far lower than in Europe, Australia or the USA. It is therefore more appropriate economically to form these floor elements conventionally and pour concrete on site, a procedure which readily allows for the varying length and radiating pattern of the beams. Chinese traditional bamboo scaffolding was used throughout!

The exterior of the building is faced with exfoliated Sardinian granite. The facade beams are white.

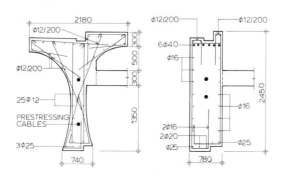

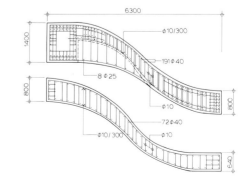

Waverley Civic Centre
Melbourne, 1982–84

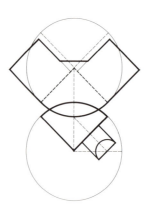

This civic centre and municipal council office building serves a population of about 130,000. The complex stands on beautifully landscaped gently sloping ground. The approach leads up from the main access road and serves as the car arrival entry. Pedestrians can also enter from the upper level of the site over a newly created plaza forecourt.

Both entries are marked by freestanding symbolic entrance porticos through which the visitor reaches the high central entrance atrium space. Different but related uses are accommodated in the new building, housed on either side of this space.

A two-storey wing contains the new council chamber, mayor's office, council facilities, function and meeting spaces. A three-storey wing houses the new council offices including future expansion space.

The high central atrium foyer can on occasions be used for large gatherings, art shows and exhibitions.

A ramp leads up from the lower entry to a freestanding elevator and an open stair which gives access to all departmental offices. A suspended bridge across the entry space connects the council chamber and its ancillary public spaces with executive offices.

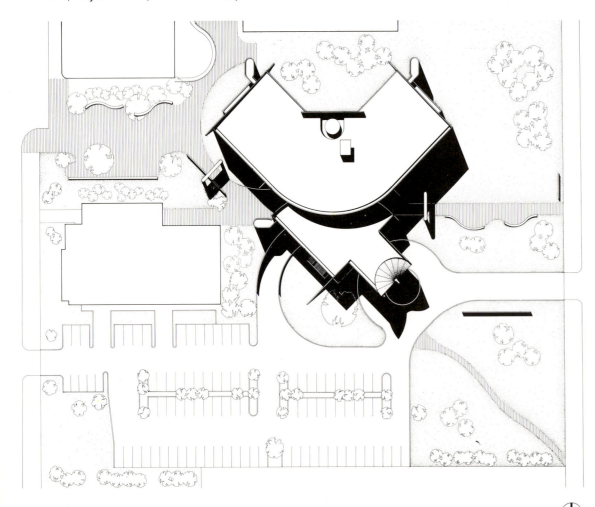

The most distinctive element in the new complex is the shape of the skylight roof over the council chamber (its form reminiscent of Veronese battlements). It consists of two opposing quadrant-shaped concrete walls forming a semicircular vault which allows overhead daylight to enter the otherwise windowless chamber. Translucent glazing admits diffused daylight, shielded by vertical sunblades. Supported on a single column standing in a circular reflecting pool, the council chamber forms the main silhouette of the new building.

The quadrant and related curved forms are used in other elements of the building such as in the opposite and intersecting plan shapes of the two wings which cross in the main entry space, the forms of the windowless stair towers, various curved screen walls and outdoor seating benches.

The building is of permanent fireproof masonry materials, mostly reinforced concrete, some of which is prestressed to allow long spans and in the cantilevered council chamber structure. The exterior of the chamber is of matt glazed white ceramic tiles and elsewhere, on floor edges and the vertical concrete sun protection louvres, it is of white epoxy. In contrast, fawn-coloured split concrete block is used for other exterior walls.

The atrium floor is of grey Norwegian quartzite.

The council chamber has tables of Indian Tamin granite and rough-textured plaster walls.

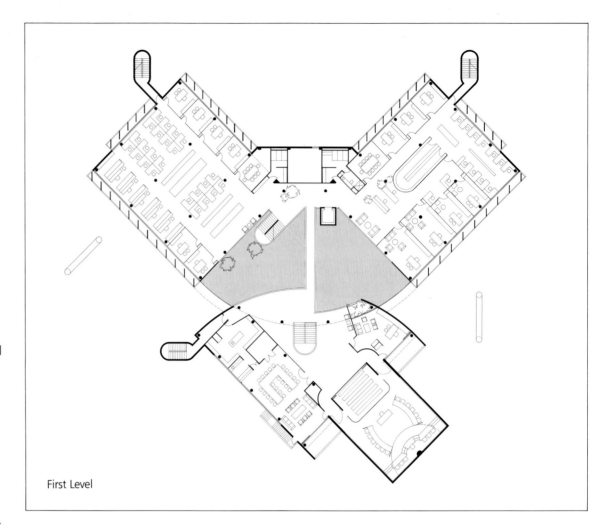

First Level

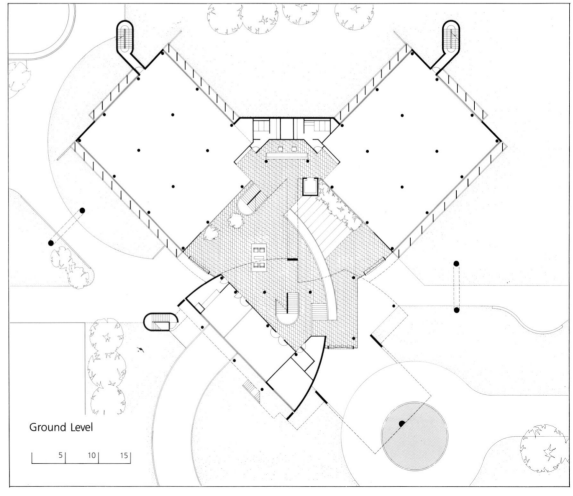

Ground Level

'... In New South Wales I have always fought with Local Government, even went to court when they objected to modern design – but in Victoria, this local Council wanted only the most progressive architecture. We built other buildings for them also – it always depends on the individuals involved...'

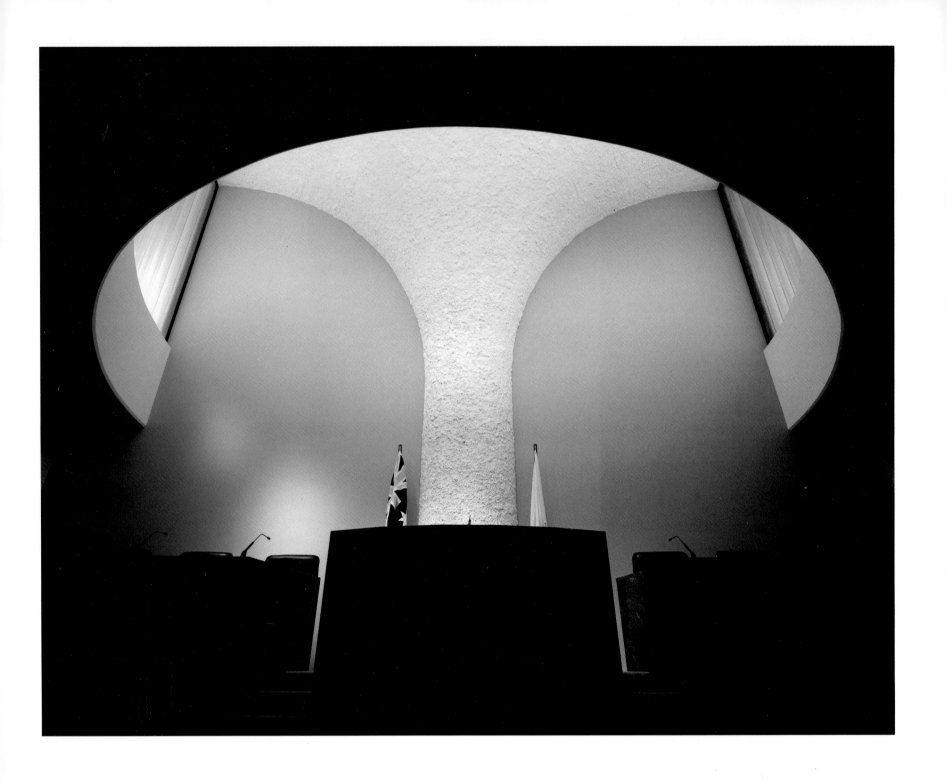
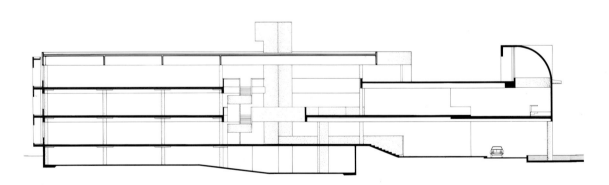

L. Basser House
Castle Cove, 1980–81

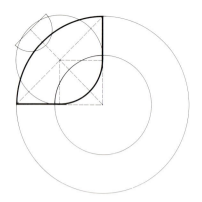

Located at the end of a cul-de-sac, the site is fan-shaped, slopes away abruptly from the road level and offers 180° views of Middle Harbour to the north. To maximise the view to the water, the plan is in the form of a quadrant with all living areas facing the view.

The 250 m² house is planned on four split-level floors adjusted to the slope of the land. The garage is level with the street at the top and a semi-circular swimming pool extends the playroom and terrace of the lower floor.

The main walls are of split-faced concrete blocks inside and out, the floor and columns off-form concrete. Living areas are covered with quartzite stone and bedrooms are carpeted. The large windows are protected by deep overhangs and downturns.

The roof is framed with regular, radial steel beams.

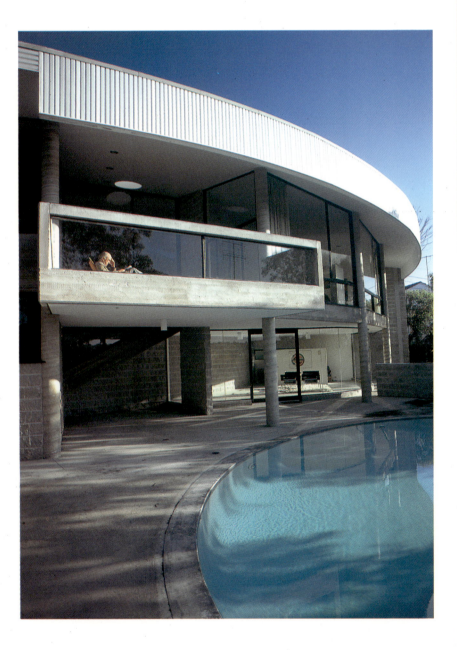

Merson House
Palm Beach, 1981–83

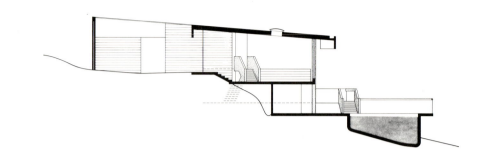

This house is built on a steeply sloping spectacular site. Below lies the full sweeping arc of Sydney's northernmost peninsula and headland beyond.

For the same reason as the L. Basser house (p. 226) the plan shape reflects the arc of the view focusing on it the north-facing central high space of the skylit garden room with its outdoor terrace projecting over the steep slope. The elliptical swimming pool is approached from this, its axial geometry being related to the terrace front.

Following the existing rock contours, the plan is divided into a high-ceilinged living area to the east extending onto an outdoor dining terrace and a two-storey bedroom wing to the west, the upper level of which is approached over a bridge from the entry area.

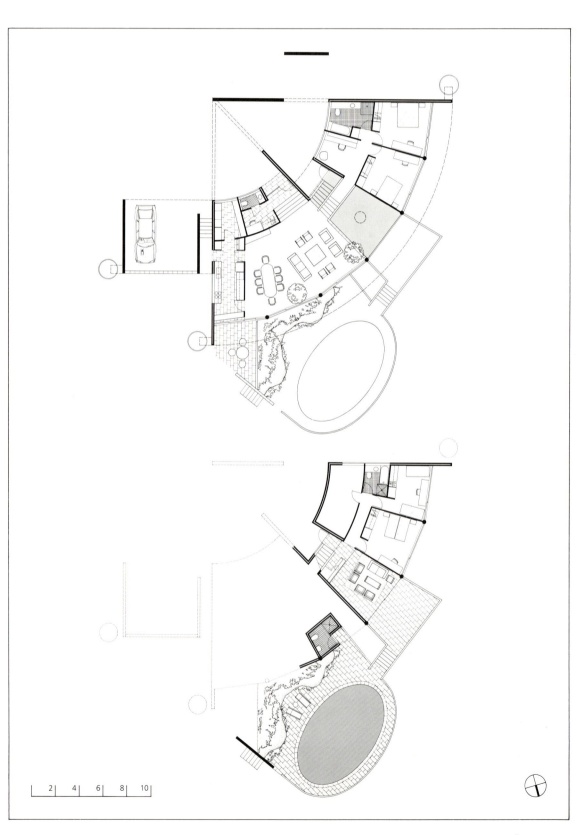

Bland House
Rose Bay, 1981–83

On the site for this 260 m² suburban home is a high rock outcrop which steeply slopes away toward the approach and the side of the land. From it there is a fine expansive view of Sydney Harbour and the city skyline toward the north-west.

This top level was chosen for the living room with a deep continuous verandah across the view side. To give some of the same view also to the dining room, it is raised behind the living area.

The entry below, adjacent to the partially excavated garage, leads into a central stair hall which connects the living with the two-storey, split-level bedroom wing.

The rectilinear form of the plan is opposed by curvilinear elements in retaining walls, the swimming pool and the freestanding fireplace.

'... the more I know your work, the better I like it. It's like beautiful music; the more you hear it, the more you understand and love it ... A "Seidler" designed home is not "fashionable", or "trendy", it has a timeless beauty about it ... It is, as the French would say, "bien dans sa peau" ("content within itself"), and this shows through on the outside ... '
Letter to the office from Bruce Bland, May 1983

Hannes House
Cammeray, 1983–84

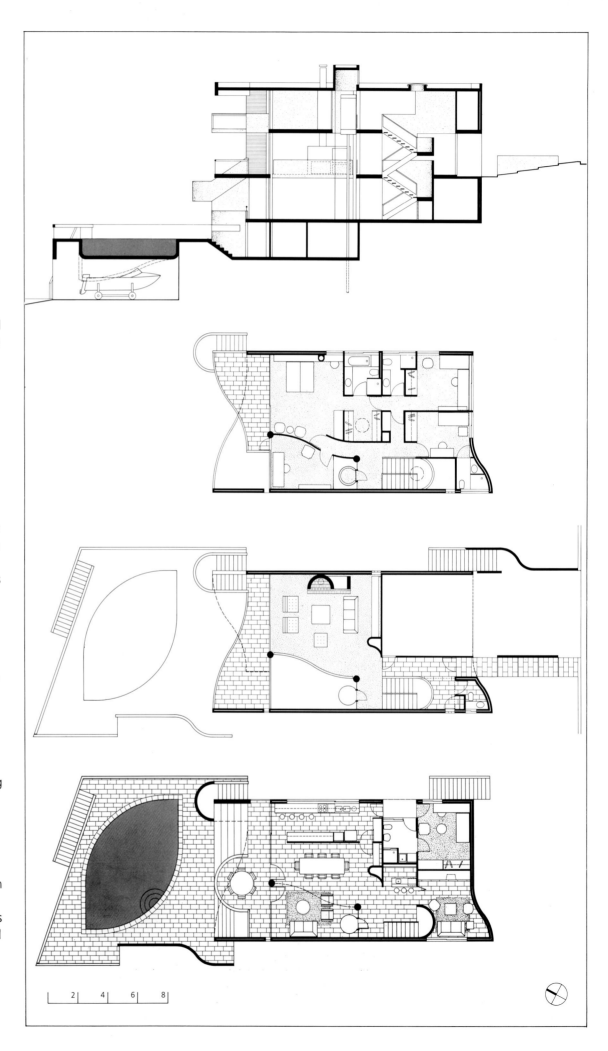

The waterfront site faces a branch of Sydney Harbour toward the north. Although narrow, it enjoys a tranquil setting with a view across moored yachts toward a public reserve and golf course on the opposite shore. It is hard to believe that such a secluded, peaceful position and natural outlook is a mere 10 minutes drive away from the centre of Sydney.

The living areas of the 350 m² house are arranged on three floors. Due to the slope of the ground, the garage, entrance and main living room are on the centre floor, the dining–family room and kitchen below, and all bedrooms above. A part-basement service floor contains a whirlpool and sauna, all connected with the outdoor pool terrace.

The three storeys of the house are joined spatially by an open void which allows views up and down from every level with drama added by the free-standing, circular glass elevator. It serves and joins the levels through the open vertical space.

The house is of reinforced concrete with grey face brick supporting walls. The lowest floor and terraces are paved in split quartzite stone slabs, others have white carpet. Surfaces on the interior and exterior are white. Granite is used on the dining table, cabinet tops, the fireplace front and kitchen counters.

Built over the steep drop to the water's edge, the swimming pool is reached from the family–dining area and has below it covered space for a boat.

The simple rectangular structure is enriched by the use of opposing undulating forms on the edges of the projecting terraces and roof overhang on the northern viewside. The resulting varying depth of terraces allows wide areas for outdoor sitting groups and creates deeper sun protection overhangs over two-storey-high glass walls. These curves and countercurves are recalled at the front of the house, on the interior, in screen and retaining wall extensions and the opposing quadrant sides of the swimming pool. Its resulting long diagonal maximises the swimming length.

237

'... the requirement for an elevator in a house was new to me. There were no acceptable standards. It had to be specially made and we had to design every detail – there was more work in this, than in the rest of the house ...'

Grosvenor Place
Sydney, 1982–88

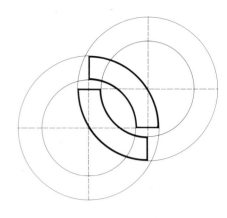

The 0.72 ha government leasehold site, at the northern end of Sydney's Central Business District, offers panoramic views toward the Harbour, the Opera House and the Bridge to the north-east and Darling Harbour to the south-west.

Pedestrian circulation diagonally through the site toward 'The Rocks' historic precinct had to be provided and existing 'heritage' buildings along the south boundary restored.

The plan form of a quadrant and its opposing configuration maximised the sweep of the best views and open space outlook. The shape, being based on clear geometry, inherently offers opportunities for a long span, column-free system of floor construction, whereby every structural span and beam are identical. It follows that every column, its space, and the floor load it carries are the same, just as is every facade element.

The brief required a pension fund's investment in rental office space totalling 90,000 m². Typical floors had to contain up to 2000 m² net flexible floor space unencumbered by internal columns. 600 cars are provided for in an underground garage.

With the tower occupying just over one-quarter of the area, the ground plan provides an appropriate amount of open plaza–recreation space for the thousands of office workers and visitors to the project. A central fountain with seating benches and outdoor eating amongst trees are contained on the northern sunny paved area. Undulating screen walls and a low restaurant and bank building (which covers the garage entry ramps) make the area secluded from surrounding streets. Circular garage ventilation shafts define the northern pedestrian entry to the plaza.

On the opposite south-western side of the tower and adjacent to the restored old buildings, a glass-covered plaza below the street offers a variety of restaurants and seating for lunchtime crowds.

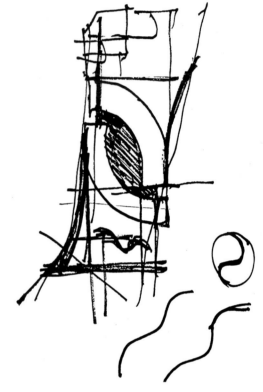

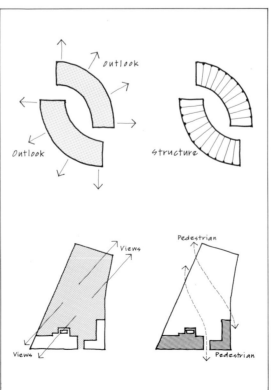

'... Realisation of a project invariably depends on one individual – a client who knows what is wanted and trusts his architect to produce it. At Grosvenor, such a person was Bob Hammond, who overcame all the hurdles... The best buildings don't emerge from consensus committee meetings...'

A building of such breadth and height warrants an entrance of consequent scale. Each three of the numerous external columns of the tower were 'gathered' together with V-shaped transfer members into a circular caisson. This changed the ground floor spacing and height of supports into a suitable larger proportion and gave importance to the circular glazed entrance lobby.

Three colourful wall-relief paintings by Frank Stella adorn the grey granite-clad core walls.

The curved facades receive a changing amount of sun radiation at different times. At the east it is the near-horizontal rising sun, at the north-west it is the medium-height morning sun, and at the north it is the high midday sun. A system of external shades has been designed to meet these conditions. They form an integral permanent fixed part of the facade and are planned to intercept the changing sun's rays around the building. Even if not subjected to direct sun, these external shades are beneficial in eliminating sky glare and avoiding the use of conventional venetian blinds inside.

Considering the superb harbour views available to the building, glass is taken from ceiling to within 30 cm of the floor so as to allow a downward angle of view.

Office occupants have often expressed the wish for outdoor terraces to be provided. Responding to this and interspersed over the tower's exterior are 'facade gardens'; deeply recessed, one or more floors high, are planted areas offering relief from the sealed air-conditioned environment of typical offices. They are provided for a certain proportion of floors, related to reception areas, boardrooms and directors' offices, usually near the approaches from elevator lobbies.

Their positioning together with the rooftop, north-facing solar collector aperture imparts a deliberate dynamic pattern of shaded interruptions to the otherwise repetitive texture of the facade.

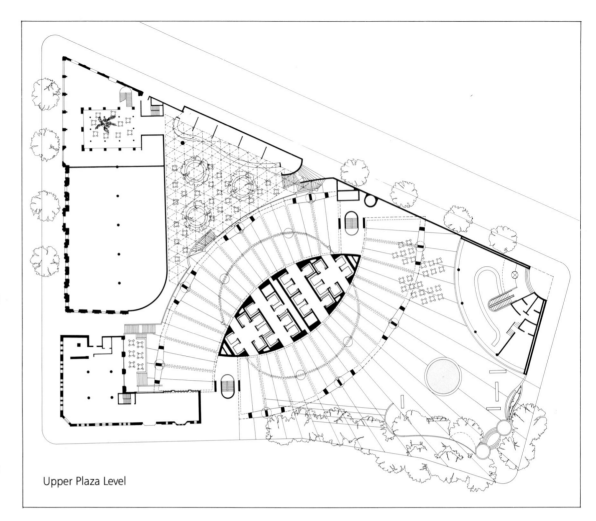

Upper Plaza Level

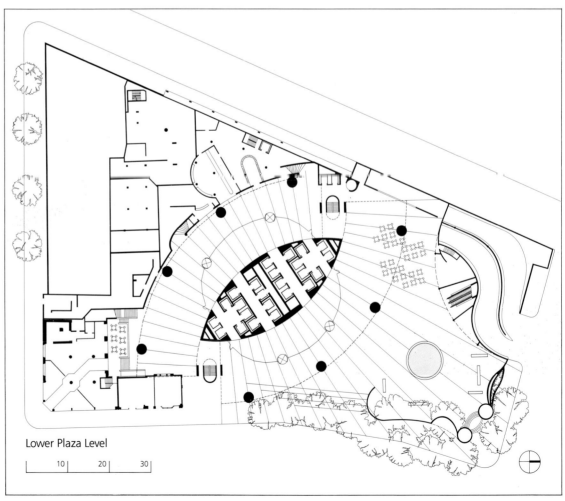

Lower Plaza Level

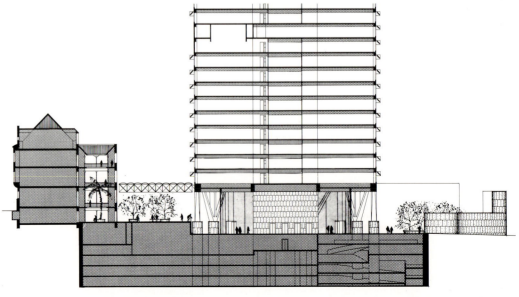

'... Ever since his protractor series of the 1960s, I have felt a rapport with Frank Stella. What I like about his work is that he doesn't stand still but is constantly exploring new visions. He liked the scale of the lobby and originally proposed six works on both sides of the core. Half of these became redundant when the authorities insisted on the preservation of the adjacent "heritage" buildings. His off-the-wall paintings bring life to the space, not only by their exuberantly colourful layered forms and textures, but by their hovering disposition in the space they control and the shadows cast within them...'

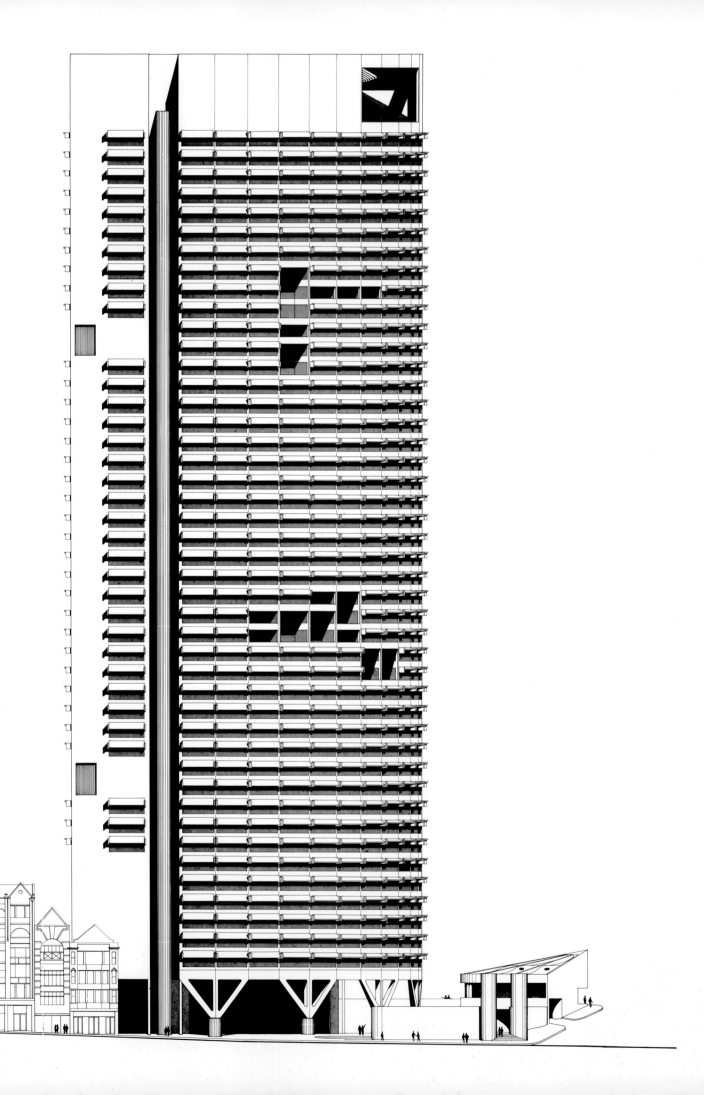

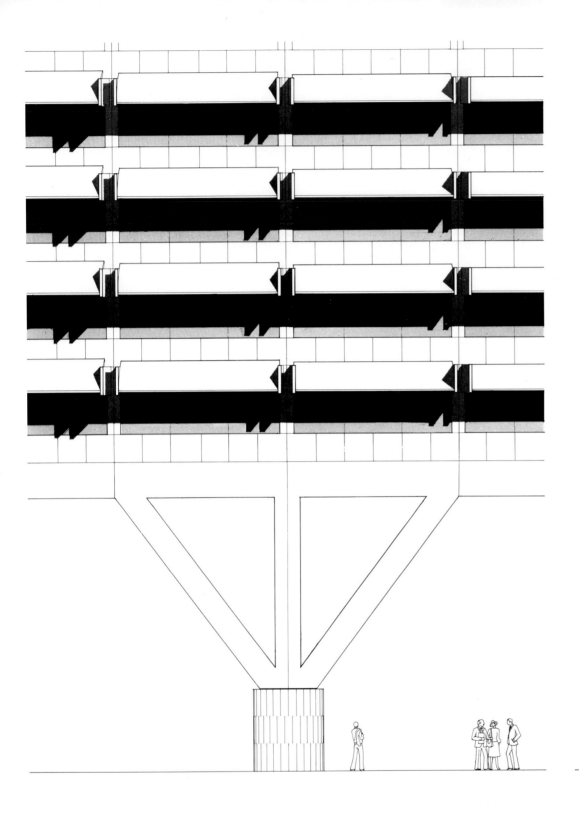
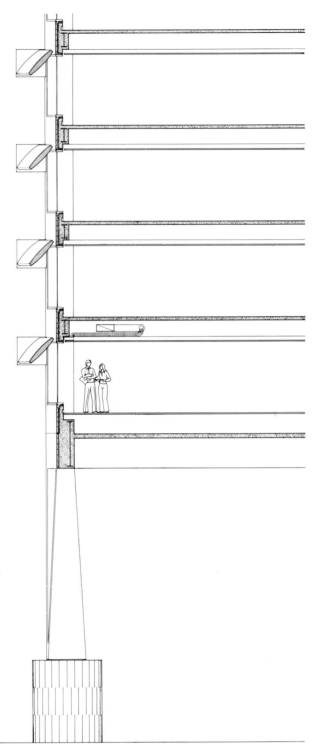
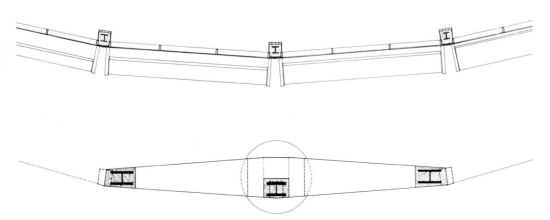

The aluminium sunshades are held at different inclines in each bay between standard side brackets, which are fixed through the grey Sardinian granite cladding of the facades.

The space between the brackets accommodates the tensioned security cables for the roof-mounted window-cleaning cradle, which can luff in and out between the sunblades to gain access to the glass.

I.E.L. Tenancy

The 14.5 m clear span of the floors allows freedom of internal planning. On one side of this tenancy are the generously planned executive offices, meeting and dining rooms, defined by curved glass, solid walls and polished stone floors. On the other side, workstations and central secretarial desks allow outward views for all occupants. In addition to elevator banks and services, the core contains kitchens, compactus and security rooms.

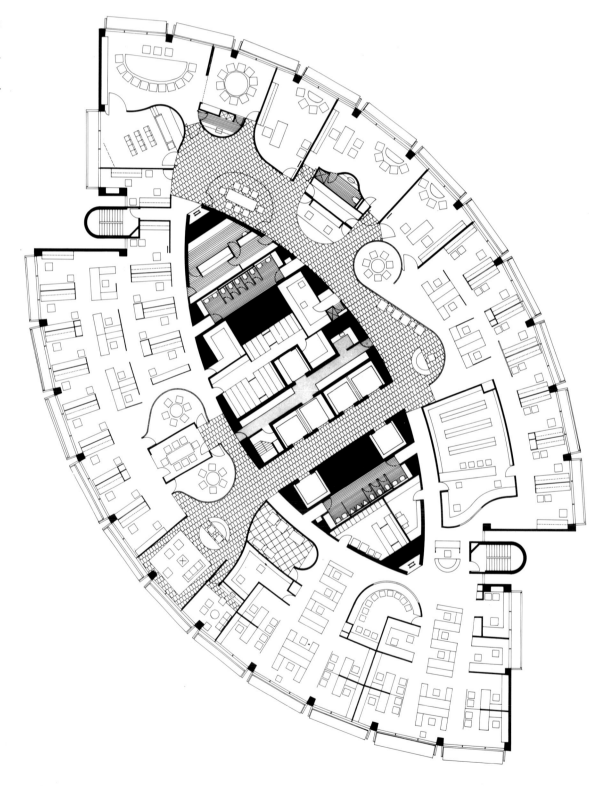

'... only one beam, one column, one spandrel and one sunshade ...'

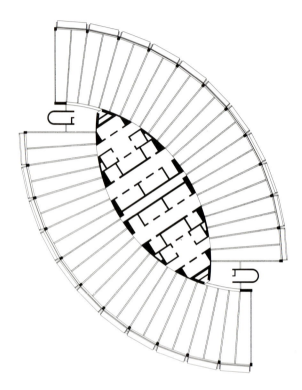

The concrete core construction went up ahead of the surrounding steel structure of identical steel beams, metal deck and external columns.

To a achieve a high fire-rated facade prefabricated spandrel panels – used as permanent forms to concrete – encase the exterior steel beams.

The panels were made of thin glass-reinforced concrete (GRC) complete with secured polished granite facings prior to hoisting.

With constantly rising energy costs, active and passive energy conservation was addressed effectively. Due to the long tenure ownership, an investment was made in energy-saving technology. Power is generated from roof-mounted inclined and tracking solar collectors. This is amplified by reusing waste heat, ranging from people, carparks, elevators, etc., and storing this energy in extensive ice banks in the basement.

To avoid peak demand charges of daytime power, economic night-time 'off-peak' electricity is used to store further energy in the ice bank for daytime use. Consequently, there are no heating boilers in the building, which compared with other buildings, has shown dramatic economy in energy consumption.

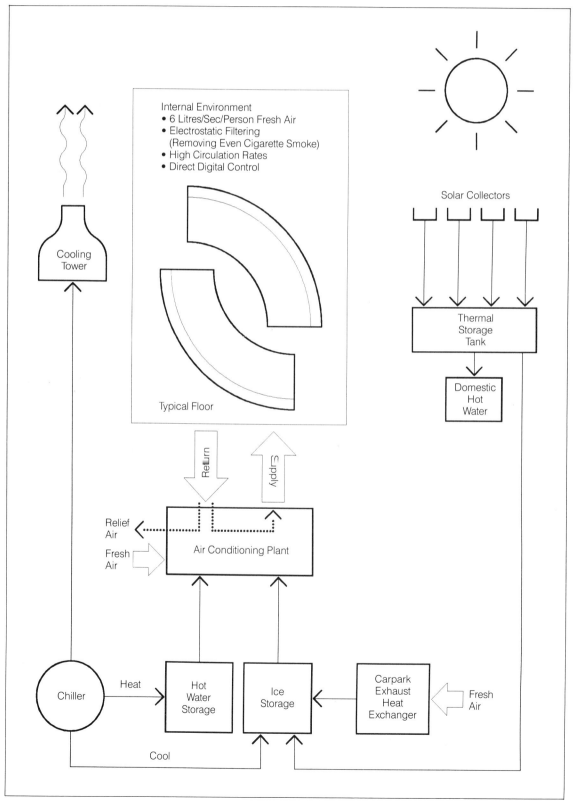

Riverside Development Stage 1
Brisbane, 1983–86

'... We first heard of this project on 1 August 1983 and final completion – the opening was in September 1986, just three years! ...'

The first stage of this two-stage project is complete. It is built on a 2 ha site fronting Brisbane's riverfront at one end of the city's business centre.

Previously blocked off by a continuous wall of low buildings and wooden wharves, the location offered the opportunity for development to open up the river's edge and make it accessible to the city. Construction was permitted to extend into the water, but covered space had to be provided for a future water-edge expressway below. Ferry wharves and a marina for private yachts had to be planned.

The site offers fine views up and down the river. This asset was maximised in the design of the 40-storey first stage tower which had to contain 50,000 m^2 net of commercial office space, with 1500 m^2 per floor free of internal columns.

The Brisbane Stock Exchange had to be housed in the base of the tower and provision was to be made for restaurants, banks, shops and an underground carpark for 500 cars. Planning had to allow for a second stage, originally to be a hotel but later changed to be offices.

Plan forms for both stages were evolved which took the greatest advantage of direct water views. Most square, round or rectangular central core plans (usually the most efficient for high-rise office towers) were discarded as offering limited water views in favour of a triangular plan which not only faced more than two-thirds of offices to the water but did so up and down the river's length. Water outlook was effective even from top floors which otherwise would look straight across the river. The shape also preserved and respected the views from a second stage without impairing privacy between the buildings.

On the waterfront a large public space is defined by lower buildings which surround the tower. A wide opening toward the riverfront is left framed by a huge curved connecting beam defining the open plaza. Steps lead down to the water under this opening, traversed by a series of ramps ('stramps') which provide the required handicapped people's access to the public ferry wharves. This public access to the water will be extended in the future on both sides beyond the site to form a continuous waterfront promenade.

The public plaza is a varied space, both horizontally and vertically, and will connect to adjacent developments. It provides both shelter and open space, containing fountains, trees, seating, outdoor restaurants, shops and a tavern. It has become a lively, popular place, crowded at lunchtime and especially on weekends when an open-air market is held.

The Stock Exchange occupies two of the three sides at the base of the tower, allowing a 15 m-high lobby to be planned across the street frontage. The surrounding floors become mezzanines overlooking this space which has a large centrally placed sculpture by Carlberg and tapestries by Calder. A continuous cantilevered glass canopy gives tropical rain protection to the entrances.

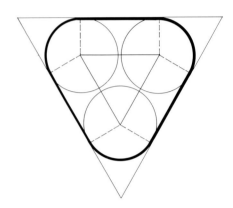

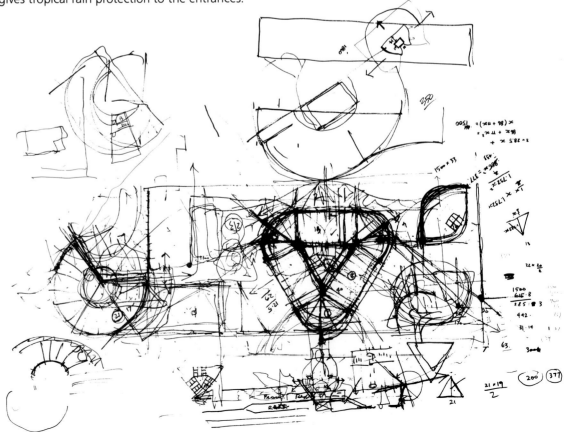

Upper Plaza Level

Lower Plaza Level

| 10 | 20 | 30 |

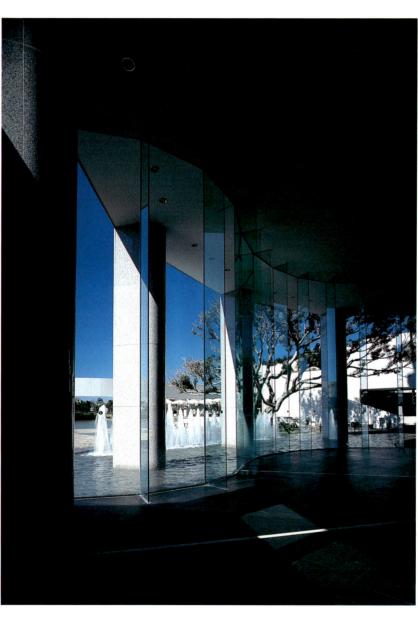

'... I was first introduced to Norman Carlberg's sculptures in Josef and Anni Albers' house in America in the 1960s. They proudly showed me one of his negative–positive reversal pieces in their living room. "It really works – doesn't it?" said Albers, which was a rare compliment – Carlberg had been one of his students at Yale.

With an assembly made of only a single, simple, quadrant-shaped element, he produced a rich and dynamic work of subtlety and yet complexity. By its presence it enriches the space and interacts beautifully with the Nervi successor Mario Desideri's radiating rib structure above...'

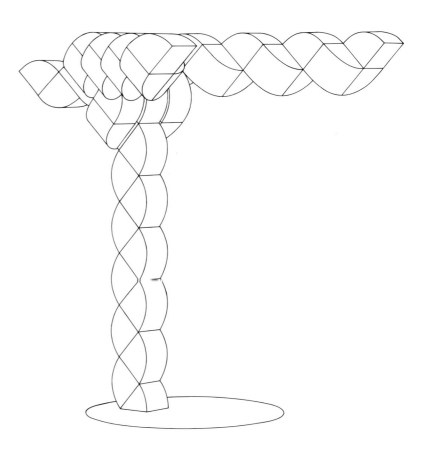

267

Rather than extending all tower columns to the ground, six columns are 'gathered' and their loads transferred into two hyperboloid-shaped supports which allow the monumentally scaled entrance to be opened up to the street. The redirection of the tower's street columns created a structural need to brace the new supports back to the rigid central core. This is done by a system of radiating and curved exposed beams which become visible on the high lobby ceiling (in consultation with Dr M. Desideri of Rome, Pier Luigi Nervi's successor).

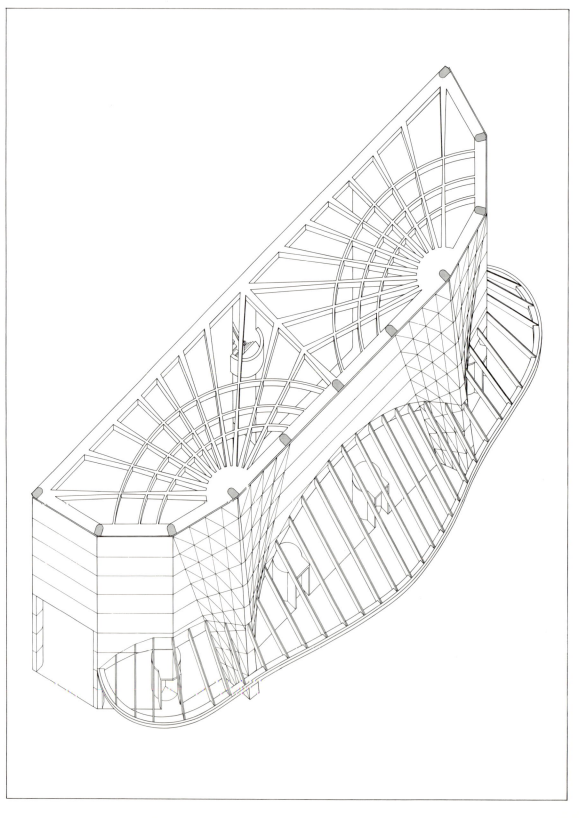

'... a fin-de-siècle glass canopy translated into late 20th-century technology...'

Traditional buildings in the area have always expressed the semitropical climate by providing sun protection awnings and verandahs. As in previous projects aluminium shades varyingly inclined protect the full-height glass walls of the two sunny sides of the tower. Recessed 'facade gardens' are interspersed over the elevations facing up and down the river.

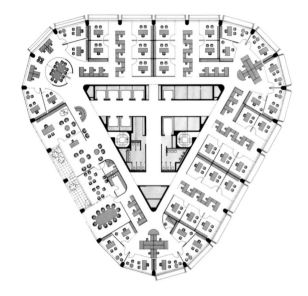

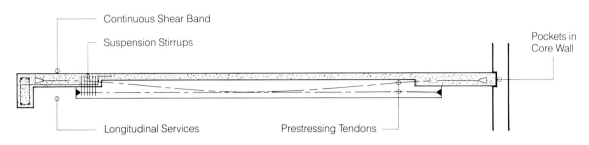

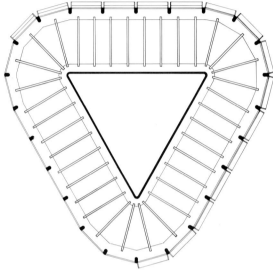

The poured-in-place concrete tower had to be built quickly and efficiently (the whole project took less than three years from commencement of design to completion). The need for a systematised cycle of construction (completing a floor every four working days) was one of the intrinsic reasons for the tower's shape. Typical floors have a clear span of 12.5 m which allows flexibility for any subdivision. All beams are the same length along the straight sides and radiating around the corners. The beam webs stop short of their supports which enabled prestressing to be done from the safety of the floor rather than from the outside. The resulting gaps along the edges of the shortened beams became longitudinal channels providing space for the passage of air-conditioning ducts within the structural floor depth.

Hydraulically operated table forms were used for speedy erection and dismantling. Every granite-faced facade element between the 6 m-spaced columns is straight and identical. The core, containing three lift rises, preceded the floor construction utilising a slip-form technique.

Riverside Development Stage 2
Brisbane, 1988

A second office tower is planned to complement the first. Its ground level development forms a sympathetic expansion of the public waterfront spaces of the existing. The promenade is extended and another plaza space is created offering outdoor dining and recreation facilities. A new common arrival and car setdown area has been planned for the whole project, located between the two towers.

The new building's semi-circular ended plan form places the services core against the non-outlook, street side, so that from almost the entire floor one can see the water. The shape of the tower and its placing does not disturb the outlook from tower 1 (p. 258).

A large glass-roofed atrium entry with visitors' seating and interior planting leads through the elevator lobbies to the waterfront spaces. As for tower 1, the second tower has clear-span floors of identical straight and radiating prestressed beams. The materials used for facades and sunshades are all the same, ensuring the aim of both stages forming a cohesive unity.

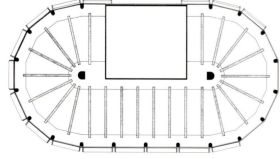

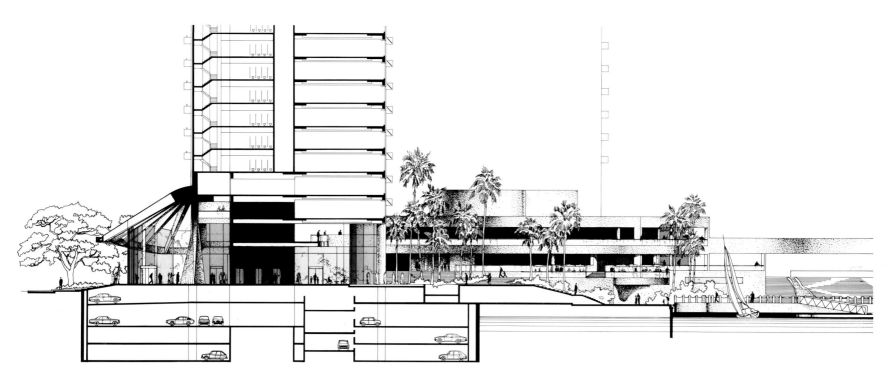
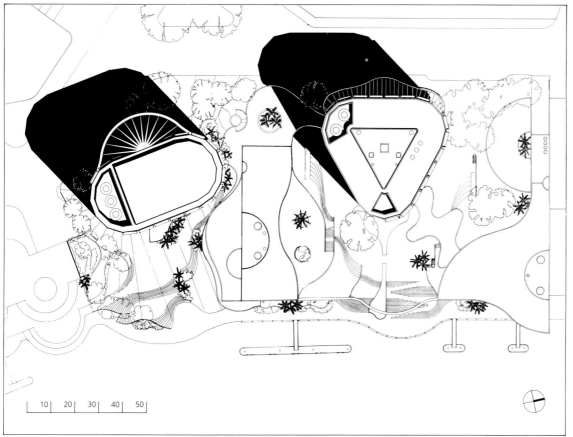

| 10 | 20 | 30 | 40 | 50 |

Hilton Hotel
Brisbane, 1984–86

The T-shaped site for this mixed development of a shopping complex and upper floors hotel is located in the hub of city life, along Brisbane's bustling pedestrian mall.

The height of the base structure relates to adjacent existing shopping buildings and has direct connection to them.

To place a hotel wing utilising the depth of the site for bedrooms would offer no desirable outlook and have them face blank walls of existing or future buildings. By planning the bedrooms across the site, distant views are opened up and podium rooftop space becomes available for the required swimming pool terrace and tennis court.

A typical vertical hotel block provides a dull, claustrophobic, routine approach to guestrooms and offers no daylit focal space for public areas of lobby, restaurants, bars, etc.

By spreading the base of the hotel rooms, an interior vertical space is created. An identity-giving central area is considered essential in a city hotel which has no outward exposure opportunities for its public spaces. It creates its own drama internally with the glass elevators' dramatic ascent. The public areas are overlooked from access galleries to the hotel rooms above, and enjoy the tapering skylit space overhead.

Individual hotel room windows look at the view through projecting planting troughs which 'filter' the harsh city rooftop outlook and also form desirable sun protection overhangs.

The podium structure is externally faced with natural stone. Dark aluminium-framed windows contain toughened heat-absorbing glass.

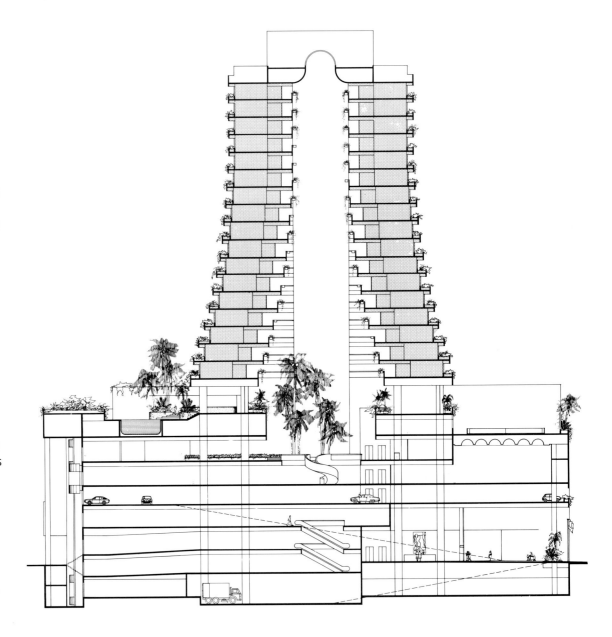

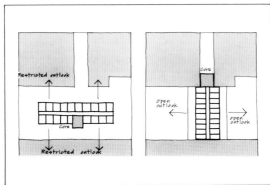

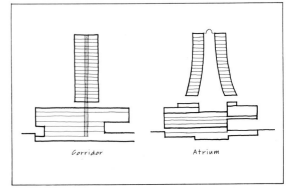

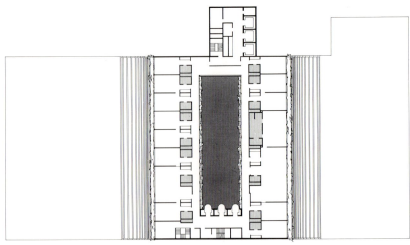
Typical High Level

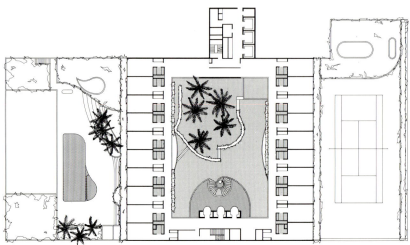
Typical Low Level

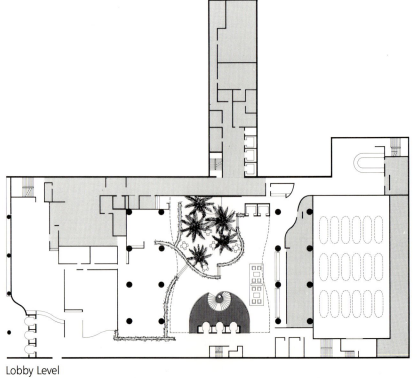
Lobby Level

Capita Centre
Sydney, 1984–89

'... When we were first approached to design on that impossibly narrow and squeezed-in site, I didn't want to get involved – but after thinking about it, I felt it was important to try to solve such an increasingly common problem in our cities ...'

In our increasingly crowded cities it is inevitable that sites are created, or rather left over, which are not desirable for development.

Even though this landlocked site is surrounded by 25–30-storey buildings on three sides, it was the wish of the owners, an insurance company, to have their headquarter offices located in this very heart of the business centre.

The 30 m-wide and 42 m-deep site has only one street frontage, and its narrow appendage is too small for office development. With only one side open, it became clear that a solution for office space on such a site would have to generate its own internal source of daylight and outlook.

The main part of the site can be divided into six square areas 12 m x 13 m. Given that the owners did not require large floor areas (they are 700 m^2), only four of the six squares are built on, and one-third of the site becomes open outdoor space onto which offices can look and from which daylight becomes available.

To create something more than a mere light well, the building is hollowed out for its full height by an open-air atrium. Changing its position from the south side, to the centre, and stepping up to the north, ledges are created and planted with trees and shrubs.

The base atrium is located against the southern boundary and forms the dramatically high entrance space.

In the middle rise of the building, the atrium is central and open to the north. It steps progressively outward toward the boundary from where sun and daylight penetrate down to the very base of the structure's hollow centre.

At the top of the building, which is above the height of adjoining multistorey buildings, the open space's width is against the northern boundary. Here views to the north and east, to the harbour, become progressively better toward the top floors.

It follows that throughout the building all resulting office areas are a maximum of 12 m from a window and overlook one of the atrium spaces, all of which are landscaped with large trees. Provision is made for sufficient soil depth for some of the trees to reach heights of 15 m or more. The stepped outline of the internal open spaces ensures that some sun and natural daylight reaches all planted terraces.

Being located between two streets, the ground floor becomes a pedestrian through-link. This is the most richly landscaped area with high palms adjacent to the wave-shaped glass-covered lobby and a porcelain tile mural by Lin Utzon.

The narrow back of the site accommodates a restaurant and mezzanine bar. The diffusing glass-vaulted roof's end wall is formed by a 10 m-high water-wall fountain.

The stepped hollowing out of the 31-storey steel-framed building created a laterally unstable structural condition, especially across the glazed street facade. Since no shear-resisting walls were possible an exposed vertical truss brace-frame is placed outside the facade, allowing passage between, for the window-cleaning cradle. The diagonal steel members across the full height of the building eliminate the central column at ground level, and create a desirably wide opening into the planted forecourt. The truss extends above the roof and supports a 30 m-high retractable flagpole.

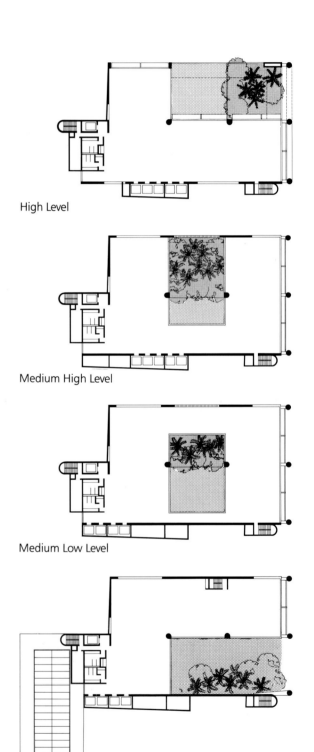

High Level

Medium High Level

Medium Low Level

Low Level

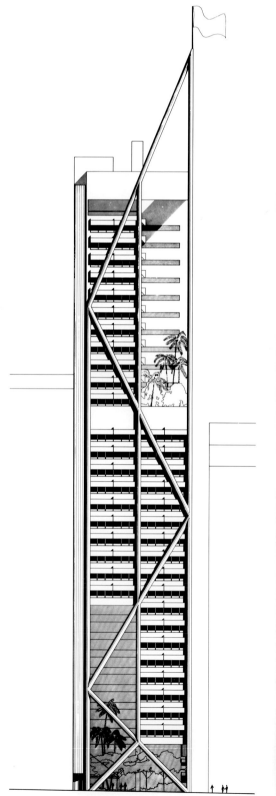
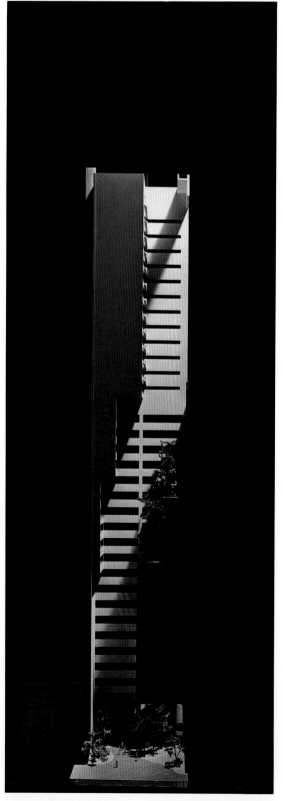
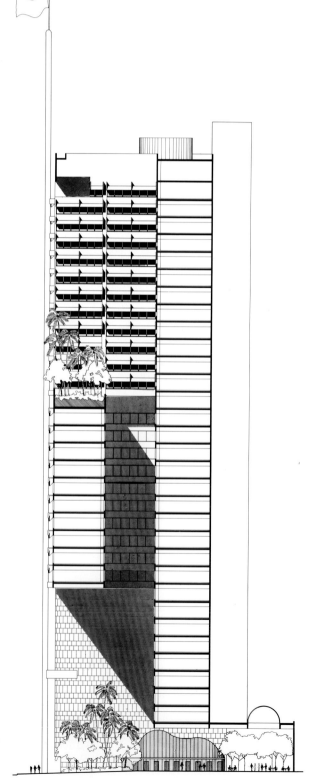

'... We had a marvellous client in David Greatorex who went all the way with us when we suggested a lush rainforest at ground level and huge trees all the way up the ledges of the atrium. Lyn Utzon's platinum and blue porcelain mural became a visual counterpoint and a magnet for the entrance...'

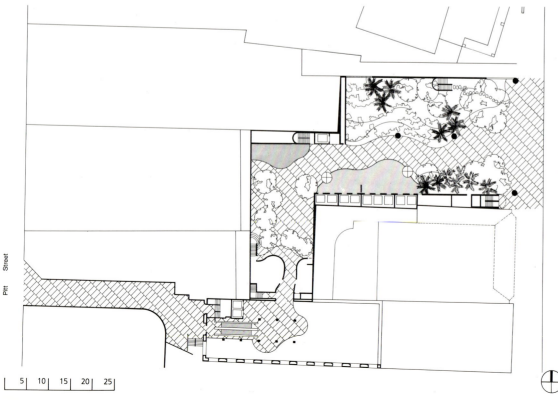

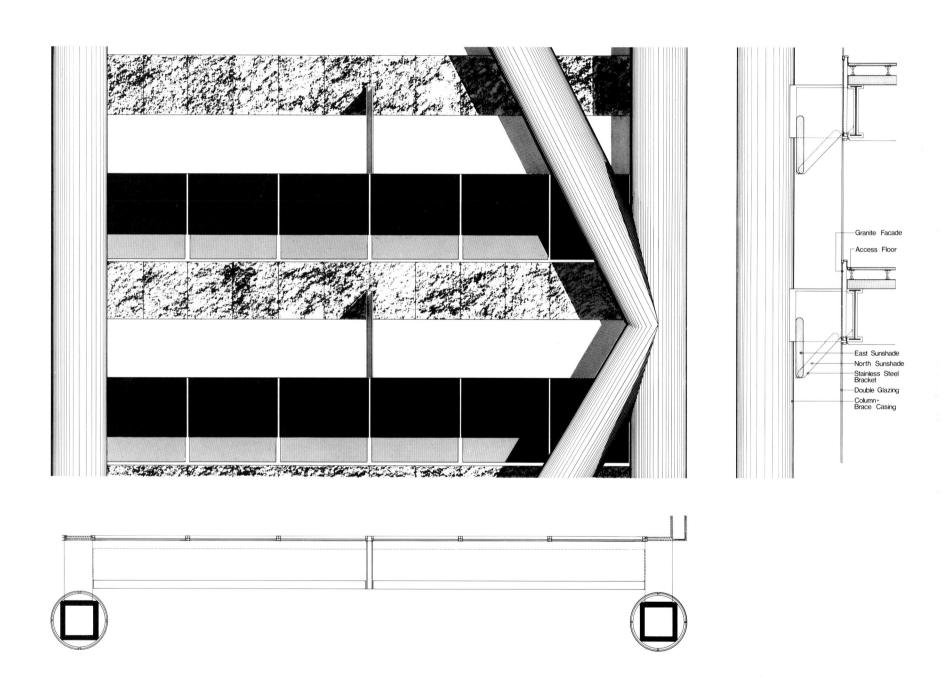

The top executive floor accommodates reception areas, board and dining rooms, opening onto a roof terrace.

The Breuer 1932 aluminium and black leather visitors' chairs are grouped around a Lin Utzon rug (she also did a gold leaf mural in the visitors' lounge).

The Charles Perry bronze is seen against the Indian Tamin granite floor and wall.

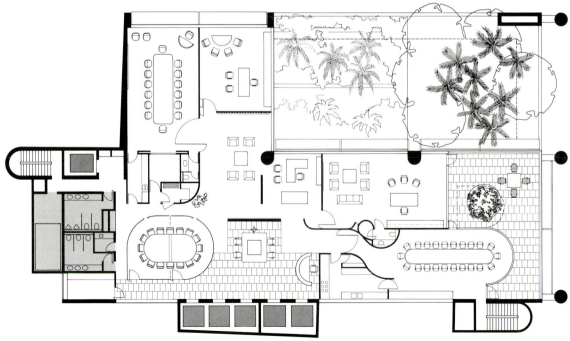

295

Shell Headquarters
Melbourne, 1985–89

Located at the extreme south-east corner of Melbourne's city centre, the site faces open space and parkland with distant mountain and water views.

The plan form of the 30,000 m^2, 28-storey building places the core on the off-view north side. The office floors wrap around the core and maximise the length of building facing toward the full sweep of the panorama. The double curve results from the aim to also face offices to the south-west view toward Port Phillip Bay. The building's shape avoids the railway tunnels cutting across below the site's corner.

The main entrance faces the corner and the axis of the diagonal street, Wellington Parade. The building's end walls are extended to the boundaries of the site at plaza level and step back as the tower rises at levels corresponding to the heights of adjacent buildings. These walls ensure mutual visual seclusion and also incorporate air intake and exhaust risers to basement carparks. Stone-paved upper and lower plaza areas between the building and street are contained by the walls and are landscaped.

At the rear of the L-shaped site, two storeys above the main lobby, a pedestrian entry court is created adjacent to a historic building which had to be maintained. Required uses which could not be contained in the office tower are accommodated in this part of the site: the theatrette for 200, a cafeteria for 300 and 11 conference rooms of different sizes, built around a fountain court. Escalators connect these public areas to the main lobby, where security screening protects the upper floors of the tower.

The typical 1100 m^2 office floors are served by two six-car lift banks and have a uniform 15 m-wide column-free depth from core to glass. 280 cars are parked in basements.

The two partial top floors of the building house executive suites and meeting rooms. They step up toward the east, to the public gardens and mountain view.

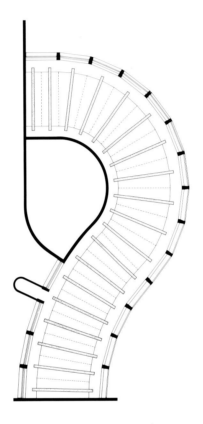

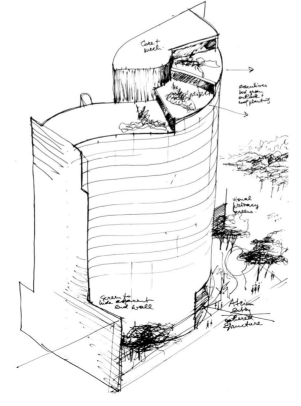

'... When Doug Scott invited me to meet the Board of Shell to discuss how I would approach the design of their new headquarters (hinting that I should show them a design) I made it clear that I do not do free sketches. Before the meeting, I could not stop myself from thinking about the building and putting an idea on paper. After showing the Board slides of our completed buildings, for a few seconds I flashed on a slide of my sketch explaining the idea of a wave-shaped building. I could tell they liked it and they asked me to leave them a copy, which I declined.

They gave us the job – and it was built just like the first sketch . . .'

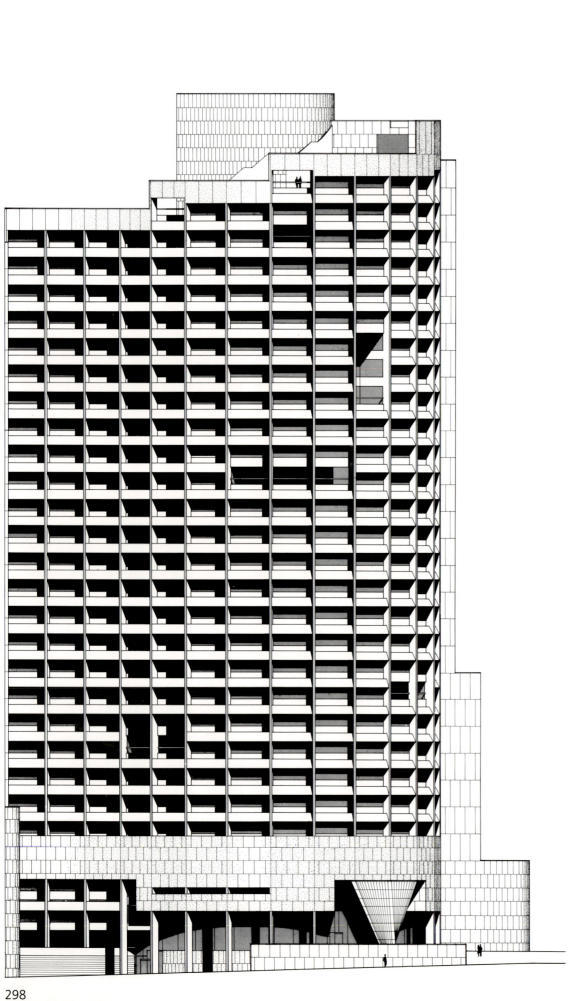

They are connected by lavishly curved granite stairs and open out onto landscaped roof gardens.

The lobby level has a generous ceiling height with a raised central section reaching 10 m above the entry doors. This space contains a porcelain mural painting by Arthur Boyd which together with the entry plaza sculpture by Charles Perry completes the approach setting. The Spring Street entry addresses the corner with a sculptured support pier on axis with Wellington Parade. This pier gathers the loads of three of the building's columns in a structurally expressive and simultaneously decorative way.

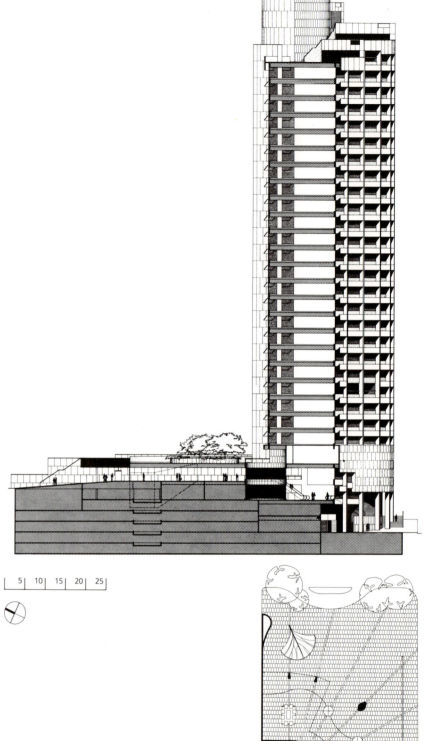

Main Lobby Level

303

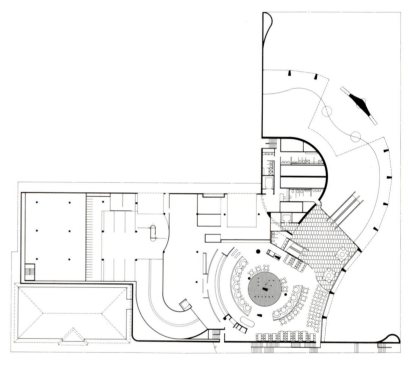

Upper Lobby Level

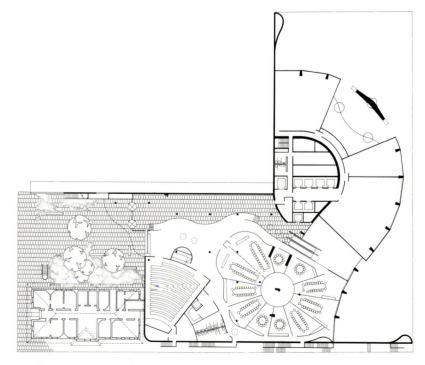

Conference Centre Level

'... Shell was a client with a determined policy of collecting art for their new building. Penelope joined their committee who commissioned the entry mural by Arthur Boyd, a wall sculpture by Hilarie Mais, weavings by Jenny Turner, paintings by John Firth-Smith, David Aspen, Jenny Watson, Mandy Martin and John Beard...'

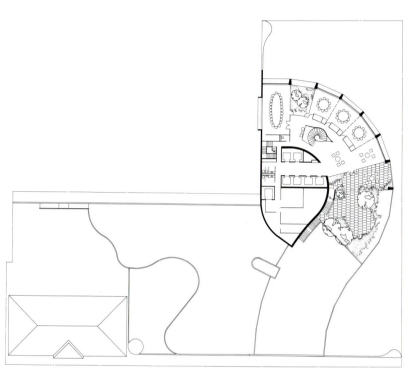

Upper Executive Level

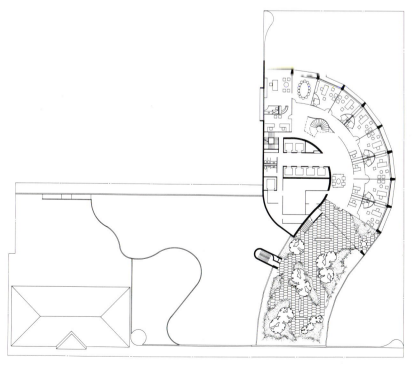

Lower Executive Level

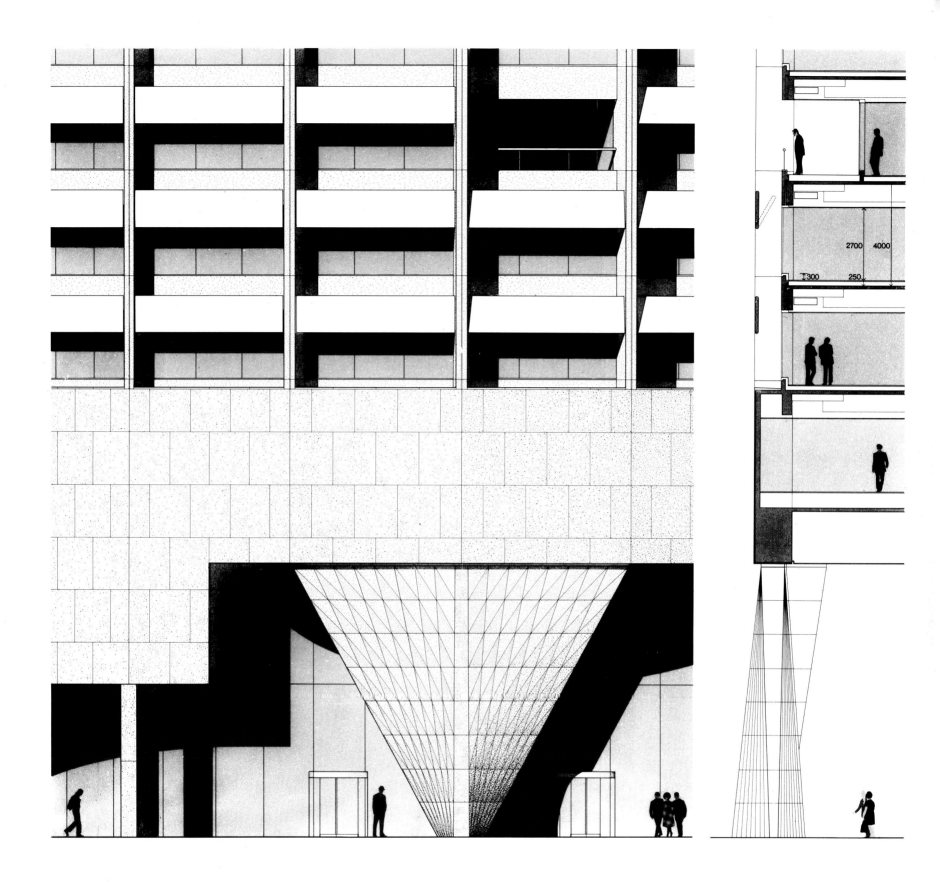

Although curvilinear, the plan-form of the tower is well suited for a repetitive floor construction system. All beams are clear-span and equal in length. Their web sections stop short of both core wall and perimeter columns, which allows services above the ceiling to pass under the shallow shear-heads within the depth of the structure. The core went up ahead of typical reusable floors using climbing formwork.

Table forms were assembled for typical floors and beams, assuring a fast construction cycle. Pre-stressing of the beams was facilitated by placing anchorages above the floor.

Both columns and spandrels were precast and made of reconstructed polished granite, matching the appearance of the natural granite facing applied to the base of the building.

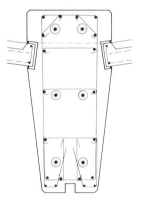

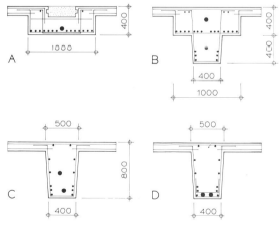
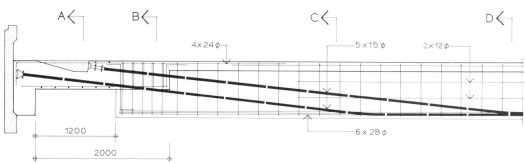

Landmark Tower
Brisbane, 1985

Being located in the centre of the arc described by the Brisbane River, the site enjoys panoramic views in all directions, and in particular, the full sweep of the river's bend. The beautiful Botanic Gardens along its banks will form the foreground of the outlook.

The client brief called for an office building with a plan configuration that would offer varying floor areas to prospective tenants, with an emphasis on large floors. These occur in the lower section and are 1650 m², with the area decreasing towards the top floors, which have rentable space of 950 m².

The 52-storey tower contains 67,000 m² net. Such a building requires a balanced structural form, especially at its base.

The central column spacing of each facade corresponds to the primary beam spans. The mid-span column loads are transferred to these for greater stiffness and lateral stability.

To achieve the variety of floor areas required, corner bays of 150 m² are progressively deleted from the typical floor plan as the tower rises in height and as lift banks terminate.

The square plan with a centre core measuring 20 m x 20 m is placed diagonally on the site so as to maximise the distance between windows and any existing or future adjacent structure.

To satisfy the requirement for long-term energy conservation, north-facing solar collectors are mounted on an inclined space frame cantilevered off the tower's columns.

Glass walls are externally sunprotected.

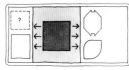 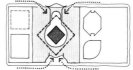

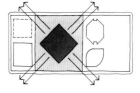

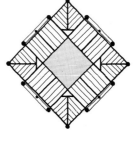

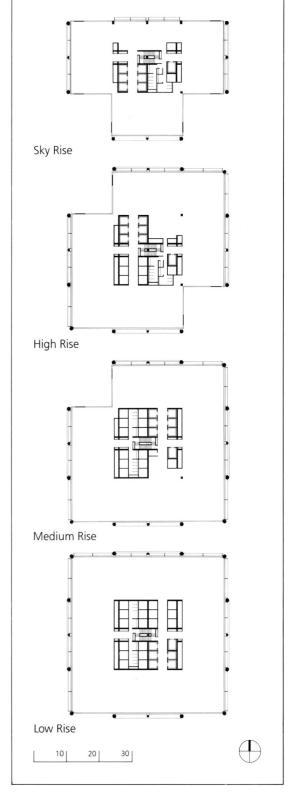

Sky Rise

High Rise

Medium Rise

Low Rise

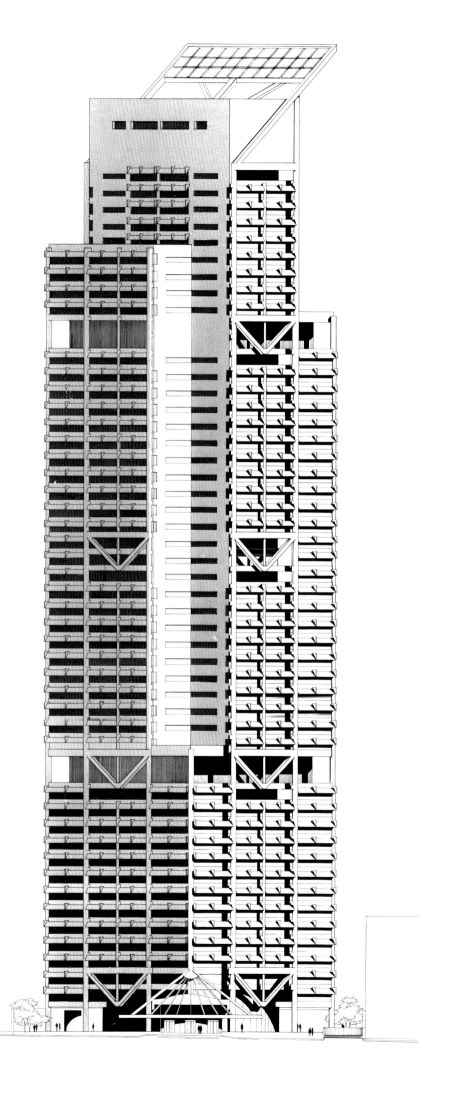

Phoenix Tower
Sydney, 1987

Since its completion in 1967, Australia Square with its public open space around the circular office tower, has become the most popular plaza in the city. The proposal for a daily newspaper office to build its headquarters on a small adjacent 1000 m² site offered an opportunity to extend both levels of this public plaza onto the adjacent Hunter Street.

The first typical floor is raised 20 m above the street, creating a monumentally scaled opening, allowing sun and view to penetrate.

The elevators are placed against the visually closed boundary and a suspension structure eliminates the columns from the resulting open portico space.

Escalators and stairs rise up from the street to the building lobby which addresses an extended upper plaza being at the same level as the adjacent circular tower's entrance.

To reduce the loads applied to the transfer structure, it is repeated at the midway point up the building. An ideal open floor is thus created for a restaurant–function centre, a mezzanine theatre, all with open terraces overlooking the Australia Square plaza.

Since a simple structural solution is preferably rectangular on plan and the site is not, additional required floor area was added by cantilevering a curvilinear extension on the east.

At the top of the building, two floors are designed for executive use with offices and boardrooms, interconnected by a spiral stair and a two-storey-high planted courtyard. Mechanical spaces above are shaped to fit closely around the needed equipment areas. The aesthetic theme of the building thus becomes a combination of structural expression with curvilinear sculptural geometric forms.

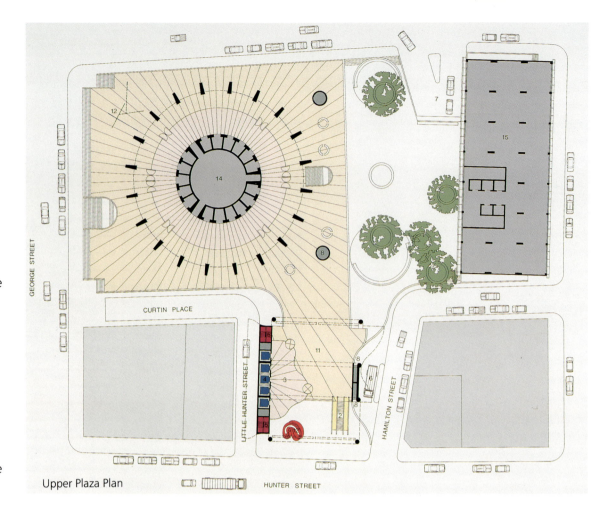

Upper Plaza Plan

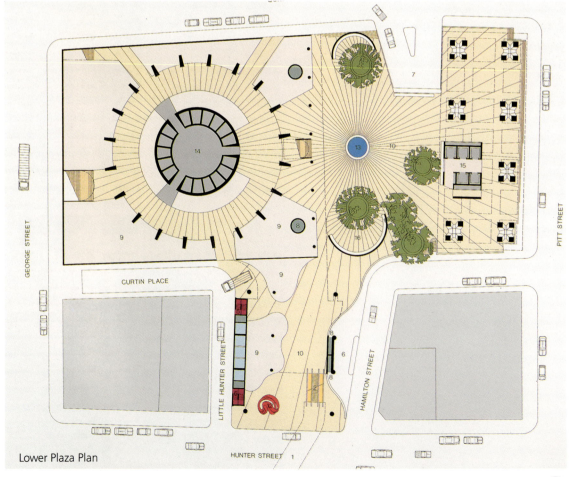

Lower Plaza Plan

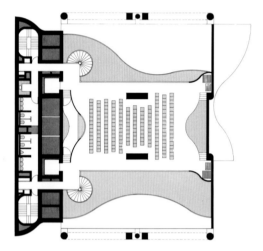
Theatrette Level 10

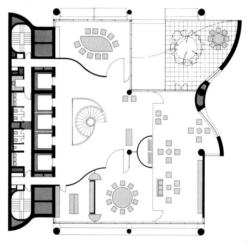
Boardroom Level 19

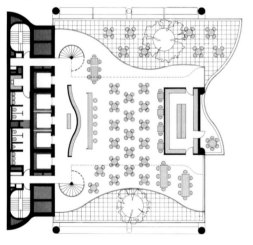
Restaurant Level 9

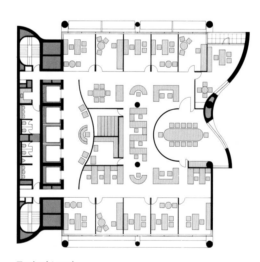
Typical Level

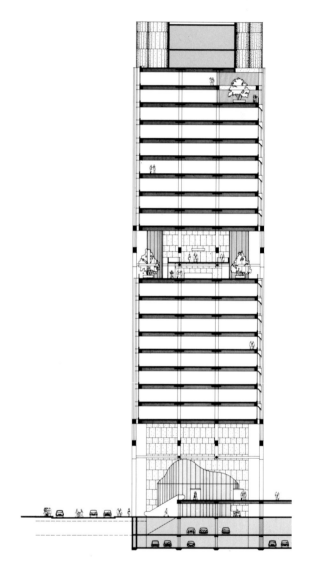

5 10 15

'... Nothing is worse than fake historicism: The authorities rejected this proposal because it did not keep the old street facades as required by the Heritage Council. Someone else propped up the facades and started to excavate. In a strong wind the facades collapsed, narrowly missing people . . . it is now an empty site . . . '

Casino and Hotel Competition
Darling Harbour, 1986

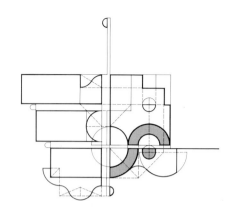

This design is in response to the NSW State Government's invitation calling for casino proposals on publicly owned land. It was prepared for the New York entrepreneur, Donald Trump, and a local developer.

The site is situated on the western edge of Sydney's business district facing the waterfront of the Darling Harbour inlet. The area is traversed by expressways, creating a barrier which separates the city from the harbour.

The structures of the large gambling halls and the 700-room hotel bridge the roadways, with the podium covering most of the site, creating a link for pedestrians to access the waterfront. Additionally, the monorail connecting Darling Harbour to the city will set down pedestrians within the site.

The casino and hotel are in separate but connected buildings; the windowless casino on the south and the hotel, to gain water outlook, on the north. To maximise exposure to the harbour, all hotel rooms face the water in an undulating plan form, with part-additional floors toward the best northern view. The centrally placed elevator core creates a 30-storey-high atrium, lit from a glazed vault above and the galleries on the city side.

The separate entrances are along Sussex Street and from pedestrian overpass bridges connecting to the city. Escalators reach the hotel's function floors, and the casino's entertainment spaces and restaurants.

The hotel's end walls project and create a stepped profile to increase the sense of identity and separation of the two facilities. This also integrates the curvilinear form of the hotel tower into the rectilinear geometry of the podium. The north-facing extension forms a monumentally scaled portico through which all pedestrians and monorail visitors must pass.

The casino's long-span structure spans the expressways and contains the back-of-house

surveillance facilities within its steel trusses. The central circulation spine connects the multiple levels of both the gambling halls and the hotel's public spaces. A bridge and freestanding elevator structure give direct access to the waterfront. Alternatively, a sinuously formed system of ramps and terraces opens onto shop arcades and landscaped zones with outdoor restaurants.

Following a change in government policy against public gambling, the project was abandoned.

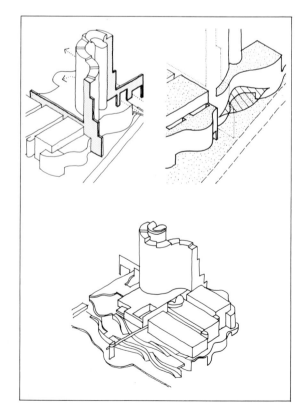

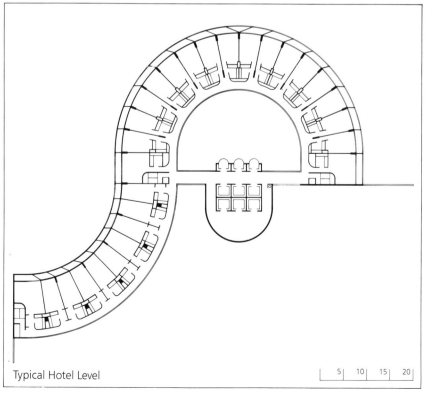

Typical Hotel Level

5 10 15 20

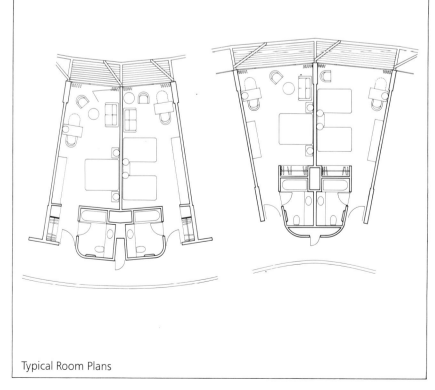

Typical Room Plans

Hotel & Casino Lobby Level

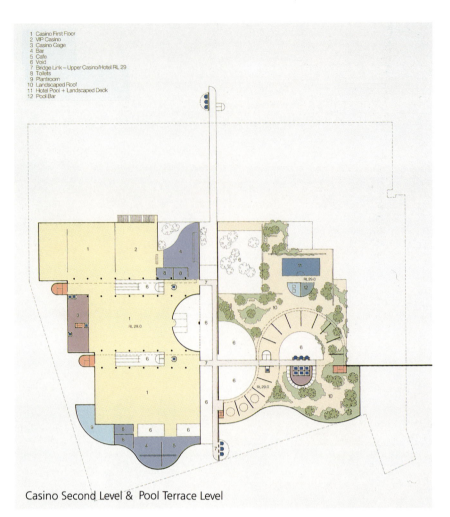

Casino Second Level & Pool Terrace Level

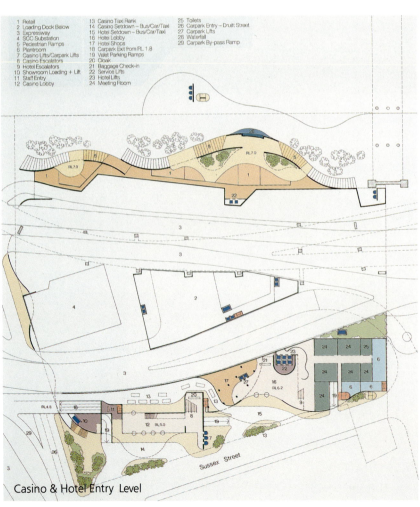

Casino & Hotel Entry Level

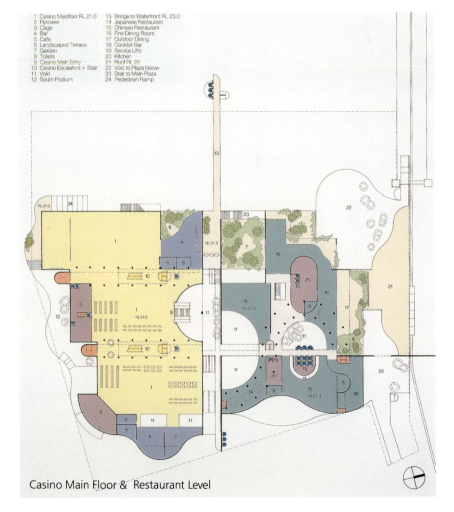

Casino Main Floor & Restaurant Level

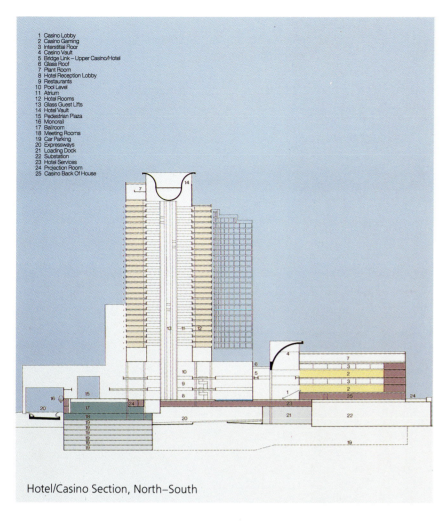

Hotel/Casino Section, North–South

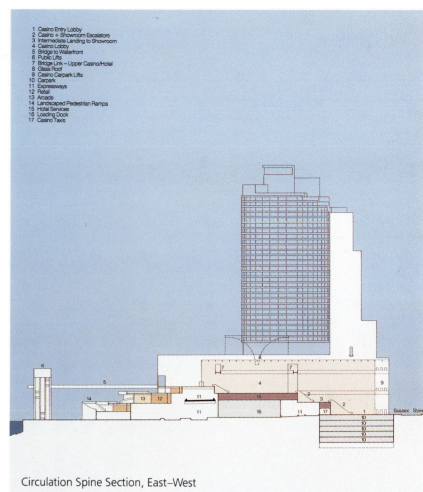

Circulation Spine Section, East–West

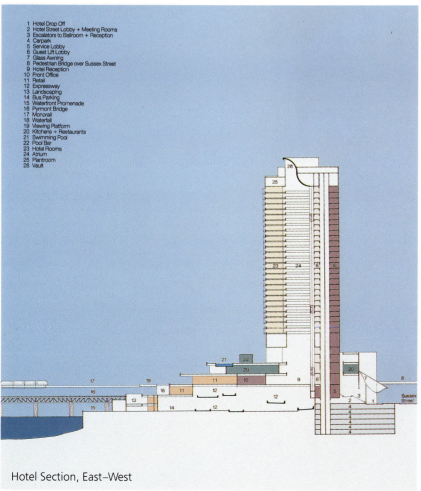

Hotel Section, East–West

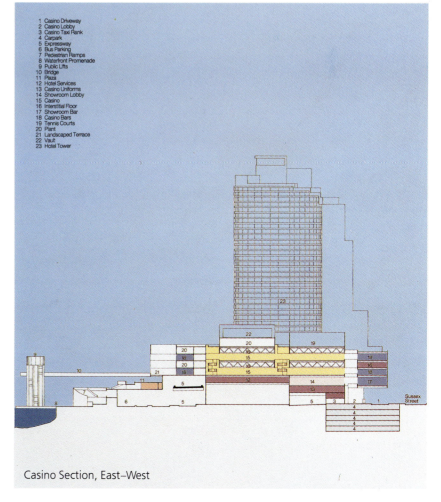

Casino Section, East–West

Harry Seidler Offices
Milsons Point, 1971–73

Located on Sydney Harbour's northern shore on top of a high sandstone cliff, the building commands panoramic views toward the harbour bridge and the city skyline in the distance with an amusement park below the cliff and large trees in the foreground.

There are five floors of offices, an executive mezzanine and two carparking levels.

Between the concrete core containing the elevator, stair and services on the north side and a system of columns and beams on the southern view side, precast prestressed concrete floor elements, 2.4 m wide, span the 11.3 m width of the building. The units vary in profile from a T-section in the centre sweeping up to a rectangular shape at the supports, expressive of the stress pattern within them. The shape of the elements allows integration of air-conditioning ducts and lighting by exposing spiral tubes between them from which indirect light illuminates the soffits between the Ts. The swept-up shape of the floor units accommodates the passage of exposed longitudinal oval ducts on typical floors.

On the east and west sides, the T-beams project beyond the glass walls and support fixed precast concrete sun blades. All precast elements were cast in smooth steel forms and are white. The poured-in-place supporting structure is of board-marked exposed concrete.

The office space is column-free and lends itself to open planning. Divisions consist of freestanding workstations and furniture units 1.5 m and 1.8 m high.

At the top of the building, the mezzanine floor houses the principal's office and boardroom with a concrete bridge connection to a wind-sheltered landscaped outdoor terrace.

The focal point in the resulting two-storey-high space is a painting by Morris Louis.

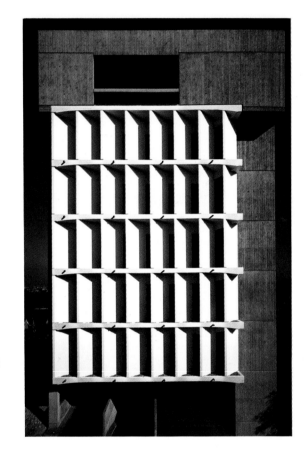

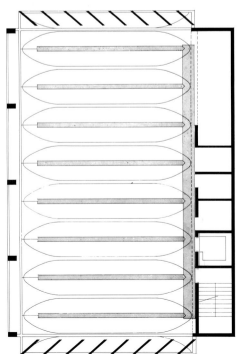

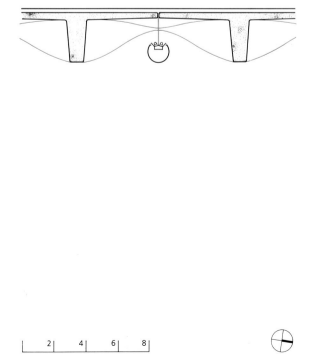

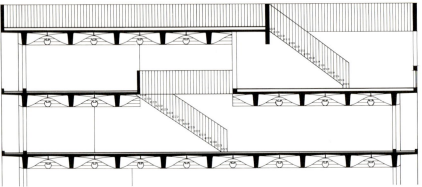

Office Extension and Penthouse Apartment
Milsons Point, 1986–88

The addition continues the existing building's architectural expression and use of materials. The old and new are the same height and form a cohesive whole when seen from the street approach side. However, the plan form and construction are different. An irregularly shaped allotment, altered building laws and the authorities' requirement for a certain proportion of waterfront development to be for residential use, all contributed to a new visual expression in the addition.

Whereas the original building is rectilinear with repetitive precast concrete T-beam floors, the addition is an irregular curvilinear building of prestressed concrete poured-in-place into flowing horizontal and vertical curve and counter-curve elements.

The new office floors have three spans with a central core on the street side and continuous sunshading terraces facing the harbour view. The two top floors accommodate a penthouse apartment attached to the original offices, with a theatre–exhibition hall forming the connection on the fifth floor. This is where drawings and models can be displayed and where audio-visual presentations to clients take place.

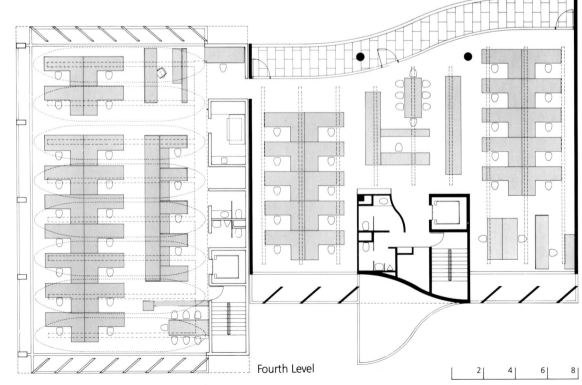

Fourth Level

'... A pavilion of seemingly limitless space defined by opposing curves. It is for presentations and entertaining – and comes to life with people – when we built this horizontal expansion to our office, the local council rules had changed to require a percentage of floor space to be for residential use – so we built this apartment ...'

The apartment is independently accessible from the new central core. Entry is into a two-storey-high space for receptions, guest accommodation and dining. The half-elliptical dining table form allows guests to sit against the curved side so that they can look at the splendid water view; the hosts sit on the opposite side and face their guests.

A dramatic curved stair leads to the upper floor lounge, study and master bedroom suite.

Within the straight outline plan, flowing curves enrich the spatially open interior and are in strong visual opposition. Only the artworks (by Albers, Stella, Lichtenstein and Noland) are colourful in contrast to the neutral grey, white and black interior.

The aim was to create an atmosphere of quietly restrained elegance and permanence. Materials have been chosen for their lasting quality; the fifth floor is paved with grey Sardinian granite slabs, also used on kitchen and bathroom walls and floors. The upper floor has natural wool carpeting. The dining table, stair treads and all horizontal furniture tops are of Indian Tamin granite. The black leather lounge, dining and teak slatted terrace chairs are Marcel Breuer's 1932 aluminium design.

Palisander cabinets and natural fur bedspreads (South American guanaco, Australian black sheep and fox) complete the restrained spacious whole.

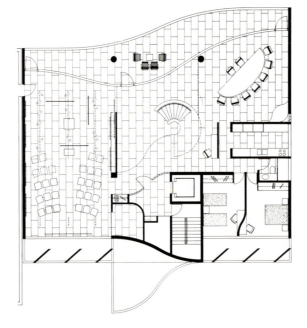

QV1 Office Tower
Perth, 1987–91

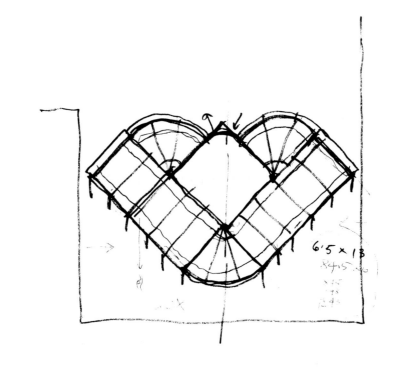
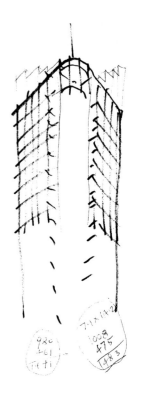

For the 10,000 m² site on Perth's main thoroughfare, St Georges Terrace, the client's brief called for an office building to contain 60,000 m² of floor area. Appropriate restaurants and service shops had to be provided. A 1000-vehicle, four-storey carpark was to be built across the street and connected to the development by a pedestrian bridge.

Spectacular panoramic views exist toward the south, to the wide expanse of the Swan River with a foreground of beautifully landscaped areas of the freeway system along the water's edge and King's Park to the west.

A 40-storey tower was located on the southern side of the site.

On the north, protected from prevailing winds, an appropriately scaled, open urban space was created on two levels, centred on a circular opening. Hay Street, the pedestrian shopping mall at the rear, merges into this space which is surrounded by restaurants and shops. Tables and chairs for outdoor eating are placed under tall palm trees facing the area's focal point – a cascading waterfall originating from a pond in the upper plaza and flowing into a shallow pool from the base of the waterfall into the centre of the circle. The landscaping is intended to convey the atmosphere of an oasis for the public in the midst of a densely built-up area.

The shape of the tower was developed, based on previous experience with similar water-view situations (see p. 258). The result is a blunted right-angled facade placed diagonally on the site, allowing most of each tower floor (of 1600 m²) to see the sweep of the river. The outlook to the north is minimised. The efficiency net-to-gross ratio is in excess of 80:20, and the plan form lends itself to a repetitive 14.3 m clear span floor system of construction. The core is placed against the north, off-view side and every span of the rectangular and quadrant-shaped sectors is identical.

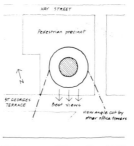
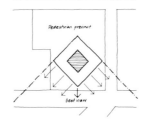
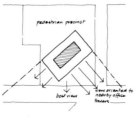
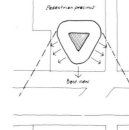
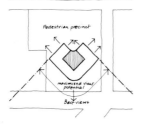
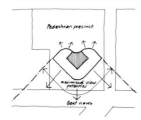
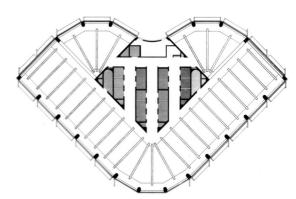

'... In Bob Williams we had a client with a sensibility in art who knew what he wanted – he challenged us to outdo anything we had previously done – the nearest thing he knew and liked was our Riverside Centre in Brisbane.

The ambitious scheme we designed was to include two live stage theatres on the site – this failed for lack of support, but instead, provision was made for a future apartment building ...'

External sunshading is applied to the glass-walled tower, similar to that developed for previous projects. In this case, however, the two longest facades face to the south-east and south-west, receiving the early morning and late afternoon sun's rays. In addition to fixed horizontal shades, angled vertical blades were introduced to protect the glass walls from low sun angle penetration. These verticals also have the effect of focusing the occupants' view onto the water and prevent looking toward less desirable views of nearby buildings.

The entrance to the tower is at the curved southernmost corner facing the main street. To give protection to visitors from semi-tropical rain, a broad suspended glazed canopy stretches across some 50 m of the frontage, reaching its highest point in the centre. Charles Perry's sculpture 'Conical Fuge' stands to the right of the entrance. To create an appropriately scaled, open and inviting three-storey-high entry, the tower's central supporting columns are turned away and fused with the adjacent supports into structurally expressive hyperboloid-shaped piers. The resulting 12 m-high space in the lobby is overlooked from progressively stepped-back mezzanine levels which contain various public meeting rooms, a theatrette and exhibition areas. The lobby offers seating for visitors and connects through directly onto both levels of the plaza at the north side.

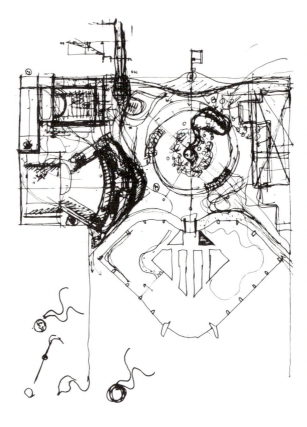

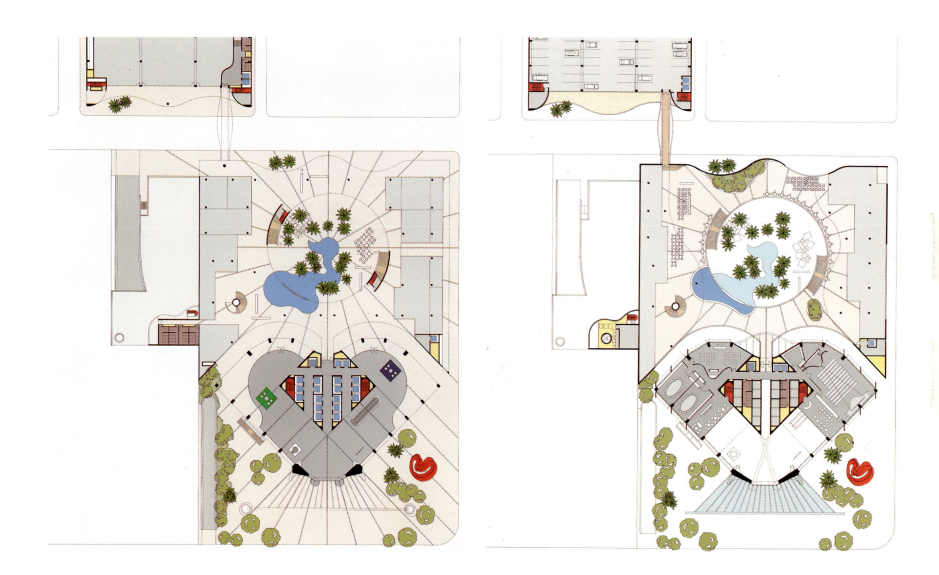

342

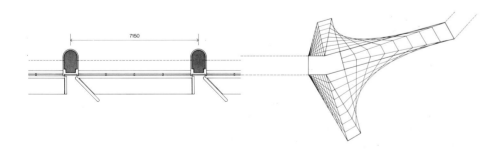

'... Other sculptors before him have hollowed out space-embracing forms, capturing inner and outer space simultaneously – but these became systematised in the hands of Perry. His works satisfy on an additional level because they are consequential and logical as well as visually enticing – great virtuosity in spatial geometry which speaks the language of our time. I find him truly a kindred spirit ...'

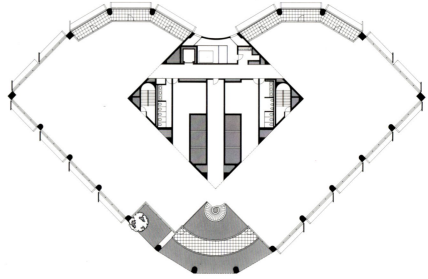
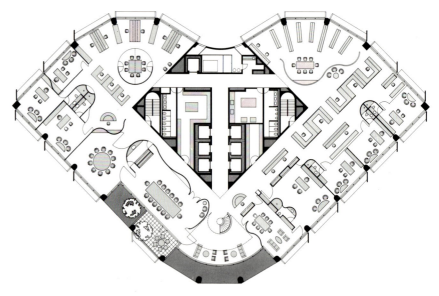

'... At night a building takes on quite a different new personality – one that I like to manipulate to create drama, especially in the public spaces; to make walls glow with the colour of their material – receiving light from virtually invisible sources and to emphasise structure by contrasting lit against non-lit surfaces. Claude Engle, our consultant, is an artist with light.

On typical office floors, low-brightness reflector sources are efficient and inconspicuous. One can have irregular and curved ceilings fully systematised so that whatever the subdivision, there is no need to move lights or sprinklers...'

Australia–Israel Friendship Forest Memorial, Israel, 1988

A gateway, plaza and monument were built within an extensive forest to be planted, commemorating 200 years of Australia and 40 years of Israel. There is a place of assembly and another of tribute to the statesmen and people who have contributed to the special understanding and bonds of friendship between the two countries.

Located at the end of the hillside village of Shorashim, two stone-paved areas are cut into the hillside and retained along the lower contours so as to afford a fine outlook to the south over the valley below and surrounding hills beyond.

The place of assembly is approached through a gateway opening formed by two opposing stone walls and a concrete lintel. A wall defining the space on the west is enlarged to carry gold-coloured metal lettering bearing the names of patrons and sponsors of the project.

From this space, steps lead down to the area containing the suspended monument wall on the east. It consists of a centrally placed, dark grey polished granite surface, with gold-coloured metal letters.

The two paved areas are defined by retaining walls of opposing forms, one straight and the other sinuously curved, placed diametrically opposite to each other. This scheme of duality, almost mirror reflection (reverse symmetry) of the two elements, is carried throughout the composition. It can be read as symbolic of the relatedness and interlocking friendship of the two countries.

Under construction 1991

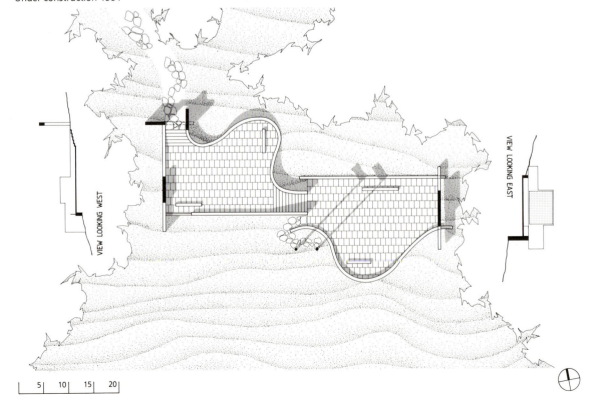

Waverley Cultural Centre
Melbourne, 1988

The new Waverley Art Gallery is only the first stage in the long-term development of this comprehensive Cultural Centre. The further components planned in the totality will consist of a live stage theatre complex, seating 750, a multi-purpose function centre, a restaurant and a new public library building.

Flowing between the rectilinear grid which forms the orientating basis of the whole development are curvilinear elements which respond to and are born of the requirements within the various parts.

When completed, the centre will be a cohesive group of structures placed around a looped access drive forming a landscaped island at its focus where a large outdoor sculpture is to be placed.

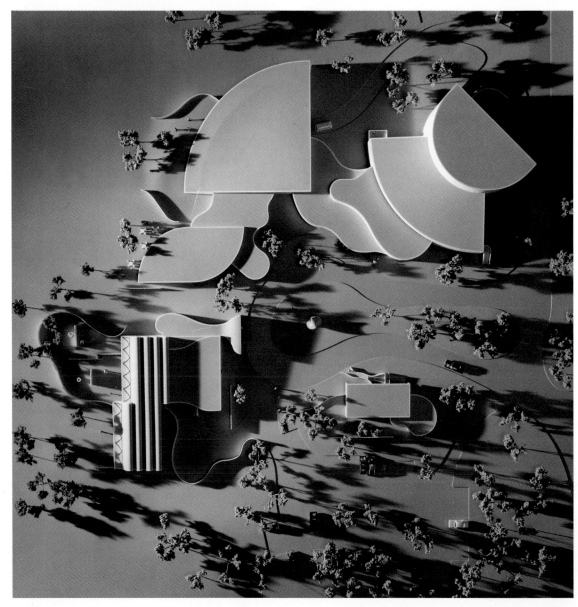

Waverley Art Gallery

The first stage of the Waverley Art Gallery consists of a rectangular flexible exhibition space in which artworks of virtually any kind can be displayed; freestanding, on walls or suspended on screens. The space is lit from S-shaped overhead south-light windows which admit diffused daylight. Depending on the artworks, natural light is controlled by means of movable vertical blades. The exhibition space will double in area in the planned second stage development toward the west.

The gallery opens to the northern-walled sculpture court through a glass wall within a deeply recessed covered terrace. This court, as yet incomplete, will be on various levels with screen walls forming controlled background display spaces for the positioning of outdoor works.

The curved funnel-like covered entry leads to a curvilinearly shaped concourse with a tea room adjunct and the focally placed entry control and sales counter.

Deliveries and loading facilities exist behind a screen wall to the west which opens into conservation, storage and administration areas.

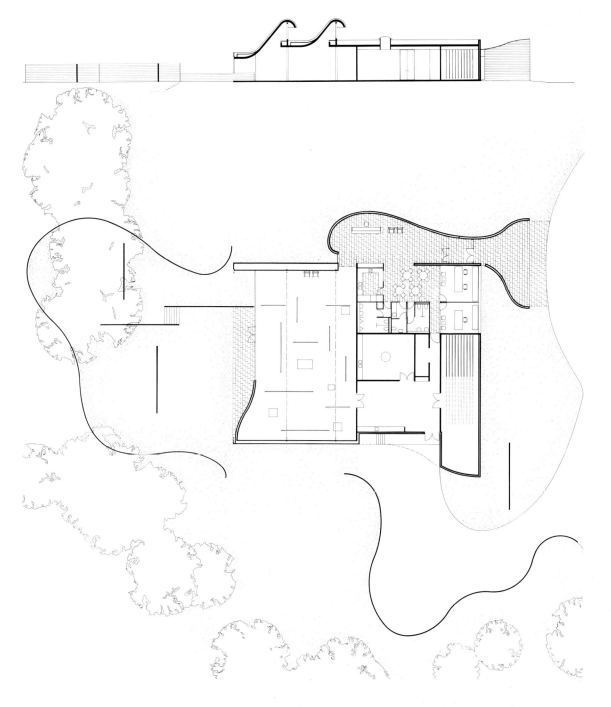

Grand Central
Melbourne, 1989

'... The angular geometry of the tower plan is reminiscent (and actually contained) in this "tensional" image by Josef Albers (from Despite Straight Lines)...'

Located in the very heart of Melbourne's central business district the 7600 m² site is at an intersection with other tall office buildings across the streets.

The architectural form of the tower is derived from responses to outlook from office floors and the rectilinear grid of Melbourne streets and buildings (favoured by the authorities). The best view from all levels is diagonal to the street grid, whereas a tower placed parallel to the street would look directly into adjacent buildings.

By rotating the tower to a diagonal, excellent outlooks are achieved south toward Port Phillip Bay and north over the historic Law Courts with their domed, rich roofscape. The shape of the tower plan responds to both these considerations. Its 57 storeys with 1400 m² to 1600 m² floors are set back from the boundaries and a four-storey podium surrounds huge top-glazed atrium spaces. An all-weather public pedestrian urban garden precinct is created, reminiscent of glass house pavilions of the Victorian era.

The project is entered from the street intersection under a glass-covered pavilion roof. The building's dark granite facing reaching into the entrance is incised with Lin Utzon's white and gold mural, which starts above, outside the glass roof and meanders down over the 9 m-high lobby's interior walls.

The top of the tower's silhouette is formed by an inclined north-facing bank of solar collectors and a satellite communications tower.

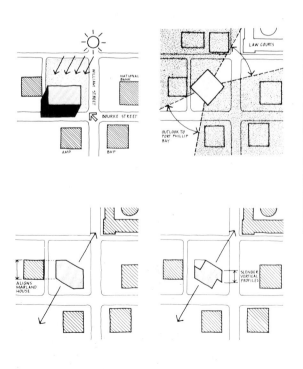

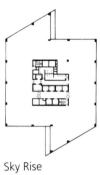

Sky Rise

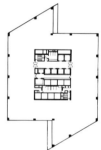

High Rise

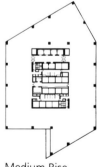

Medium Rise

Low Rise

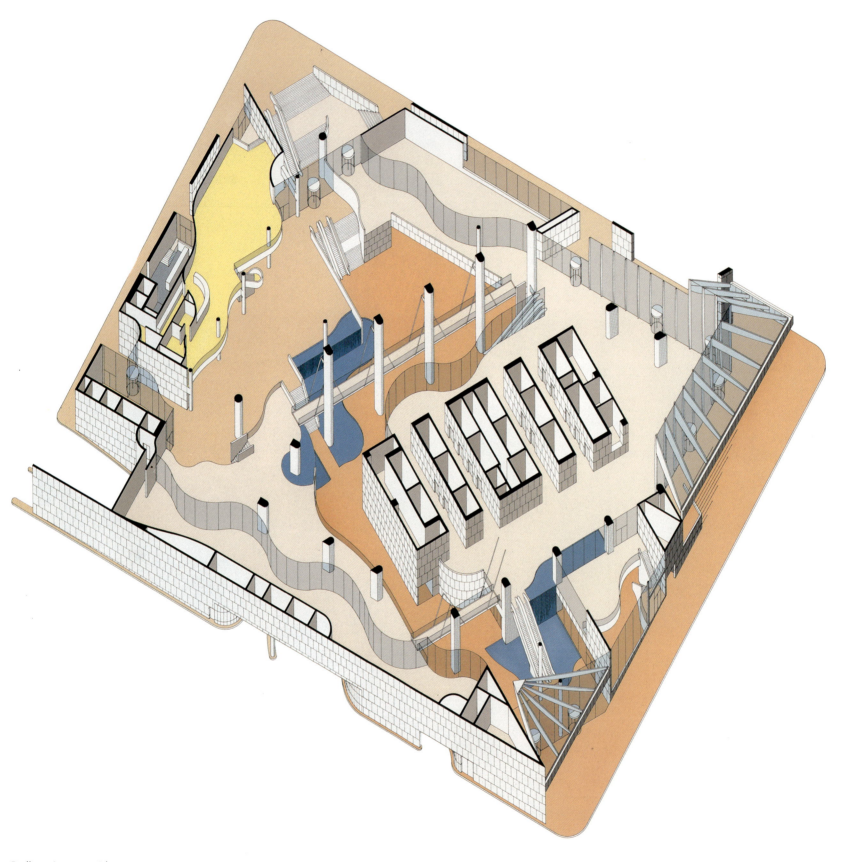

Podium Axonometric

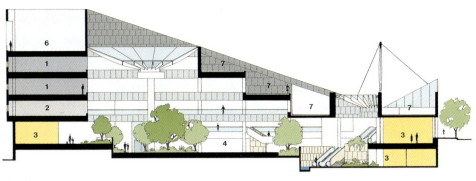

Section AA

Section BB

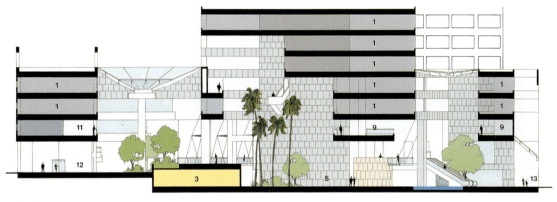

Section CC

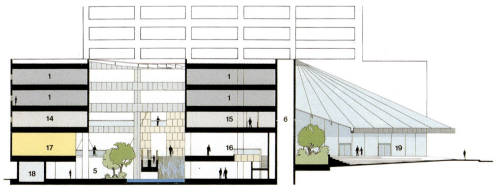

Section DD

1 Office Space
2 Professional Suites
3 Retail
4 Plaza Eatery
5 Main Plaza Level
6 Plant
7 Open Terrace
8 Main Lobby
9 Theatrette Balcony
10 Storeroom
11 Restaurant
12 Little Bourke St Entry
13 Bourke St Lower Entry
14 Theatrette
15 Video Conference Room
16 Exhibition Space
17 Cocktail Bar
18 Car Ramp
19 Tower Lobby
20 Law Courts Entry

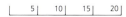

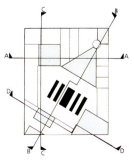

'... Lin Utzon lived in Sydney when her father's Opera House was in construction. Years later her work as an artist became known through the beautiful porcelain she designed for Royal Copenhagen. After visiting her studio in Denmark and seeing the large scale work for public spaces she was planning, we commissioned the porcelain mural for Capita – which led to her giving us these lyrical forms for Grand Central.

I see them as essential in animating the intricate geometries of the architecture...'

Hamilton House, Vaucluse 1989–91

Set on a large hilltop in Sydney's premier suburb, the site commands spectacular views of the city skyline to the west and the opposite shoreline to the north.

The owners had always lived on the site and their old house was demolished, maintaining a magnificent old Angophora tree in the centre of the entrance drive courtyard. The house is positioned behind the tree at the top of the site.

Solidity, the use of permanent materials, and luxuriously proportioned spaces set the keynote for the design of this three-storey, 700 m^2 house. The essentially rectangular plan is surrounded by sumptuously curved forms which respond to needs: balconies widen for outdoor furniture groups, the study 'scoops in' more city views, and the focal spiral stair is lit from a circular roof dome. Over the entrance the roof projects in an S-shape horizontally and down vertically to give protection – its form mirrored in the two-storey-high space inside, above the front doors.

Exterior walls made of polished precast concrete blocks support prestressed concrete floors. All living areas are paved with highly polished Indian Tamin granite slabs, also used on the fireplace wall and tops of furniture units.

The living-room sculpture is by Inge King.

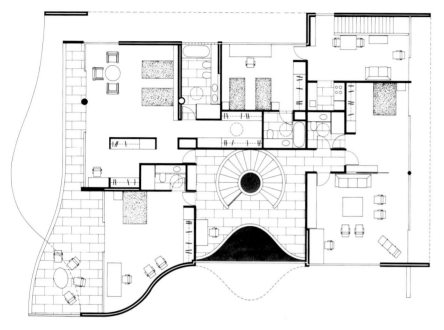

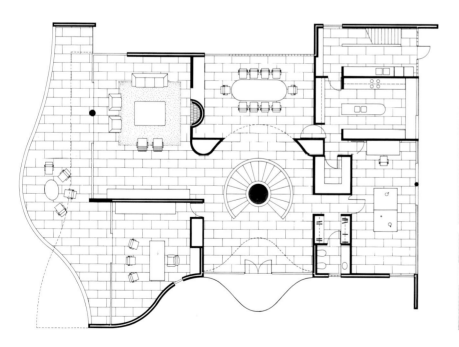

369

ABC Apartments
Darlinghurst, 1990

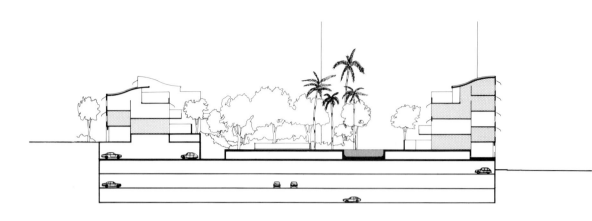

Located on a hillside in an inner-city suburb, the 7000 m² site enjoys fine views of the harbour and city to the north and west. Development is to an index of 4:1.

The 43-storey tower is placed at the southern end of the site and shaped to gain the greatest exposure sweep of outlook centred on Sydney's landmarks, the Opera House and the harbour bridge.

The rest of the site, excavated to house a five-storey, 500-car garage, accommodates on its deck a large swimming pool and tennis court, overlooked from the terraces of surrounding low-rise small apartments. These act as screens for the densely planted private gardens of the development. To blend the low-rise street-fronting base structures into the 19th-century terrace houses of the neighbourhood, the design has matching sandstone bases, brick walls and compatible stepping silhouettes.

The apartment tower planning divides the floor space evenly between living and bedroom portions, making these interchangeable in plan. The regular, speedily built cross-wall construction allows for equally shaped projecting terraces to be attached to any of the cross-wall spans.

Freedom results for creating combinations and side reversal of two-bedroom and three-bedroom apartments as well as penthouses on the top two floors.

Since the views get more dramatic with increased height, all the way out to the Pacific Ocean, the orientation of balconies changes to face outward in the top quarter of the tower which contains the larger apartments.

Each of the four luxurious three-storey penthouses has its own rooftop swimming pool.

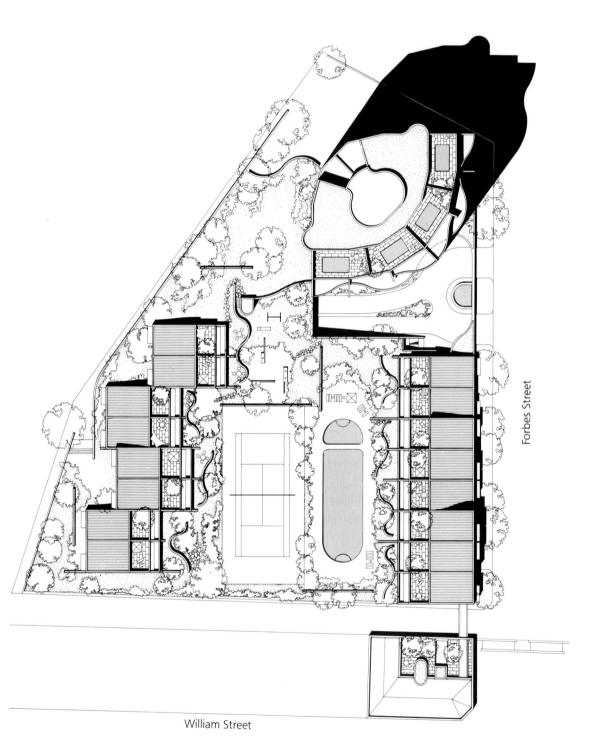

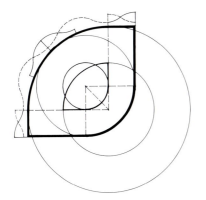

1 Lift Lobby
2 Fire Stair
3 Services
4 Entry
5 Dining
6 Living
7 Terrace
8 Kitchen
9 Laundry
10 Powder Room
11 Bed 1
12 Bed 2
13 Bed 3
14 Bed 4
15 Walk-in Wardrobe
16 En Suite
17 Bathroom

Levels 31–41

Penthouses Level 43

Levels 1–30

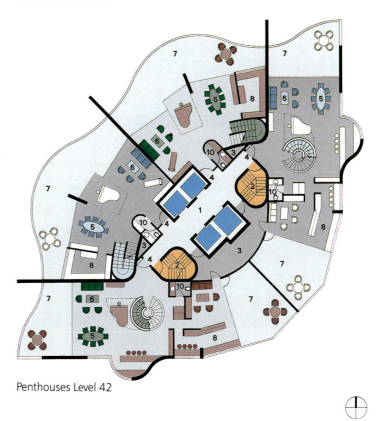

Penthouses Level 42

Planning and Architecture at the End of our Century

by Harry Seidler

Disenchantment must surely be the appropriate word to describe what most people in cities of the Western world feel about the newly built developments taking place around them. Not only are the physical problems obvious – the overbuilding with excessive bulk, the consequent pollution, traffic and pedestrian congestion – but the visual impact is undistinguished at best, oppressive at worst. Due to increasing urbanisation it is an environment that is being added to constantly and which will, almost certainly, worsen in time. Indexes of how much is allowed to be built are based on political decisions taken by elected city governments after lobbying by pressure groups of landholders and developers. The latter see their role as purely one of responding to the growing market demand for floor space. What flows from this are long-term profits and capital growth for investment in a time of inflationary devaluation of liquid assets.

Given immense thrust through the media, the emerging new laws and images make us believe that the direction of development in the last 80 years or so has been totally ill-oriented – that it has created nothing but environmental and visual chaos. It is put to us forcefully that the time has come for a complete turnabout; we should abandon all past notions of city planning, discard theories of architecture developed in our time and change direction. This anti-intellectual stance is an irrational turning back of the clock away from the gradual advancement, the logical and consequential development that has taken place. To understand how deeply this reaction has permeated current attitudes toward the built environment, let us examine two areas of concern – first, what is allowed to be built in our cities and second, what architects choose to build.

The Urban Dilemma
In the realm of urban planning, it seems that all the proposed utopian schemes for guiding three-dimensional physical planning after World War II have not been pursued. The enlightenment needed to grasp the benefits and consequent rewards to the community was too much to expect, given a system of decision-making by local government bureaucrats. Landholders fought against constraints on building bulk for fear of depreciated property values without compensation. Politicians found the necessary actions of resumption and re-subdivision 'untenable'. So, laissez-faire attitudes prevailed, and development has lurched forward on the assumption that market forces alone are best left to guide it.

The physical results of rejecting far-sighted policy has led, inevitably, to a negative public reaction. This, in turn, has been given widespread momentum by the media which purvey and encourage 'heritage' conservation modes. The outcome is that any proposal to build something new is immediately put on the defensive. The call is either for abandonment of entire projects or the preservation of existing buildings and their re-use. Where this policy is applied to worthy structures of the past it is obviously desirable and to be encouraged. But the form it has taken is the adoption of an historicist attitude which asserts that keeping old facades and hiding any new building behind them is better than anything totally new. The results are pitiful and border on the absurd. Old and new become caricatures, embodying the worst of both. 'Facadism' represents a shallow, provincial view of history; it robs the old of any character and prevents the new from being itself, let alone great.

The present mood against new development has also inspired the most amazing and arbitrary 'rules'. For example, one can cite the objections of authorities in Melbourne, Australia, to a large city building. They quote, verbatim, a recently proposed San Francisco plan and insist that this reactionary set of new rules, imported from halfway around the world, be adopted. This plan calls for the prohibition of buildings with flat roofs, of blank walls and for a 'generous use of decorative embellishments'. To demonstrate what benefits are offered to builders in return for compliance, these decorations are even allowed to protrude outside the zoning envelope! The San Francisco plan further requires buildings to be 'shaped to appear delicate and of complex visual imagery'. Worst of all, there is a dictate to 'retain the street wall'; tall buildings are to have distinctive tops and shafts and there must be 'street-fronting bases' for all tall buildings.

Prevalent rules discourage limits to site coverage and, in fact, outlaw any towers which leave large portions of the ground level unbuilt. The irrationality of insisting that urban development be built to a ratio between floor space to site area of 14:1, while at the same time having 100 per cent site coverage, is obvious. To allow an increase in the population on a city block to that extent and then to strangulate pedestrian circulation by restricting it to 3 m-wide footpaths, is inhuman and unworkable. It is socially irresponsible to build to high indexes of 12 or 14 unless there is a limit on site cover of no more than 25 to 35 per cent. This should be so, not only for the sake of health and clarity of the inevitably huge structure that results, but also to generate some breathing space for the additional thousands of people who work in such buildings. In our increasingly crowded cities the aim should be to create as much genuinely useful open space (open to the sky or glass covered) on private land as possible, places of repose and recreation (1, 2). Such urban pedestrian spaces have been the delight of European cities for centuries (3, 4, 5).

The fashion of solid street-fronting bases for towers is also highly questionable. One must reject it for practical and aesthetic reasons because it forces architects to design huge, deep, windowless, commercially unviable podium spaces which are structurally and constructionally undesirable.

What lies behind all of this is a misguided form of romanticism – an attempt to re-create 18th and 19th-century urban patterns which evolved when population densities were much lower than today and when buildings were rarely more than three or four storeys high. By all means let there be enlightened, that is flexible, three-dimensional control strategies that protect the community from excesses; controls which make the intent understood and which can be amended with

1

2

3

4

5

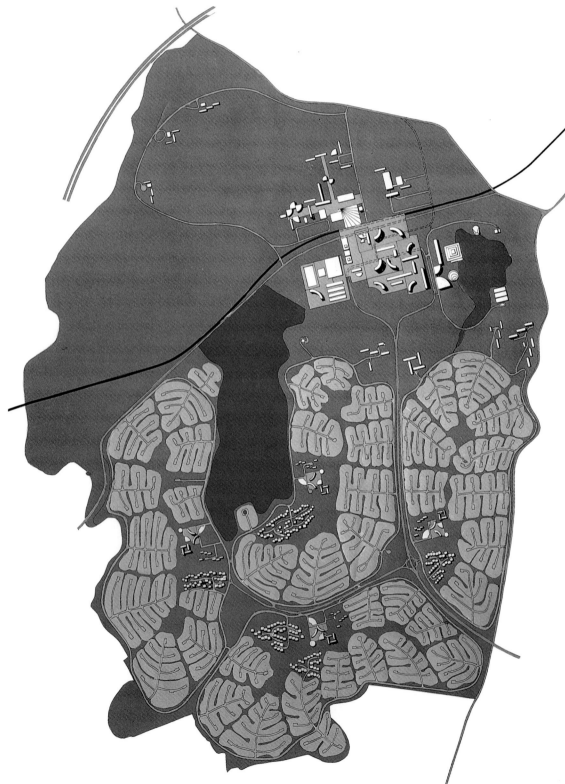

time. The design professions must, however, as a matter of principle, fight against governments being given the right to codify and thereby dictate design in detail. To allow such rules is absurd and contrary to fundamental freedom of action, freedom for the advancement and development of architecture. To stifle creativeness by law is intolerable. We should want no part of a system in which bureaucrats become powerful arbiters of taste, imposing a dictatorship over the language of form.

Simplistic restrictive rules govern the rampant urban sprawl, the creation of seemingly endless dormitory suburbs which extend the infrastructure of our big cities to stretching point. Following minimal standards of allotment size and road widths, agricultural land is usurped without any organically functional plan of self-contained communities. Such plans were proposed decades ago showing circumferential traffic-carrying roads surrounding neighbourhood units of 5000 inhabitants. In these proposals, a variety of housing densities are provided with single-family houses on cul-de-sacs so that every child can go to primary schools, located in the centre, without crossing any streets. Community halls, shopping and medium-density group housing completes the core of each neighbourhood which in groups create a regional satellite urban centre. This in turn supports strategically placed high schools, hospitals and high-density housing placed in spacious open surroundings. Architects must lead the community in the planning of such hierarchically organised neighbourhoods (6). These would stimulate a greater sense of belonging and of community spirit than exists in the haphazard, endless, isolated dormitory suburbs being built without integral community planning.

Opposition to Modern Architecture
On the subject of architectural theory, taste and the issue of what architects choose to build, we find the reaction has been equally thoughtless and devastating as in planning. There is no stronger evidence of cultural insecurity, nothing more pitiful than re-heated, fake history, and yet much wordy journalism tells us that it is time to revert

6

to the past and suggests that we go back to the 1930s and other fragmentary earlier sources in history for inspiration. Lumping together and labelling everything built in our time under the much-maligned term 'International Style', the media distort historical facts with great abandon.

The term 'International Style' is a misnomer. It was anathema to the methodology expounded by the pioneers of the Modern movement in architecture. Walter Gropius himself expressed contempt for its use. To him the only structures which could truly be labelled international in style were *'those classic colonnades, borrowed from the Greeks, placed in front of important buildings anywhere from Chicago to Moscow to Tokyo'*.[1]

Modern architecture, as conceived by its pioneers, was not a fixed set of forms but rather a way of thinking. It is an approach which *'allows one to tackle a problem according to its peculiar conditions, not by ready-made dogma nor stylistic formula, but by an attitude towards the problems of our generation which is unbiased, original and elastic'*.[2] Modern architecture could never be a style per se. It must remain in constant flux, responding not only to regional differences and social demands but also reflecting the changing visual language of art and the ever-expanding wealth of technological means. As the form-determining factors change, so too must the architectural expression.

This methodology is simply a framework on which to hang very different and potentially changing images – the opposite to frozen stylistic moulds. It is an attitude towards design which can grow and mutate with the cultural essentials of time and place.

The clarity of this concept and the consequent changing aesthetic, built upon the study of visual fundamentals,[3] never became the guiding principle for designing buildings in our time. Instead, what had originally started as a fight against traditional 'style' was utterly misunderstood and was imitated insensitively until it became so banal that it could itself be termed a style. Since the last war, unskilled, superficial images with hideous clichés have covered Western cities. The understandable public distaste for these ubiquitous results finds its voice in the present media war on the so-called 'International Style'. The attack is misdirected. Journalists and opportunistic writers deliberately misrepresent facts, re-write history and cowardly discredit the dead pioneering initiators. They blame those whose work originated a long-overdue movement away from the superficial 'art for art's sake' architecture of the fin de siècle era.

Ironically, by Gropius' definition, those who today perpetrate and practise the 'International Style' are none other than the 'rats, posts and other pests' that Aldo van Eyck aptly referred to in his 1981 RIBA Annual Discourse. Who else but those he so lucidly describes would proceed from doing parodies of Le Corbusier to blending Speers' Reichskanzlei with Mussolini's visions and dish them up in Portland, Oregon, or suggest variations of the Mausoleum at Halicarnassos be put on top of Breuer's Whitney Museum in New York?

What is now proposed, seemingly unchallenged, is the very antithesis of the visual and technical concerns of our time. We are shown ponderous, earthbound, pyramidal compositions standing flatfootedly, exposing their childish broken pediment 'metaphors' in order to make us feel closer to 'history'! Ignoring and defying all constructional, let alone structural logic, they are the tantrums of a rich spoilt child delighting in being contrary and shocking us with corny stylistic idioms, not to say ludicrous bad taste (7, 8, 9, 10).

The labels abound, supported by inept and obtuse verbiage: Adhocism, Pluralism, Contectualism, Post-Modernism, Inclusivism, Late-Modern, Post-Modern Classicism, Deconstructivism, etc. The current schizophrenia oscillates in adulation between Post-Modernism and 'Modernistic' Stylism (that painful fad of the 1930s) to the exhibitionistic display of technological acrobatics for its own sake. Rather than serving any constructional needs, the latter which exposes the vulnerable

7

8

9

10

11

12

arteries of a building to the elements ensuring anything but permanent life for the structure.

These, as any fashion, cloy the appetite. They are transient and self-extinguishing, grating and annoying the senses in the end. They are regressive, anti-intellectual modes – defying reason, art and technics. They are not a worthy product of our time whose creed should be one of restraint and disdain for wilful waste or physical or visual extravagance.

The degeneration has indeed gone full circle. One need only remember the Western architectural world's outrage at the 'cultural inferiority' of then communist East Berlin's Stalinallee, erected after the war at the same time Le Corbusier was building his first 'Unite' in Marseille. And now, in a complete reversal of roles, East Germany has rebuilt the Bauhaus structures better than new and Czechoslovakia has restored the Tugendhat House. They declared them national shrines while, in the West, Bofill builds a public housing scheme which boasts new classical orders made of glass or precast concrete and gigantic fluted Roman columns for fire stairs (10). It is the kind of architecture that totalitarian regimes of both left and right have always favoured.

It could all be ignored if there were not the danger, due to all the wordy journalism surrounding and justifying it, of being taken literally by the young and uninitiated; of being blown up and catapulted into the significance of a new design philosophy.

A remark Marcel Breuer made to me in the 1950s puts these things in perspective. In discussing his reaction to the then fashionable classicism – that sugar-coated, misunderstood Miesian mode prevalent in North America at that time – he said, in German, 'Nur abwarten' (just wait patiently). And who remembers or takes that fad seriously now? Or who remembers the Brutalists in England with their pathetic imitations of Le Corbusier's rough concrete of the 1940s? With that record what lasting validity can be ascribed to the 'metaphors' so verbosely elaborated to describe the present reversions to licentious decorative caprice?

Looking Forward

There is a discernible visual direction in our time. It permeates the work of many painters and sculptors and is manifested in our immediate history. The essence of it is best defined by the painter Josef Albers: '*Where the discrepancy between physical fact and psychic effect is maximised, there lies the threshold of art*' and '*One plus one is three – in art*'.[4] This credo of getting the most aesthetically and physically for the least in effort and material is directly applicable to architecture. Not only is it valid for economic reasons, but it will heighten the value of that which, by a shortcut of the mind and with penetrating insight, finds 'Gordian Knot' simultaneous solutions to aesthetic, planning and constructional problems.

The simplistic way in which this essential element has been misinterpreted is the cause for much of the harm that has been done in the name of Modern architecture. To do the minimal *only* leads to dullness, stagnation and rejection, but to do little in such a way that riches result, both visually and tangibly – that is where our direction lies!

From its earliest days the Modern movement has emphasised the study of visual fundamentals of just how our eyes respond in predictable ways to visual phenomena. A study of these principles will make us realise how we see changes as other areas of our existence change. What was valid in 1930 can no longer be actively so today because our senses will respond differently due to the altered social conditions and to advances in art and technology. Thus our notions of appropriate construction, of the way space should be ordered, of visual expression and the forms that derive out of these concerns must, of necessity, be different from those of the past or of other cultural milieus.

For example, however much we may admire Le Corbusier's buildings, their 6 m grid structures (which was all they could do economically then) are superseded today just as is their planning, plumbing and everything else about them. We may still find his spatial flow poetic, enticing and valid, though even if achieving it meant the use of excessive hand labour or constructional devices no longer realistically plausible.

We live in a world of vastly varying social and economic climates. I have built on four different continents. What is possible and in fact desirable in one country with ample, willing and undemanding labour but poor technology is unthinkable in a location with advanced industrial potential and high labour costs (11, 12). Such considerations will inevitably produce regional differences in buildings even if the common aim is to create a subtle orchestration of spatial intricacies.

It is also evident that 20th-century man's concept of space and how it should be organised has changed in a way which only our advancing technology can muster. Instead of the assemblies of connected finite volumes of the past, we now seek a sense of the infinite and yet simultaneously the intimate – a sense of the beyond in the immediacy of the present.

Likewise in the search for appropriate form our horizons have broadened considerably with time. The initial puritanical rigidity has been allowed to widen into an all-encompassing search which today is yielding a wealth of new expression. We have learned to borrow from the art forms of our time just as we have learned not to exclude history. By 'history', of course, I do not mean the puerile adaptation of decorative paraphernalia but rather a study of the essential forces behind the images of the past. For instance, the subtly brilliant geometric systems that came into being in the 17th and 18th centuries (13, 14) can inform our approach to developing system-oriented methods of construction. But the visual language must be new. I believe that visual tension, not the phlegmatic earthbound images of the past, speaks to our time; the channelling of space and surfaces in opposition, curve against countercurve, sun and shadow, the juxtaposition of compression to the surprise of release.

Even if the expression is exuberant or flamboyant, an economy of visual means will heighten the value of the result. Instead of creating an arbitrary assemblage of unrelated geometries, single-form elements should be evolved and transformed, finding their echo throughout the work at every scale – a set of variations on limited visual themes.

Free rein must be given to the expression of the laws of nature, not what is 'imagined' to be so by many structurally naive architects, but the unassailable physical truth of statics. Being born of the immutable and irrevocable truth of nature, the richness of expression which can result from such a search will have the irreplaceable quality of longevity, of remaining authentic as times change.

In our approach to constructional systems architects generally have been far too simplistic, accepting any dull repetitiveness to be economically valid. Just as the revivalist architecture at the end of the last century was out of tune with the emerging industrial means, so I believe the design profession today is not responding adequately to either current technological and manpower conditions or new construction methodologies. That is why we are losing the grip on vital decision-making and are being replaced by hustling technicians. To design a tall building today, which simply takes too long to build, is a self-arresting process, a hollow victory realised only on paper.

It is our task to maximise systems of mechanisation appropriate to and 'in tune' with the particular task. Even though these must vary in different socio-economic and industrial climates, one must not stop at the consideration of structure and covering only, as is so often the limit of prevalent thought. Rather, one must encompass simultaneously integral solutions to the problems posed by all the services required in a project, thereby avoiding the usual nightmarish afterthought complications of most modern buildings. Flexibly planned, fireproof structures can be built to last indefinitely. Even if the 'arteries' of services wear out, they should be designed for inevitable replacement in time.

True Modern architecture is not dead as some will have us believe. We have hardly started to

13

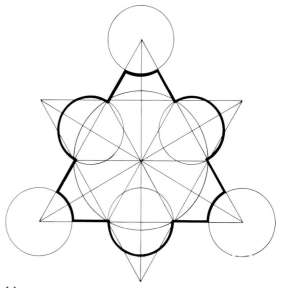

14

explore the potential of its methodology. The high principles and clear moral consequentiality of the pioneers needs to be constantly interpreted anew. They demanded basic integrity and an intrinsic honesty of approach. Only by making these part of our work will the frontiers of development be pushed forward.

Finally
In dealing with the problems of our environment today it is not possible to ignore the much-publicised, embarrassing notions expressed by, let us say, a less than erudite member of the English Royal Family. Nor can one ignore certain self-appointed critics, even from the realm of academia, who speak and write in his defence. Nothing demonstrates more clearly the provincial and insensitive view of the visual arts in our time, than the insistent proposal to return to 18th- and 19th-century imagery, coupled with the claim that such a fossilised view of our culture is shared by the 'masses'.

No-one would wish to condone the massive misdeeds perpetrated in much of the Anglo-Saxon world since World War II. With very few exceptions, England has consistently rejected and been generally immune to expressions of the visual language of our time. America achieved much for some decades (during the working presence of European pioneers) but finally only played at imitating superficial phenomena, ultimately showing its true cultural colours: reactionary provincialism. Unfortunately Australia is falling victim to the anti-Modernist hysteria supported by the American architectural media.

Significantly this debased reversion in Western culture is not shared in Scandinavian and other European countries that have a history of early developments in Modernism.

Near the end of our century it may be well for us to take heed of the almost 100-year-old inscription above the entrance to the Sezession Building in Vienna:

DER ZEIT IHRE KUNST
DER KUNST IHRE FREIHEIT

(To each time its art
to art its freedom)

One would think that this simple wisdom should not need to be stated again.

(Based on the 1984 lecture at the RIBA in London and the 1987 Habitat Lecture at the Centre for Human Settlements, University of British Columbia, Vancouver.)

Notes
1. *Design* magazine (USA), April 1946, Vol. 47, No. 8.
2. Walter Gropius, *Apollo in the Democracy*, McGraw-Hill, 1968.
3. As taught at the Bauhaus by Itten, Albers and Klee in the 1920s and later by Albers at Black Mountain College, N.C., USA 1934–50.
4. *Despite Straight Lines*, Josef Albers, Yale University Press, 1961.

Biographical Chronology

**Biographical Chronology:
Text by Philip Drew**

This Biographical Chronology juxtaposes Seidler's life and work against significant architectural developments around the world. The chronology is divided into two horizontal bands: above the black time line is the international framework and influences; below this, Seidler's life and work are illustrated. (His recollections and comments are shown in italics.)

Despite widespread economic chaos, a wave of Utopian optimism arose in Europe after the First World War which produced what has come to be known as the 'heroic' period of Modern architecture. **Walter Gropius** (Seidler's first great mentor) founded the **Bauhaus** in Weimar. This became a leading focus for the visual arts in Central Europe. Its aim was to bridge the gulf between the craftsman and the artist and thereby unite the useful and the 'fine' arts. Many young artists were appointed to teach at the Bauhaus in the early 1920s, notably Johannes Itten, Paul Klee, Wassily Kandinsky, Laszlo Moholy-Nagy, including the architect Adolf Meyer. The Dutch De Stijl group, especially Theo van Doesburg, had an influence on the Bauhaus.

The Bauhaus moved to Dessau in 1925; there, Gropius designed and built its now famous building. Five former students were appointed to teach; they included **Marcel Breuer** and **Josef Albers** (two further mentors of Seidler). Under Marcel Breuer's direction, the Bauhaus workshops produced the first tubular steel lightweight chairs which have become classics of 20th-century design. Light fittings, woven fabrics and new industrialised products were developed for interiors; typography was revolutionised. The contribution of the Bauhaus is evident throughout the Western world to the present day.

Walter Gropius

Marcel Breuer

Josef Albers

Le Corbusier: Garches

Brinkmann & Van der Vlugt: Van Nelle Factory

Gropius: Bauhaus

Gropius: Chicago Tribune Tower

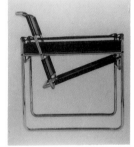
Breuer: Wassily chair

Breuer: Cesca chair

Gropius: Siemensstadt

Albers: Scintillation

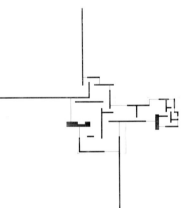
Theo van Doesburg

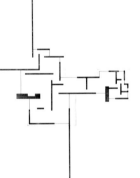
Mies van der Rohe: Brick country house

1920–1929

Harry Seidler was born the second son in a middle-class Viennese family. The family lived at first in an apartment on the corner of Grundlgasse, Vienna IX. His upbringing was strict, with rigorous training in ancient Greek and Latin at the 'Wasa-gymnasium' classical high school.

Born 25 June 1923, Vienna

Mies van der Rohe was the last director of the Bauhaus before the Nazis closed it in 1933. His Barcelona Pavilion subsequently became an icon in the history of architecture, as have the early houses of **Le Corbusier**, his Villa Savoye at Poissy, Villa Stein at Garches and Villa La Roche in Paris (now the Foundation Corbusier). His visionary schemes of 'Ville Radieuse' and the plan for Algiers had immense influence. Breuer went on to build in Switzerland, and developed laminated timber furniture for Isokon

Bauhaus closed by Nazis

in England, where he exhibited his vision of a city centre.

All over Europe there was response with daring new buildings – in Holland the Van Nelle factory, in Stuttgart, a celebrated housing development built under the guidance of Mies van der Rohe (Weissenhof Siedlung) and a great many other public housing schemes by Gropius such as Siemensstadt in Berlin and other cities in Germany.

Le Corbusier: Algiers

Le Corbusier: Student dormitory

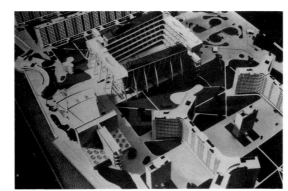
Breuer: Civic Centre

Frank Lloyd Wright: Falling Water

Gropius House, Lincoln

Hagerty House, Cohasset

Breuer House, Lincoln

Le Corbusier: Poissy

Maillart: Thur Bridge

Breuer: Doldertal Apartments

Breuer: Isokon recliner

Le Corbusier: Poissy

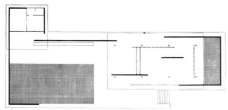
Mies van der Rohe: Barcelona Pavilion

'... In the mid-1930s, I recall seeing a film which made a deep impression on me. It showed dramatic visions of the world of tomorrow – soaring huge spaces in clear-cut machine-made structures. Its imagery haunted me for a long time and stimulated my interest in building...'

Moholy-Nagy: sets for V. Korda's film *Things to Come*

1930–1939

Family holidays were spent skiing in Austria alternated by summer vacations in Italy.

Vienna offered a wide range of activities for a boy growing up, from cycling in the woods that surrounded the city, to the city itself with its theatres and restaurants. Seidler took his bicycle, pictured, with him to England.

In Mariazell

Wasagymnasium

In Venice

389

Parallel developments took place in engineering, with bridges by the Swiss, **Maillart**, and the Italian, **Nervi**. With the onset of the Second World War and the emigration of Gropius, Breuer, Mies van der Rohe and Albers to the USA, Modern architecture and design became established in America. Very little was built, however, other than in Brazil, which developed its own form of Modern architecture especially exemplified in the work of Oscar Niemeyer.

Bauhaus teaching was continued in the USA by Albers at Black Mountain College and by Moholy-Nagy at the New Bauhaus in Chicago.

Sigfried Giedion, who acted as the spokesman for the Modern movement and lectured Harry Seidler at Harvard, signed the frontispiece of Seidler's copy of *Space, Time and Architecture*.

1945
Germany surrenders.

Breuer: Chamberlain Cottage

Nervi: Hangar at Orbetello

Niemeyer: Ministry of Education

Niemeyer: Casino

Niemeyer: Pampulha Yacht Club

Niemeyer: Restaurant

1940–1945

Six months after the Nazi occupation of Austria in 1938, Seidler escaped to **England**, attended a polytechnic school at Cambridge and lived in the home of Lady MacAlister, who taught him to speak English.

Soon after the Second World War began in May 1940, Seidler, along with other aliens born in enemy countries, was **interned**, initially in England and the Isle of Man, prior to transportation to Canada on board the prison ship S.S. *Ettrick*.

It was traumatic for a 17- to 18-year old, brought to a new continent and kept behind barbed wire. Seidler spent his time studying with fellow inmate architects and historians. His reactions are vividly presented in a diary he kept in German. An edited translation in English was later published. (*The Diaries of Harry Seidler, May 1940–Oct. 1941*, edited by Janis Wilton, Allen & Unwin, 1986.).

He was released 'on parole' in October 1941 to continue his studies at the **University of Manitoba**. It was renowned for its excellent school of architecture under design professor John Russell. The high level of structural engineering subjects taught in the school of civil engineering proved of considerable value to Seidler in later years. He graduated in 1944.

Winning a scholarship to Harvard's Graduate School of Design, Seidler attended **Walter Gropius' Master Class** in 1945–46. Among his contemporaries were I.M. Pei, Ulrich Frazen, Henry Cobb, Don Olsen, John Parkin, Paul Rudolph and Edward L. Barnes.

'. . . Gropius instilled in us students the firm belief that we are to bring about vital changes to the physical environment – to better the man-made world.

He never took a pencil in his hand "to show you how", but by questioning broad aspects of the problem to be solved, he made students dissatisfied with everything around them including their own work. He demanded consequential thinking – a three-sided simultaneous design process which brings into happy marriage considerations of social use, aesthetics and technology. He had no patience with inadequate one-sided thinking . . .'

In Cambridge

At 'Barrmore' with Lady MacAlister

Interned

Watchtower, Camp 'L' Quebec

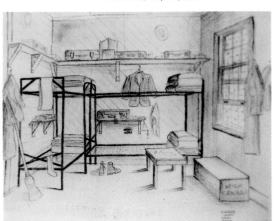
Sleeping hut, Camp 'L' Quebec

At University of Manitoba

Graduation 1944

Gropius Master Class (Harvard, G.S.D. 1946)

The earlier powerful influence in the USA was the work of **Frank Lloyd Wright** who, since the turn of the century, had produced some of the country's most distinguished domestic 'organic' architecture, culminating in his breathtaking design of the Kaufmann House at Bear Run, Pennsylvania (Falling Water). **Neutra**, the Viennese-born Californian architect, built a house for the same family in Palm Springs.

'... I remember, in 1947, a prestigious event at the Museum of Modern Art – the Mies van der Rohe exhibition. It was a dramatic display of architecture with ceiling-height photographs and full-scale steel and brick details built on the floor.

Frank Lloyd Wright was at the opening, complete with cape and cane. I heard him say to a companion that this was the work of one of his more talented disciples! ...'

Mies van der Rohe and Philip Johnson

Neutra: Kaufmann House, Palm Springs

Mies van der Rohe: Farnsworth House

1946–1947

On graduation in 1946, at Gropius' suggestion, Seidler attended Josef Albers' Design Course at Black Mountain College, N.C.

'... I found out more about visual perception at Black Mountain than at any architecture school. We learned by tangible experience why we prefer certain images to others: it is because our eyes respond differently from those of people at other times in history ...'

Albers made us think through spatial-visual problems posed verbally and only then did he encourage us actually to test our answers physically (only to find out we were usually wrong!). He taught us to think spatially around and through objects by setting puzzling tasks. His method of teaching was tantalising because he made his students participate in exploring phenomena of vision ...'

Seidler's parents and brother leaving USA for Australia, 1946

Marcel Breuer had earlier befriended Seidler at Harvard and when he established an office in **New York**, he asked Seidler to be his first assistant. Seidler worked on Breuer's own house at New Canaan, Robinson House at Williamstown, Geller House on Long Island, Thompson House at Ligonier, etc.

'... I became intimately involved with his methodology of approach. Each building design had as its theme a single strong idea. Plans were always basically direct in organisation and resulted in related sculptural masses. Detailing was consequential and universally applicable. It was continually refined and carried forward from one project to the next ...'

During his spare time Seidler worked on projects for friends, such as the Pickard House in Toronto: an addition of a sunroom and terrace.

Studio Building, Black Mountain College

Albers teaching

Breuer: Geller House

Breuer House, New Canaan

Breuer: Robinson House

Seidler: Pickard addition

Albers' class

Seidler, Varda and students

Breuer & Seidler on site

Breuer: Robinson House

Breuer: Fischer House

Breuer: Robinson House

Seidler Studio Apartment
222 Riverside Drive
New York

Rudolph: Florida House

1948

The excitement generated by the new architecture of Brazil brought Seidler to **Rio de Janeiro**; there he associated with **Oscar Niemeyer** and worked on housing for the Aeronautical Training Centre at San José dos Campos.

'... The exuberant sculptural forms of Brazilian buildings were new to me and I remember Gropius referring to Niemeyer as architecture's "Paradiesvogel" (bird of paradise). Structures were of tough concrete, very different technically from the lightweight timber used in the USA. I learned about sun protection in a warm climate. The experience there came back to me in my work, years later...'

Nervi: Exhibition Hall, Turin

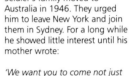

Seidler's family moved to Australia in 1946. They urged him to leave New York and join them in Sydney. For a long while he showed little interest until his mother wrote:

'We want you to come not just as a visitor, but to accept a commission to design us a house.'

The thought of bringing his own ideas to reality was compelling and after working in Brazil he came to Sydney.

'... Even though I found the sea of red brick and tile suburbia oppressive, the expanse of Sydney Harbour was a delight and surprise. With its warm climate, clear blue skies, beaches and palm trees, it seemed like a place for holidays.

Just as most of the Breuer Houses in Connecticut were built on large tracts of land, in the search for a site, I chose a virgin area of bushland. It was secluded from development and

Studio-Apartment
Point Piper

The remodelled bottom floor of a waterfront building at 4 Wolseley Crescent, Point Piper, Sydney. Seidler's studio and living quarters, 1948–60. Seidler used it as his office until his marriage in 1958, and his domicile until 1960.

Rose Seidler House
Turramurra

see p. 34

Photographer brother Marcell, builder Bret Lake and Seidler on site

Dupré, Seidler, Niemeyer, Fenandez in Sao Paolo

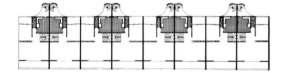

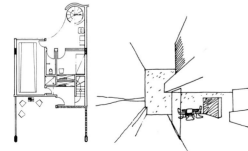
Niemeyer: San José dos Campos Housing

Sir John Sulman Medal
RAIA 1951

Niemeyer: Tremaine House

Breuer House, New Canaan

Breuer: Exhibition House, MOMA Garden

The Snowy Mountains Scheme is begun. It signals Australia's plans for expanding and developing its industrial and manufacturing capacity.

1949 | 1950

likely to remain so, being at the edge of a valley of public reserve, Ku-ring-gai Chase.

Although official obstacles made themselves felt almost immediately, support came from local architects who were experiencing the same problems. I found Sydney Ancher, Arthur Baldwinson and Douglas Snelling, who were kindred spirits, ready to exchange views and information. Ancher suggested a builder, Bret Lake, and soon work was started on my parents' house. Periods of inactivity caused by the shortage of building materials were usual.

When completed, the house caused quite a stir; sightseers and press reports abounded. On weekends, people swarmed around the house, sometimes four deep, looking through the glass walls! . . .'

Commissions to design houses regularly brought about confrontation with local councils on matters of design, which often ended in litigation.

'. . . Much public attention was drawn to arguments and court cases about the design of unconventional houses. The legal precedent quoted often was the case brought by the architect, Sydney Ancher, against Warringah Shire Council who refused a permit for a flat-roofed house.

The *judgment* handed down by Justice **Sugerman** in March 1948 ruled in favour of the architect's design. After expert evidence, he considered encouragement for **progressive architecture** to be in the **national interest,** which in his view must be put before the parochial interest of the local community.

In spite of this, Councils continued to object to designs of Modern houses, which resulted in me having to fight in court to have my designs declared innocent! . . .'

Rose House
Turramurra

Marcus Seidler House
Turramurra

Waks House 1
Northbridge

Dr. Fink House
Newport

Bowden House
Canberra

see p. 42

see p. 46

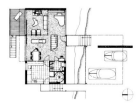

COUNCIL WON'T PASS MODERNISTIC ROOF

COUNCIL YIELDS OVER HOME

393

Johnson House, New Canaan

Breuer: Vassar College Dormitory

Seidler settled into Sydney with ease. The local profession was eager to learn about his American experiences and helped him with builders. This was the decade of the glass box as epitomised by Philip Johnson's house at New Canaan, Connecticut, 1949.

'... After the first year in Sydney, quite a number of people wanted me to design houses for them. They were average people, at first, mostly Europeans, German and Austrian migrants who had experienced Modern buildings before. Then there were Australians seeking something other than the traditional brick house. They responded to the idea of houses designed to be more open to the outdoors, the warm climate, and to reflect an informal lifestyle. What wonderful people, I thought, and how different from the very few clients Breuer had in New York who were wealthy and wanted Modern houses mainly for élitist–visual reasons.

But here they had one thing in common: severe cost restraints. The houses had to be straightforward in concept, simple and economic to build. The building industry was starting up slowly after a period of inactivity during the war.

It was difficult to find competent builders, who were prepared to state a firm construction price and a number of owners decided to become builders themselves. They employed tradesmen and labour of their own choice, a procedure that complicated and intensified my work and limited control...'

The search for a standard house flexible enough in its planning to be easily adapted to different sites led Seidler to design the Universal House.

'... The challenge put to me often was the design of a "universal" house for the average family, able to be built for minimal cost on any site.

The response was a three-bedroom, 100 m² house, with courtyards, screen walls and garage varyingly arranged so that the living area was always private and faced north regardless of the site's orientation...'

T. Meller House
Castlecrag

see p. 48

Lowe House
Mosman (Demolished 1989)

Universal House
(Project)

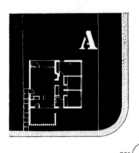 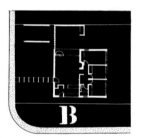

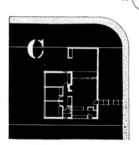 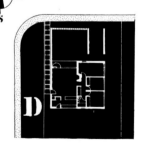

394

Frank Lloyd Wright: Johnson Wax Administration Building

Gropius with T.A.C.: Harvard Graduate Centre

1951

'... I welcomed the imposition of economy on the design of houses – I felt that it is only by making progressive design available to people of average means, that Modern design would become universally accepted. To achieve reality, buildability, meant employing direct and minimal means, which also seemed in line with the zeal instilled in us by Gropius, to help build a better world for everyone ...'

Already by 1950 Seidler was involved in larger projects:

'... My many attempts at designing large projects here did not materialise beyond the scale model stage ...'

Rose Seidler House receives the Sir John Sulman Medal from the RAIA. This is the first of many such design awards.

Tuck House
Gordon

Sydney University Student Hostel Camperdown (Project)

Ithaca Gardens Apartments 1 Elizabeth Bay (Project)

Williamson House Mosman

Rubensohn House Quirindi (Project)

see p. 50

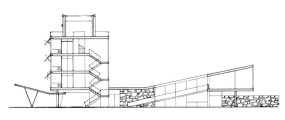
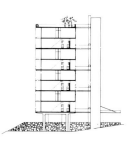

REMARKABLE HOUSE AT THE SPIT

A remarkable house which Sydney's John Sulman medallist Harry Seidler is building near The Spit is so arresting in appearance that the builder has erected a warning notice to keep sightseers away.

Mr. Seidler has designed the house so that the owner can garage his cars on his roof—in two dome-shaped shells that look like Eskimo igloos.

Local residents describe it as the "strangest house in Sydney." Builders and architects say its construction is "revolutionary."

PRECIPICE EDGE

Mr. Seidler said yesterday: "We had to get exceptional strength and lightness to fix the house to such an extremely steep slope—it runs away at an angle of more than 45 degrees down to the sea rocks below."

To achieve this double aim he used what structural engineers know as the flat-slab principle, that is, a flat slab of reinforced concrete, built without beams and supported by columns.

Engineers say it is the first time that this principle has been adapted to domestic architecture in Australia.

To put the idea into effect Mr. Seidler obtained the co-operation of Mr. P. O. Miller, consulting civil engineer, who produced and tested for him a special concrete of high-compression strength, strong enough to support a weight of 3,000lb to the square inch, compared with 2,000lb for ordinary concrete.

DEADLOCK ON HOSTEL
Minister Powerless

Plans for the construction of the, by now, almost legendary S.R.C. hostel have again come to a deadlock in the three-cornered game between the S.R.C., the Minister for Housing (Mr. Clive Evatt), and the City Council.

Model constructed by S.R.C. architect Harry Seidler of his proposed student hostel. Reports this week indicate that the hostel looks like fading right out of existence.

395

Le Corbusier: Unité, Marseilles

1952

This was the decade of the small house. Seidler was kept busy with many small low-cost and a few larger commissions. It was a far cry from America with its wealthy patronage of architecture. By this time Seidler was enjoying wide recognition, socially as well as professionally.

'. . . At that time, Breuer was receiving larger commissions other than houses. In 1948, he had tried to discourage me from coming to Australia and in 1952 he wrote to me asking if I would return to the USA and open an office for him in California, to work on a big project. It was a great temptation, but finally there was really no choice, because I had so much work and houses in construction, that I decided to stay . . .'

Sussman House
Kurrajong Heights

Thurlow House
Blakehurst

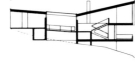

Hutter House
Turramurra

see p. 52

Landau House Whale Beach
(Demolished 1989)

Barnes House
Lane Cove (Project)

396

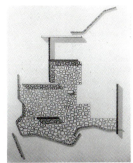
Breuer: Neumann House space

Breuer: Clarke House

1953

Seidler stayed in the public eye with a series of controversial court cases on behalf of architectural innovation.

'... One of the most protracted and bitter fights was with Ku-ring-gai Council who refused to permit a house with walls of glass rather than masonry. The absurdity of their argument became clear when they capitulated after five months, at the threshold of the court. But the little house was never built – the clients could not wait and bought a house elsewhere...'

The depressed state of the post-war Australian economy lasted well into the 1950s until revived by the Korean War. The Korean War ended in July 1953. Basic materials in building which were previously in short supply except for essential works began to become more widely available.

Waterman House
Palm Beach

Bluhdorn House
Roseville (Project)

Currie House
Newport

Lessing House
Pymble

397

London County Council: Roehampton

Le Corbusier: Millowners Building, Ahmedabad

1954

At Seidler's suggestion Walter Gropius was invited to visit Sydney.

'... I suggested to the Institute of Architects that they should invite Walter Gropius for their 1954 convention. He gave illustrated lectures which were a great success and his public comments, rejecting Councils' aesthetic control, were most topical. Gropius and his wife, Ise, loved Sydney, especially the beaches. My mother and I entertained them in her Turramurra house – speaking German and serving ''Belegte Brötchen''...'

PROF. OPPOSES RESTRICTIONS

Local governing bodies should not tell architects the kind of houses they should build, Professor Walter Gropius said last night.

Professor Gropius, one of the world's most famous architects, arrived in Sydney from America yesterday by Pan-American Clipper.

Mr. Seidler smiled when a reporter asked Professor Gropius whether councils should direct architects on house design.

Several suburban councils have opposed Mr. Seidler's radical designs.

Professor Gropius answered: "I do not believe that design and problems of art can be governed by governments at all.

"All I have seen along that line has been a failure.

"The best they can do is hinder something ugly being built.

"Art and good architecture are creative.

"Governments and committees cannot create – they can only regulate."

Piper House Ryde

Klausner Duplex Hunters Hill

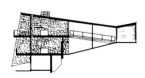

RAIA Convention Exhibition & Model House Sydney

Modern architects continue to see the industrialisation of building as the key to satisfying the community's requirement for mass housing. Seidler designed the Exhibition House for the Sydney Town Hall. This sought to demonstrate the general idea of an industrialised house made of standard components as advocated by Walter Gropius in his General Panel System.

Newton House Palm Beach (Project)

Horwitz Office Building Sydney

Mies van der Rohe: Crown Hall I.I.T.

Le Corbusier: Ronchamp

Ronchamp introduced a new plasticity of form, a voluptuous element and a scenographic management of natural light.

Television broadcasting begins and the Olympic Games are held in Melbourne.

'... Gropius, who admired Le Corbusier, always said that it would take one or two generations to fully understand and absorb his inventive work. After seeing Ronchamp in 1955, I visited Gropius and spoke enthusiastically about my impressions of it. He responded with great doubts about the validity of such highly sculptural expression in architecture...'

1955

The international public was mesmerised by Modern architecture. In Australia architecture was topical.

'... After long urging by the Horwitz publishing group, to make photographs of my houses available to them for a book, I agreed. The early photographs were all taken by my brother Marcell, who had been a professional photographer, but due to his other activities he suggested that Max Dupain provide the latest images. Soon afterwards I built an office building for the publishers; my first. After the book appeared I felt the need to see work being done in other parts of the world. It was the first of almost yearly circumnavigations of the world since then, sometimes to work with consultants, but always to explore the newest as well as the treasurehouse of historic monuments through the ages...'

1956

Harry Seidler met Le Corbusier at Chandigarh.

'... He was generous with his time and showed us the Secretariat building in construction – a human chain of mostly women was carrying buckets of concrete up the ramps.

The few completed Capital buildings were wonderful sculpturally and inventive, given the limited means...'

Olympic Stadium
Melbourne (Competition)

Olympic Swimming Pool
Melbourne (Competition)

Group Housing
Kurnell

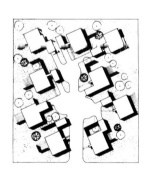

Amenities and Workshop Building Banksmeadow

Breakspear House
Clontarf

Council Objects To Design Of Clontarf House

Manly Council has issued a stop-work order against a house designed by Mr. Harry Seidler and being built in Peronne Avenue, Clontarf.

ARCHITECT ACCUSED OVER NEW HOUSE

SEIDLER WINS IN CLASH WITH COUNCIL

A prosecution launched by Manly Council against Harry Seidler, well-known Sydney architect, failed in Manly Court yesterday.

Le Corbusier: Shodan House, Ahmedabad

1957

'... One of the smallest houses built was for a signwriter. He was a man of acute visual sense who was determined that he just had to have a Modern house. The result is this 80 m², three-bedroom house which was built for the lowest cost ever, of £2,000!...'

Jørn Utzon of Denmark wins the competition for the design of the Sydney Opera House. Saarinen rescued Utzon's design from the pile of rejected drawings.
'... Saarinen came to Sydney as one of the judges for the Opera House – he arrived late and insisted on going through the pile of drawings the other judges had eliminated. He pulled out Utzon's design and spent the rest of the week persuading the others that this was IT...'

Seidler commends Sydney Opera House jury.

"I Am Quite Staggered."
Mr Harry Seidler, the Sydney architect who collaborated in one of the designs: "The winning design is poetic. It is a piece of poetry. It is magnificent. I am quite staggered by it. The jury should be commended for having the courage to award the prize to it."

With Saarinen

'... after the judging, we gave him a party for young local architects at my parents' house. It pleased him to see his "womb" chair there. He showed slides of his latest work – the General Motors Centre in Detroit...'

Heyden House
Miranda

J. Meller House
Double Bay

Sydney Opera House
Sydney (Competition)

Bowling Club
Canberra

Glass House
Chatswood

Tyree House
Clifton Gardens (Project)

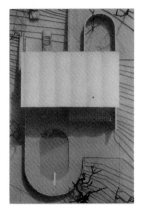

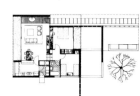
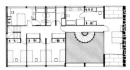

Sydney Opera House
International Competition
'honourable mention' 1957

400

Breuer: UNESCO

Mies van der Rohe: Seagram

Le Corbusier: Chandigarh

Applying the Gropius' team approach to Australian urban design problems – McMahons Point. A new vision for Sydney. Seidler looked to the future.

The McMahons Point team

The office moved from the Point Piper studio to Caltex House at 167 Kent Street where Dusseldorp had his offices.

J. Bland House
Coogee (Demolished 1988)

Basser House
Cammeray

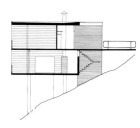

Moloney House
Kangaroo Point

McMahons Point Development
North Sydney (Project)

see p. 70

Hogbin House
Avalon

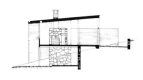

401

Candela: Restaurant, Mexico

Frank Lloyd Wright: Guggenheim Museum

1958

On 15 December 1958 Seidler married Penelope Evatt on her 20th birthday. Next to her is her uncle, Dr H.V. Evatt, and her father, Clive, behind.

'... When I married Penelope we went to Japan for our honeymoon, staying at the original Imperial Hotel built by Frank Lloyd Wright. It had incomparable public spaces. Postwar reconstruction had not yet fully started in Japan – we met Maekawa and saw his and Tange's early work in Takamatsu. Seeing the Katsura summer palace and its garden was memorable. We were some of the first visitors to Red China – in Hong Kong harbour people still lived in boats...'

1959

The Ithaca Gardens Apartments 2, Blues Point Tower Apartments commissioned by Dusseldorp and CIBA Administration and Warehouse were the first major commissions that mark the decline of the small single house as the major focus of the practice.

Kalowski House
Dover Heights

Exley House
Warrawee

Luursema House
Castlecrag

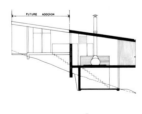

Talmudical College
Bondi

Blues Point Tower Apartments
North Sydney

see p. 72

Waks House 2
Northbridge

Frank Lloyd Wright's death on 9 April 1959 was followed by Le Corbusier's death six years later on 27 August 1965. These departures signalled a new phase in Modern architecture, a changing of the baton. A younger generation was waiting in the wings. The New Brutalism which arose in Europe was a serious attempt to reform Modernism.

Le Corbusier: La Tourette

Breuer: St John's Abbey, Minnesota

City Council Apartments
Camperdown (Competition)

Paspaley House
Darwin

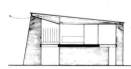

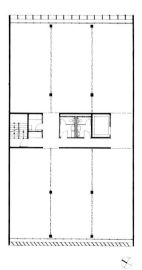

Architecture and Arts Award 1962

Printers Union Building
Sydney

CIBA Admin. & Warehouse Building Lane Cove

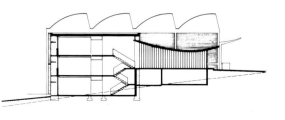

Apartments
Avalon

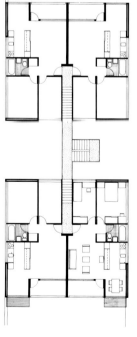

403

Nervi: Palazzetto dello Sport

Niemeyer: Brasilia

Breuer: Flaine

1960

After initially being impressed by the intellectual brilliance of Philip Johnson, Seidler was later to become increasingly disenchanted by him.

'... While working with Pei, I met many old friends from my student days and Philip Johnson, who had built some very elegant buildings including the Seagram Tower with Mies van der Rohe. He was most hospitable and generous to us, entertaining us in his New Canaan glass house. However, the admiration I felt for him then has waned in recent years, since he espoused Post-Modernism as an acceptable direction for architecture to take ...'

After completing the first multi-storey building for G.J. Dusseldorp's organisation, he asked Seidler to work on an ambitious city centre development – Australia Square. Dusseldorp admired the New York developer Zeckendorf whose architect I.M. Pei was Seidler's former classmate at Harvard. He arranged for Seidler and Pei to collaborate on the first proposal. It was later abandoned, requiring more site area than Dusseldorp owned.

Silvers Building Ultimo

Grimson & Rose Exhibition House Pennant Hills

Long House Wahroonga

Ithaca Gardens Apartments 2 Elizabeth Bay

Australia Square 1 Sydney (with I.M. Pei, Project)

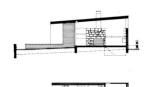

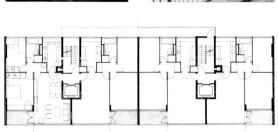

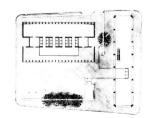

Architecture and Arts Award 1960

Saarinen: TWA Terminal

Saarinen: Dulles Airport

1961

First real recession since World War Two. Menzies came close to losing the federal election.

Australia Square passed through many vicissitudes before it became a reality.

In the same year Seidler moved his office to Lend Lease House at 47 Macquarie Street, Sydney.

In the early 1960s medium and high-density housing replaced the single dwelling as the design focus.

Lend Lease House Offices
Sydney

Weinreich House
Vaucluse

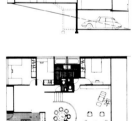

Wood House
Penrith

Two Exhibition Houses
Carlingford

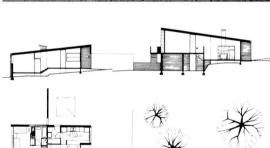
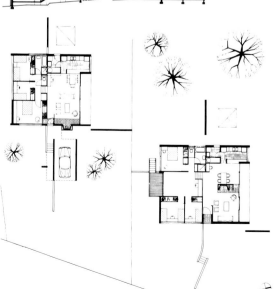

City Council Apartments
Paddington

405

Ellwood: Rosen House

Le Corbusier: Carpenter Centre, Harvard

1962

This year marks the beginning of Harry Seidler's CBD high rise when his career takes off with the design of Australia Square.

Australia Square was a source of controversy when it was first proposed as a 600 ft 58-storey tower. To many people it represented the beginning of the Manhattanisation of Sydney.

Harry Seidler visits Nervi's office in Rome. This was to have a lasting effect on his subsequent development with Nervi acting as his consultant and adviser for some of the architect's most innovative structures.

Australia Square 2
Sydney

Sir John Sulman Medal
RAIA 1967

Civic Design Award
RAIA 1967

Welfare Centre for the Aged
Alexandria

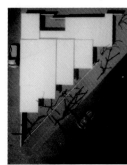

Ski Lodge
Thredbo

Wilkinson Award
RAIA 1965

Victoria Tower Apartments
Potts Point

Sydney Cove Redevelopment
'The Rocks' Sydney (Comp'n)

Nervi: Palace of Labour, Turin

Nervi: Burgo Paper Mill, Mantua

Sert: Harvard Student Housing

1963

'. . . I had met Nervi in Paris on the Unesco site in 1955. When he accepted my invitation to act as structural consultant on Australia Square, I spent some weeks in his Rome office. It was a great education, learning to understand the clear underlying logic and his way of expressing nature's forces beautifully.

It all became tangible when seeing his projects in construction: the Olympic structures, the paper factory in Mantua, the Turin exhibition building and the Pope's audience hall in the Vatican . . .'

Harry Seidler re-establishes contact with his early mentors, Gropius, Breuer and Albers, on one of his many visits to New York.

Diamond Bay Apartments
Dover Heights

Ercildoune Apartments
Elizabeth Bay

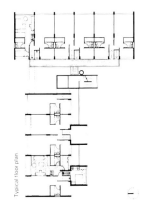

Muller House
Port Hacking

see p. 54

Monahan House
Castlecrag

Wilkinson Award
RAIA 1966

Breuer: Whitney Museum

Breuer: Muskegan Church

Tange: Olympic Arenas

1964

Seidler discovers family life with the birth of his son Timothy Evatt Seidler on 22 August 1964.

The first tri-lingual publication introduced Seidler to an international audience.

Apartments
Rushcutters Bay

see p. 74

Apartments
Earlwood

Eros House Offices
Canberra

Campbell Group Housing
Canberra

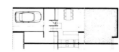

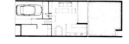

Garran Group Housing
Canberra

see p. 78

Breuer: Koerfer House

Kahn: Salk Institute

Aalto: Otaniemi University

1965

... The search for a sculptor to do a work for Australia Square came to an end at Saché in the Loire Valley – at Calder's delightful old farm house. I showed him slides of the project and he was keen to do a stabile. His studio was a charmingly messy place ...

NSW Housing Commission Apartments Rosebery

see p. 76

Apartments Double Bay

NSW Government Stores Alexandria

Horwitz Sloop

409

'... Tapiola is planning in our century at its best, its vision and implementation due to one man – a banker: Dr Heikki Von Hertzen.

The fact that different architects can create unity and yet diversity is proven there. Their designs are all built following Aarne Ervi's winning competition town plan.

The rest of the world should learn from this ...'

Ervi: Tapiola

Tange: Yamanashi Centre

1966–1967

Prime Minister Sir Robert Menzies retires. The Australian economy slows in 1966–67. The Sydney Opera House crisis brought together many segments of the Sydney artistic community in a common cause and focused world concern over the future of the monument. Students, architects, academics and many others protested at the NSW Government's precipitate acceptance of Utzon's resignation outside the gates of the Bennelong Point construction site.

Harry Seidler visited the Utzons at Copenhagen. This was after Jørn Utzon's resignation from the Sydney Opera House project.

Honorary Fellow
AIA (Hon FAIA) 1966

Harry & Penelope Seidler House Killara

see p. 60

Wilkinson Award
RAIA 1967

Daily Telegraph, Friday March 4, 1966
CALLING FOR PEACE

Daily Mirror, Thursday March 3, 1966
1000 marchers call for Utzon

JOERN UTZON

The Australian, Saturday March 12, 1966
Utzon asks time to think again

Tuesday March 15, 1966
Utzon scapegoat move planned, says architect

The Sydney Morning Herald, Tues., March 15, 1966
ARCHITECTS AT WAR
YOUNG REBELS LEAD FIGHT TO KEEP UTZON IN CHARGE

SEIDLER

Daily Mirror, Monday, March 14, 1966
'DELIBERATE CAMPAIGN' TO OUST UTZON

dear Penelope!
a good man fights for his ideas!
but a great man is a man who fights for other people and for ideals –
such a man is your Harry, and I have come to respect him deeply – he has taught me a lot because I have never been able to do what he has done in the last month...
to experience this – his marvellous friendship outweighs completely any disappointment and bitterness in me.
love from Jørn.

Arlington Apartments Edgecliff

see p. 80

Pei: Everson Museum, Syracuse

Candela: Olympic Stadium, Mexico

Breuer: Stillman House

Breuer: IBM Research Centre, France

1968

International and Australian recognition attended the completion of Australia Square.

Pan Pacific Architectural Citation AIA 1968

1969

Artist Christo proposed to wrap Australia Square Tower, then in a project called *Wrapped Coast – One Million Square Feet, Little Bay, Sydney, Australia*, wrapped Little Bay, south of the city, with fabric.

Pauline Rose Seidler born 19 January 1969.

Ling Apartments
Elizabeth Bay

International Trade Centre
Milsons Point (Project)

National Art Gallery
Canberra (Competition)

Campbelltown Planning
Campbelltown

Condominium Apartments
Acapulco Mexico

see p. 82

Gropius: Gropiusstadt

Mies van der Rohe dies 17 August 1969.

Nervi: Bridge, Verona

S.O.M.: Hancock Tower

1970

Gropius dies 5 July 1969. Some years before his death, he left this 'testament' to his students:

'For whatever profession, your inner devotion to the tasks you have set yourself must be so deep that you can never be deflected from your aim. However often the thread may be torn out of your hands, you must develop enough patience to wind it up again and again. Act as if you were going to live forever and cast your plans way ahead. By this I mean that you must feel responsible without time limitation, and the consideration whether you may or may not be around to see the results should never enter your thoughts. If your contribution has been vital, there will always be somebody to pick up where you left off, and that will be your claim to immortality.'

During the 1960s Sydney led the Western world in providing architect-designed modern houses for average families through merchant builders such as Pettit Sevitt. No similar product was available elsewhere. Local pulp 'fashion' magazines which promoted neo-historic-style houses instead ended this.

26 September 1969. Seidler office moved to 7 Ridge Street, North Sydney, a centre for creative activity.

Mass demonstrations against Australian participation in the Vietnam War.

City Centre Planning
Sydney (Project)

Memorial to Martyrs
Rookwood

Pettit & Sevitt Exhibition House Westleigh

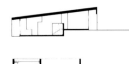

Chevron Development
Melbourne (Project)

Hotel & Office Tower
Sydney (Project)

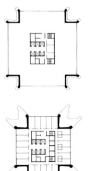

Resort Hotel
Fitzroy Is., Qld (Project)

Project House Award
RAIA 1969

412

The Sydney Opera House demonstrated that architecture was both a functional art and sculpture meant to be seen in the round, from every side and from above. The prominence of the building fabric in the city made it an influence on local architects well before its completion in 1973.

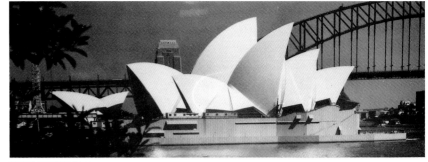

Utzon: Sydney Opera House

1971

Life Fellow
RAIA (LFRAIA) 1970

Perry and Seidler in Rome with bronze 'Double Knot'

Renault House
Castle Cove

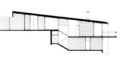

Trade Group Offices
Canberra

see p. 126

Ten Eyck Development
Albany, NY (Project)

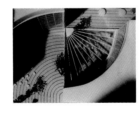

RAIA Exhibition Pavilion
Hyde Park, Sydney

see p. 124

Harry Seidler Offices
Milsons Point

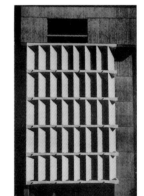

see p. 322

MLC Centre
Sydney

see p. 140

Merit Award
RAIA 1974

Sir John Sulman Medal
RAIA 1981

Merit Award
RAIA 1979

Civic Design Award
RAIA 1981

Sir John Sulman Medal
RAIA 1983

Meier: Douglas House

Kahn: Kimbell Museum

1972

Public recognition: Seidler is made an Officer, Order of the British Empire (OBE).

With brother Marcell at investiture

Seidler meets Breuer and Blake in New York. Blake subsequently wrote the text of *Architecture for the New World* on Seidler, published 1973.

Gissing House
Wahroonga

McLaren Street Offices
North Sydney

High Court of Australia
Canberra (Competition)

CRA Development 1
Melbourne (Project)

see p. 68

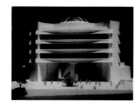

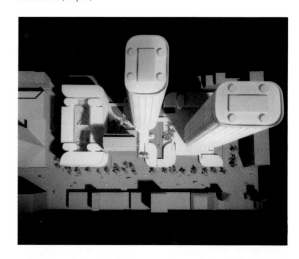

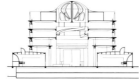

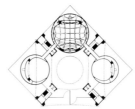

414

S.O.M.: Sears Tower

Patrick White is awarded the Nobel Prize for literature. The Queen opens the Sydney Opera House.

Rudolph: Bass House

Piano & Rogers: Pompidou Centre

1973–1974

1975

The Australian Labor Party wins a federal election after being out of office since 1949. Gough Whitlam, who showed great interest in the arts, becomes Prime Minister.

10 March 1973. Office moved to 2 Glen Street, Milsons Point, North Sydney, in a specially designed building by Seidler.

The Australian Embassy showcased Seidler's architecture on a site that called for the greatest urban sensitivity. It came through with flying colours and recognition from the French.

Team lunch in the Breuer office at 48 Rue Chapon, Paris 2

With Breuer

A constitutional crisis occurs when the Senate defers its decision on two Appropriation Bills. The Governor-General, Sir John Kerr, dismissed the Whitlam Government and appointed Malcolm Fraser as a caretaker Prime Minister until elections could be held. The Australian economy was hit by recession in 1974–75. Seidler's practice was affected in 1976 and staff numbers fell from around 14 to six or seven and thereafter gradually increased to 20 in 1981.

Bushey Park Housing
Singapore (Project)

The Australian Embassy
Paris

Torin Co. Factory Penrith
(Design: Marcel Breuer)

Tuggeranong Offices
Canberra (Project)

Tuggeranong Energy Plant
Canberra (Project)

see p. 154
see p. 134

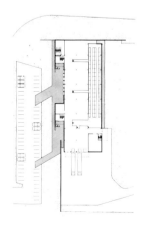

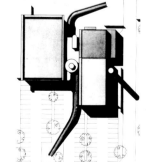
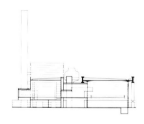

415

Utzon: Bagsvaerd Church

Erikson: Anthropological Museum

Meier: Atheneum

1976

Letter from Mrs Walter Gropius to Harry Seidler after she attended his illustrated lecture at the Graduate School of Design at Harvard, during his term as Visiting Critic in Design.

1977

During the Fall Semester of 1976–77 Seidler taught at Harvard's Graduate School of Design; followed a year later by periods spent at the University of British Columbia and the University of Virginia. In 1980 he was the Inaugural Visiting Professor at the University of New South Wales.

1978

... I have rarely seen architecture and sculpture interact so successfully as the retrospective Calder show in Breuer's Whitney Museum ...

Fairfield Municipal Library
Fairfield

Baranduda Town Centre
Albury-Wodonga (Project)

see p. 172

Council Offices
North Sydney

Apartments
Broadbeach

Ringwood Cultural Centre
Melbourne

see p. 176

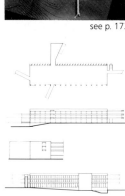

Merit Award
RAIA 1977

Victorian Architectural Medal
RAIA 1980

Pei: National Gallery

Foster: Hong Kong Bank

1979

The former Governor-General of Australia, Sir John Kerr, is proposed as Australian Ambassador to Unesco in Paris. Seidler protests publicly at Kerr's plan to replace the furnishings with antique furniture. The appointment falls through and the integrity of the interiors is saved.

Fellow Australian Academy of Technological Sciences (FTS) 1979

State College of Victoria
Rusden (Project)

Australian Parliament House
Canberra (Competition)

Mid-City Shopping Centre
Sydney

Hillside Housing
Kooralbyn

Hong Kong-Shanghai Bank
Hong Kong (Competition)

see p. 180

see p. 204

see p. 192

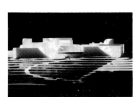

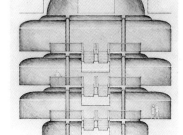

Prizewinner 1980

Honourable Mention
RAIA Qld 1982

Tange: Bologna Development

Bayer: Convolutions

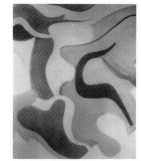
De Kooning: Painting

1980

Simple and sensuous: in the 1980s Seidler switched to curvilinear themes, 'S' profiles and discovered the subtle complex geometrical schemes inspired by such diverse influences as De Kooning, Stella, Herbert Bayer and Baroque architecture.

1981

Marcel Breuer dies on 2 July 1981. Seidler attended a simple memorial gathering held at the Whitney Museum in New York held on 21 September and contributes an obituary for the *AIA Journal*, August 1981.

'. . . The one overwhelming recollection about Lajko is the warmth and lack of pretention he exuded. One had a feeling of well-being, of comfort with him – just as one had in his houses.

To us students at Harvard in the 1940s he was the taste maker with his exquisite visual understatements – that were at once lyrically romantic but also disarmingly simple solutions to planning and building.

L. Basser House
Castle Cove

see p. 226

McGregor Townhouses
Canberra

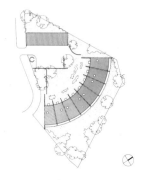

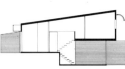

Navy Weapons Workshop
Garden Island, Sydney

see p. 194

Offices & Apartments
Kuala Lumpur, Malaysia (Project)

see p. 202

Hong Kong Club & Offices
Hong Kong

see p. 206

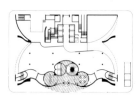

Merson House
Palm Beach

see p. 230

Merit Award
RAIA 1983

Kahn: Institute of Management, Ahmedabad

1982

But the world takes a long time to distinguish between works of art and shallow visual thrills. Just as it took half a century for his furniture to be universally rediscovered, so it may take as long again for the inherent genius in his architecture to be fully understood and rediscovered . . .'

'. . . Stella sent black-and-white, three-dimensional scale models of his painting/wall sculptures for the Grosvenor Place entrance hall. I asked him whether the final works will also be black-and-white – he answered "there might be a bit of colour". Little did we suspect what he had in mind – works with brilliantly vibrant colouring which gave life to the granite-clad lobby! . . .'

Bland House
Rose Bay

see p. 232

Waverley Civic Centre
Melbourne

see p. 218

Grosvenor Place
Sydney

see p. 240

New World Development
Singapore (Project)

Lustig & Moar
National Architecture Prize 1989

Yarralumla Group Houses
Canberra

see p. 188

Merit Award
RAIA 1984

Merit Award
RAIA 1985

Sir John Sulman Medal
RAIA 1991

Merit Award
RAIA 1985

Foster: Renault Factory

Meier: Atlanta Museum

1983

Seidler cutting the traditional piglet at the structural completion ceremony, Hong Kong Club

Seidler family gathered together: Timothy, Penelope, Harry and Polly.

National Archives
Canberra (Competition)

Hannes House
Cammeray

see p. 234

Margaret St Offices
Brisbane

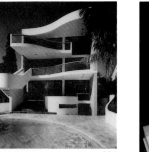

Frankston Cultural Centre
Melbourne (Project)

Riverside Development
Stage 1 Brisbane

see p. 258

Robin Dods Triennial
RAIA Medal 1989

National Award
RAIA (Sir Zelman Cowen Award)
1987

Merit Award
RAIA 1985

Niemeyer: Le Havre Development

Utzon: Kuwait Parliament

1984

In 1984 Seidler becomes the first Australian to be elected a Member of the Académie d'Architecture, Paris.

With Claude Engle at lighting test, Hong Kong Club

Jacoby was used by the Seidler office many times, the Australian Embassy, Paris, being the first:

'... I met Helmut Jacoby in Germany, who is without doubt one of the world's great architectural delineators. Hours are spent with him discussing and describing every material used, its special quality, so that he can represent it life-like with his inimitable artistry. His drawings both emphasise abstract design qualities, but are also uncannily realistic when finally compared to the completed building ...'

CRA Development 2
Melbourne (Project)

Circular Quay East Development Sydney (Project)

Hilton Hotel
Brisbane

see p. 278

Capita Centre
Sydney

see p. 282

Merit Award
RAIA 1991

Rogers: Lloyds

Piano: The Menil Collection

'... **Harry Seidler**, Breuer's long-time assistant and now the doyen of Australian architecture, has just launched an attack on Graves of quite out of the ordinary bitterness. His submission to the New York Landmark Commission's hearing on the Graves' scheme last month called Post-Modernism architectural AIDS – showing exceptional tastelessness. He described Graves' design as 'an act of vandalism', and an 'obscene offence which will bring upon its perpetrators

1985

1986

1986 was a peak period for the Seidler office with five major projects under construction by the middle of 1986. By conventional standards Seidler's office was always small. In the 1950s it consisted of Seidler by himself and possibly one assistant; in the 1960s it grew to six and consisted of upwards of 10 to 12 at Ridge Street. By July 1981 it had grown to 20, it increased to 39 people by 1986 and expanded to a maximum of 42 in 1987. It went down to 15 at the end of 1991 with the loss of Darling Park. These figures indicate a highly efficient and productive office. A strong commitment and loyalty to Modernism explains the low staff turnover.

Sydney Morning Herald, 29 November 1985
Cartoon following the controversy with City Council's initial disapproval of the S-shaped Shell Building.

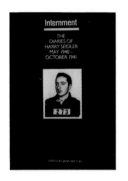

Shell Headquarters
Melbourne

Landmark Tower
Brisbane (Project)

Westpac Bank & Offices
Melbourne (Project)

Office Extension & Penthouse Milsons Point

Silver Table Candelabra
(Competition)

see p. 296

see p. 310

see p. 326

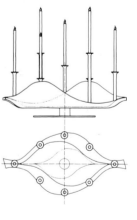

Merit Award
RAIA Vic. 1991

National Award
RAIA 1991

Merit Award
RAIA 1991

National Award
RAIA 1991

the ridicule and wrath of the thinking world for allowing such an outrage to proceed'. His whole submission is peppered with insults; clumsy, flatfooted, primitive, pitifully inept, dull, insensitive, incongruous and insulting are only some of the milder epithets.

Graves is, however, quite capable of giving as good as he gets: 'Breuer is dead, but his wife lives, and speaks to him daily. I've asked my parents to have a word with him, but they're not architects,' he told listeners in London . . .'
Blueprint, June 1987 (London)

Jahn: United Air Terminal

Niemeyer: Communist Headquarters, Paris

1987

1988

One of Seidler's enduring hates in the 1980s was Post-Modernism. He actively campaigned against it, lending his opposition to plans by Michael Graves to build an addition to the Whitney Museum; by fighting facadism; and by opposing the indiscriminate retention of old buildings.

'. . . Together with many friends in New York, I joined the fight to stop the desecration of Breuer's Whitney Museum – Graves wanted to put up something resembling the Mausoleum of Halicarnassos on top of it – but we won! . . .'

In 1987 Seidler was honoured by the Companion Order of Australia, its highest honour.

The Bicentennial celebrations on 26 January 1988 provided an important impetus for the renewal of Sydney in such ambitious undertakings as the refurbishment of Circular Quay, Macquarie Street and the re-construction of Darling Harbour.

Seidler attends the 50th anniversary of Gropius' Lincoln House and donates the Rose Seidler House to the Historic Houses Trust of NSW as a museum open to the public.

Casino & Hotel
Darling Harbour, Sydney (Comp'n)

Phoenix Tower
Sydney (Project)

QVI Office Tower
Perth

Mitchell House
Manly (Project)

La Plage Apartments
Manly (Project)

see p. 316

see p. 312

see p. 336

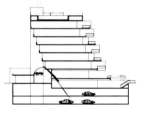

Pei: Louvre Pyramid

Pei: Bank of China

Speckelsen: Tete Defense

1989

Many observers, including the renowned English architectural historian-critic Professor Kenneth Frampton of Columbia University, New York, consider Riverside with its splendid public plaza to be one of Seidler's most accomplished office tower projects.

Academician of the International Academy of Architects, Sofia 1987

Honorary Doctorate, LLD University of Manitoba, Canada 1988

Seidler is honoured by his home city with the award of the Gold Medal of Vienna by the Bürgermeister, Dr H. Zilk.

SBS Television reconstructs his formative years in Vienna in a programme entitled *Nostalgia*.

Grand Central 1
Melbourne (Project)

Australia-Israel Friendship Forest Memorial Israel

Waverley Cultural Centre
Melbourne

Waverley Art Gallery
Melbourne

Riverside Development Stage 2 Brisbane (Project)

Grand Central 2
Melbourne (Project)

see p. 354

see p. 356

see p. 276

see p. 360

424

Piano: Airport

Foster: Stansted Airport

Foster: Offices, Tokyo

Meier: Offices, Paris

1990

1991

1st prize
Marble Architectural Awards
1989

The 'R' word is used by Federal Treasurer, Paul Keating, and Australia enters its worst recession since the 1930s.

At 68 years, Seidler is alert, active and looking forward with optimism to the future. His commitment to principle unimpaired; there is no sign of him slowing down.

Honorary Degree
(Doctor of Letters)
University of Technology, Sydney
1991

Hamilton House
Vaucluse

Darling Park Development
Darling Harbour, Sydney

ABC Apartments
Darlinghurst

Restored & Remodelled House Mondavio, Italy

see p. 366

see p. 372

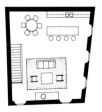

Selected Bibliography

Books on or by Harry Seidler

BLAKE, Peter, *Architecture for the New World: The work of Harry Seidler*, Horwitz, Sydney; Wittenborn, New York; Karl Kraemer, Stuttgart, 1973
——, *Harry Seidler, Australian Embassy/Ambassade d'Australie, Paris*, Horwitz, Sydney; Wittenborn, New York; Karl Kraemer, Stuttgart, 1979
BOYD, R., afterword by Harry Seidler, *The Australian Ugliness*, 2nd revised edn, Penguin, Melbourne, 1980, pp. 253–63
DREW, Philip, *Two Towers. Harry Seidler: Australia Square, MLC Centre*, Horwitz, Sydney; Karl Kraemer, Stuttgart, 1980
FRAMPTON, Kenneth, *Riverside Centre*, Horwitz, Sydney; Karl Kraemer, Stuttgart, 1988
Harry Seidler 1955–63, Introd. Reyner Banham, Horwitz, Sydney; Freal, Paris; Hatje, Stuttgart, 1963
SEIDLER, Harry, *Houses, Interiors, Projects*, Associated General Publications, Sydney, 1954, 2nd edn, Horwitz, Sydney, 1959
——, *Australia Square*, Horwitz, Sydney, 1969
——, *(Human Settlement Issues 2) Planning and Building Down Under*, University of British Columbia Press, Vancouver, 1978
Towers in the City, introd. Peter Murray, Edizioni Tecno, Milan, 1988
WILTON, Janis, ed., *Internment: The Diaries of Harry Seidler May 1940–October 1941*, Allen & Unwin, Australia, 1986

Books containing articles on Harry Seidler

ALOI, R., *50 Ville del Nostro Tempo*, Hoepli, Milan, 1970, pp. 99–106 (H. & P. Seidler House, Killara)
——, *Ville D'Oggi*, Hoepli, Milan, 1963
——, *Nuove Ville*, Hoepli, Milan, 1971
ALOI, G., *Case di Abitazione*, Hoepli, Milan, 1972, pp. 215–22 (NSW Housing Commission Apartments, Rosebery), pp. 223–30 (Arlington Apartments), pp. 231–8 (Rushcutters Bay Apartments)
BARRAN, Fritz, R., *Der Offene Kamin*, Hoffmann, Stuttgart, 1962, p. 54 (Lessing House), p. 134 (Waks House II), p. 159 (Heyden House)
——, *Der Offene Kamin Folge 3*, Julius Hoffman, Stuttgart, 1976, p. 84 (Gissing House), p. 85 (H. & P. Seidler House, Killara), p. 88 (Ski Lodge)
BOLOGNA, G., *Cembureau*, Aitec, Rome, 1974
BOYD, R., *The Australian Ugliness*, Cheshire, Melbourne, 1960, pp. 124–5 (design theory)
——, afterword by Harry Seidler, *The Australian Ugliness*, 2nd revised edn, Penguin, Melbourne, 1980, pp. 253–63 (On planning)
——, *Australia's Home*, Melbourne University Press, 1952, pp. 180–2 (design theory), pp. 186–9 (court cases)
CHUNG, Wah Nan, *Contemporary Architecture in Hong Kong*, Joint Publishing Hong Kong, 1989, pp. 70–73.
CLEREHAN, N., *Best Australian Houses*, Cheshire, Melbourne, 1961, (Waks II House)
CURTIS, William, J.R., *Modern Architecture Since 1900*, Phaidon Press, Oxford, 1982, pp. 334–6 (Rose Seidler House)
DANZ, E., *Kamine*, Hatje, Stuttgart, 1964, p. 34 (RAIA Convention Exhibition & Model House), p. 73 (Glass House)
——, *Sonnenschutz*, Hatje, Stuttgart, 1967, pp. 88–9 (Horwitz Office), pp. 106–7 (Lend Lease House), p. 148 (Printers Union)
DEILMANN, Harald, and Andreas, *Gebaude fur die Öffentliche Verwaltung*, Alexander Koch, Stuttgart, 1979, pp. 177–80 (Australian Embassy, Paris), pp. 186–9 (Trade Group Offices)
——, KIRSCHENMANN and PFEIFFER, *Wohnungsbau*, Krämer, Stuttgart, 1973
EMANUEL, Muriel, *Contemporary Architects*, Macmillan Press, London, 1980, pp. 118–9 (On Breuer), pp. 588–9 (On Niemeyer), pp. 734–6 (design theory)
FLETCHER, Sir Banister, *A History of Architecture*, Butterworths, 1987
FREELAND, J.M., *Architecture in Australia*, Cheshire, Melbourne, 1968, pp. 272–3, 276, p. 281 (Rose Seidler House), p. 302, pp. 304–5 (Australia Square)
FUTAGAWA, Y., *GA. Houses 2*, Edita Tokyo, 1977, pp. 152–7 (H. & P. Seidler House, Killara)
HARRIS, M.E., *The Arts at Black Mountain College*, MIT Press, Cambridge, Mass., 1987
HASSENPFLUG-PETERS, *Scheibe Punkt und Hügel*, Callwey, Munich, 1966, pp. 80–2 (Ithaca Gardens), p. 83 (Diamond Bay Apartments)

HATJE, G., *Encyclopaedia of Modern Architecture*, Thames & Hudson, London, 1963, p. 40 (Austrian architects), p. 255 (design theory), p. 312 (on Sydney Opera House by Utzon)
HAYES, B., *Australian Style*, Hamlyn, London, 1970, pp. 204–15 (H. & P. Seidler House, Killara, and design theory)
HOHL, R., *Office Buildings*, Architectural Press, London, 1968, pp. 116–9 (Lend Lease House), pp. 156–61 (Australia Square)
IRVING, R. and KINSTLER, J., *Fine Houses of Sydney*, Methuen, Australia, 1982, pp. 170–2, pp. 74–5, pp. 77–81 (H. & P. Seidler House, Killara)
JACOBY, Helmut, *Architekturdarstellung*, Hatje, Germany, 1971 (National Art Gallery Competition)
JENSEN, R., *High Density Living*, Leonard Hill, London, 1966, p. 70 (City Council Apartments, Camperdown, competition), p. 67 (Blues Point Tower), p. 69 (Ithaca Gardens)
JOHNSON, Donald, L., *Australian Architecture 1901–51 Sources of Modernism*, Macarthur Press, 1980, pp. 172–208 (design theory)
JUDD, B. and DEAN, J., *Medium Density Housing in Australia*, RAIA, Canberra, 1983, pp. 112–4 (Kooralbyn)
KASPAR, K., *Ferienhäuser–International*, Hatje, Stuttgart, 1967, pp. 110–3 (Ski lodge)
KOBOSIL, F. and KOLACED, S., *Rodinné domky v Zahranici*, SNTL, Prague, 1972, pp. 284–93 (H. & P. Seidler House, Killara)
KOHLER, W. and LUCKHART, W., *Lightarchitektur*, Ullstein, Berlin, 1956
KRAFFT, A., *Architecture Formes Fonctions*, Krafft, Lausanne, No. 10, 1963, pp. 160–1 (Blues Point Tower), p. 162 (Sydney Cove Redevelopment Competition); No. 11, 1964; No. 13, 1966; No. 15, 1969; No. 16, 1971
——, *Contemporary Architecture*, Krafft, Lausanne, Vol. 1 1979–80, pp. 69–74 (Australian Embassy, Paris); Vol. 5 1983–84, pp. 107–10 (Mid-City Centre), pp. 179–84 (Kooralbyn); Vol. 9 1987–88, pp. 148–53 (Hong Kong Club); Vol. 11 1989–90, pp. 200–6 (Riverside Centre)
LOHSE, SCHADER, ZIETSCHMANN, *Neues Bauen, Gutes Wohnen*, Bauen & Wohnen, Zurich, 1954, pp. 20–25 (Rose Seidler House), pp. 26–29 (Waks House I)
LUCK, Peter, *A time to Remember*, William Heinemann, Australia, 1988, pp. 32–3 (Rose Seidler House, Australia Square)
Maisons de Vacances, Hachette, Paris, 1964, pp. 48–9, pp. 174–5, pp. 246–7 (Ski Lodge, Thredbo)
McCOY, E., *Arts & Architecture – the Entenza years*, MIT Press, Cambridge, Mass., 1990, pp. 151–3 (Rose Seidler House)
McGREGOR, Craig, *Headliners*, University of Queensland Press, Australia, 1990 (social portrait)
McKAY, BOYD, STRETTON and MANT, *Living & Partly Living*, Nelson, Melbourne, 1972, p. 128 (Pettit & Sevitt Exhibition House), pp. 142–3 (Garran Group Housing), pp. 180–5 (Victoria Tower Apartments), pp. 186–9 (Apartments, Rushcutters Bay)
MEYER-BOHE, W., *Vorgefertigte Wohnhäuser*, Callwey, Munich, 1959, pp. 89–93 (RAIA Convention Exhibition & Model House)
MILLS, E.D., *The Modern Factory*, The Architectural Press, London, 1959, pp. 149–50 (Amenities & Workshop Building)
MODES, A. and KULTERMANN, U., *Das Schöne Heim*, Thiemig, Munich, 1981, pp. 61–70 (H. & P. Seidler House, Killara)
MORGAN, A.L. and NAYLOR, C., *Contemporay Architects*, 2nd edn; St James Press, London, 1987 (on Breuer), (on Niemeyer), pp. 818–21 (design theory)
MURPHY, Mary, *The Challenges of Change, The Lend Lease Story*, Lend Lease, Sydney, 1984, pp. 33–5 (Ithaca Gardens), pp. 115–9 (Australia Square), pp. 132–7 (MLC Centre), p. 164 (Riverside Centre)
NAGEL, S. and LINKE, S., *Einfamilienhäuser, Bungalows, Ferienhäuser*, 1968, pp. 104–5 (Basser House), pp. 140–2 (Muller House); *Reihenhäuser, Gruppenhäuser, Hochhäuser*, 1968, p. 38 (Victoria Tower Apartments), p. 39 (Apartments, Double Bay), pp. 204–5 (Sydney Cove Redevelopment Competition), pp. 206–8 (Apartments, Rushcutters Bay); *Verwaltungsbauten*, 1969, pp. 84–7 (Lend Lease House Office); *Heimbauten*, 1970, pp. 200–1 (Welfare Centre for the Aged); *Kleine Wohnhäuser*, 1972, pp. 42–3 (Rose House), pp. 68–9 (Monahan House), Bertelsmann, Gütersloh
NELSON, G., *Living Spaces*, Whitney Publications Inc., New York, 1952, p. 20 (Rose Seidler House), p. 21 (Waks House I)
PAROISSIEN, Leon and GRIGGS, Michael, eds, *Old Continent New Building*, David Ell Press & Design Arts Committee of the Australia Council, Sydney, 1983, pp. 26–7, p. 35 (Turramurra houses), p. 64 (L. Basser House), p. 75 (Kooralbyn), p. 82 (Australia Square), p. 83 (MLC Centre), p. 25, p. 85 (Trade Group Offices), p. 86 (Mid-City Shopping Centre)

PAUL, S., *Apartments*, Reinhold, New York, 1967, p. 88 (Diamond Bay), p. 193 (Blues Point Tower)
PEHNT, W., *Encyclopaedia of Modern Architecture*, Abrams, New York, 1964, p. 40 (Austrian architects), p. 255 (design theory), p. 312 (on Sydney Opera House by Utzon)
PFAU-ZIETSCHMANN, *Einfamilienhäuser 33 Architekten*, Bauen & Wohnen, Zurich, 1964
PHILLIPS, Alan, *The best in office interior design*, Batsford, London, 1991 (Capita, Grosvenor Place, Riverside Centre, Shell Headquarters)
PIDGEON, M. and CROSBY, T., *An Anthology of Houses*, Batsford, London, 1960, pp. 164–5 (Bassser House), pp. 166–7 (Sussmann House)
PLUMB, Barbara, *Houses Architects Live In*, The Viking Press, New York, 1977 (H. & P. Seidler House, Killara)
Quaternario 88: International Award for Innovative Technology in Architecture (Sydney 1988), le Grafiche Lema–Maniago, Italy, 1988, pp. 222–39 (Riverside Centre)
RICHARDS, J.M., *New Buildings in the Commonwealth*, Architectural Press, London; F. Praeger, New York, 1962, p. 32 (Amenities & Workshop Building), pp. 40–1 (Lessing House), p. 42 (Waks House I)
SEDLAK, Vincenz, *Membrane Structures in Australia 2*, LSRU, NSW University, 1982
SHARP, Dennis ed., *The Illustrated Encylopaedia of Architects and Architecture*, Quarto Publishing, London 1991, p. 139
SOWDEN, H., *Towards an Australian Architecture*, Ure Smith, Sydney, 1968, pp. 218–9 (design theory), pp. 220–1 (Rose Seidler House), p. 219, pp. 222–9 (Australia Square), pp. 230–41 (H. & P. Seidler House, Killara)
SUCKLE, Abby, *By Their Own Design*, Whitney Library of Design, USA & Canada, 1980, pp. 122–35 (design theory)
TAYLOR, Jennifer, *Australian Architecture Since 1960*, Law Book Co., Sydney, 1986 (design theory)
TENTTAGEN, N.V., *International Architektur Dokumentation*, Vols. 1, 2, 3, Bauverlag, The Hague, 1972
WAGNER Jr, Walter F. and SCHLEGEL, Karen, eds, *Houses Architects Design for Themselves*, McGraw-Hill, 1974, pp. 100–3 (H. & P. Seidler House, Killara)
WALTER, Betsy and WRIGHT, Jean, *Australian Style*, Weldon Publishing, Sydney, 1991, pp. 92–5 (penthouse, Milsons Point)
WEBBER, Peter, *The Design of Sydney: Three Decades of Change in the City Centre*, Law Book Co., Sydney, 1988, pp. 165,175 (Circular Quay East Development project)
WEIDERT, W., *Einfamilienhäuser–International*, Hatje, Stuttgart, 1967, pp. 40–3 (Lessing House), pp. 110–3 (Two Exhibition Houses)
ZUMPE, M., *Wohnhochhäuser*, Bauwesen, East Berlin, 1967, pp. 167–8 (Diamond Bay), pp. 175–7 (Ithaca Gardens), p. 251 (Sydney Cove Redevelopment Competition)

Theses and Reports

BEAVAN, Allan, *The Australian House Since 1900: Rose Seidler House, Turramurra 1949*, thesis, University of NSW, 1984
EMMETT, Peter, *Conservation Plan. Mid-century Modern. Rose Seidler House 1948–50*, report, Historic Houses Trust of NSW, November 1989
BUNCELL, David R., *Harry Seidler: Space, Structure and Form. The Architecture of Harry Seidler: An analysis of the expression of space, structure and form in relation to twentieth century artistic movements*, thesis, University of Sydney, 1983
VIVIAN, Philip, *Three Values and Deep Seated Convictions*, thesis, University of WA, 1987

Reports by Harry Seidler
(Held at Mitchell Library, Sydney)

Multiple Dwellings, A study prepared for Civil & Civic Contractors Pty Limited, May 1958
Seidler Studio, Faculty of Architecture, University of New South Wales, 1980

Illustrated Project Reports by Harry Seidler & Associates
(Held at Mitchell Library, Sydney)

Urban Redevelopment Concerns You (McMahons Point Development)	—	1957
Australia Square, Sydney	—	1962
Australia Square, Sydney	April	1964
Housing Commission, Rosebery, Sydney	May	1964
NCDC Group Housing, Campbell, ACT	Aug.	1964
NSW Government Stores	March	1965
Flats at 351 Edgecliff Road, Woollahra (Arlington Apartments), Sydney	—	1965
Martin Plaza Block 2, Sydney	Dec.	1969
Ten Eyck Redevelopment, Albany, New York	—	1970
Trade Group Offices, Barton, ACT	June	1970
CRA Redevelopment, Melbourne	Feb.	1972
Mid City Centre, Office, Sydney	March	1973
Ambassade D'Australie, Paris	Jan.	1974
State College of Victoria, Rusden	Oct.	1974
Ambassade D'Australie, Paris	Oct.	1974
Tuggeranong 2, Offices, ACT	Nov.	1974
Mid City Centre, Retail, Sydney	Oct.	1975
Australian Embassy, Paris, Furniture	—	1975
Australian Embassy, Paris, Site Visit and Construction Reports	Jan./Feb. May/June	1976 1976
Australian Embassy, Peking, Site Negotiation Local Building Study	Feb.	1976
MLC Centre, Construction Achievement Award, Sydney	—	1978
New Parliament House, Canberra	Aug.	1979
Hong Kong & Shanghai Banking Corp.	Oct.	1979
Office Building, Kuala Lumpur	Dec.	1980
The Gateway Lend Lease Rocks Site, Sydney	April	1981
The Hong Kong Club Redevelopment	May	1981
New World Development, Singapore	March	1982
The Rocks Gateway, Kern (Grosvenor Place), Sydney	June	1982
Margaret Street Office Development, Brisbane	Oct.	1982
National Archives Headquarters	Feb.	1983
CRA Redevelopment, Melbourne	June	1984
City Mutual Life Assurance Office (Capita), Sydney	May	1985
Landmark Tower, Brisbane	Aug.	1985
Shell House, Melbourne	Nov.	1985
Westpac, Melbourne	May	1986
Hotel Casino, Darling Harbour, Sydney	Dec.	1986
QV1 Office, Perth (Theatre)	Oct.	1987
Grand Central, Melbourne	March	1989
QV1 Office, Perth (Apartments)	Aug.	1989
Darling Park Joint Venture, Sydney	Oct.	1989
ABC Apartments, Darlinghurst, Sydney		1991

Structural Reports by L'Industria Italiana del Cemento, Rome

Australia Square, Sydney Dr Ing. Mario De Santis	March	1969
2 Glen Street, Milsons Point, Sydney Dr Ing. Gianbattista Quirico Dr Ing. Carlo Bongiovanni	April	1979
Australian Embassy, Paris Dr Ing. Claudio Di Luzio	Nov.	1979
MLC Centre, Sydney Dott. Ing. Claudio Di Luzio	Dec.	1982
Trade Group Offices, ACT Dott. Ing. Nicola Alberto Barone	Feb.	1984
Hong Kong Club Dr Arch Riccardo Spagnoli	Dec.	1986
Waverley Council, Melbourne Dr Ing. Claudio Greco	Nov.	1988
Riverside, Brisbane Prof. Ing. Mario Desideri	Oct.	1989
Garden Island, Sydney Dr Ing. Claudio Greco	Nov.	1990

Cassettes and Videos
(Held at Mitchell Library, Sydney)

Lectures and seminars given at Harvard University, University of British Columbia, University of Manitoba, University of NSW, University of Technology, and various interviews

Key to Periodicals referred to in Bibliography

A	*Arts and Architecture*, Los Angeles
AA	*Architecture in Australia*, Sydney
AAQ	*Architectural Association Quarterly*, London
A&A	*Australian Journal of Architecture and Arts*, Melbourne
AB	*Architecture Bulletin*, RAIA NSW, Sydney
Abit	*Abitare*, Milan
AD	*Architectural Design*, London
AF	*Architectural Forum*, New York
AIA	*AIA Journal*, Washington
AIT	*Architektur Innenarchitektur Technischer Ausbau*, Stuttgart
AAk	*Architektur Aktuell*, Vienna
AP	*Architecture Plus*, New York
AR	*Architectural Review*, London
ArSA	*Architecture SA*, Cape Town
ARec	*Architectural Record*, New York
A+U	*Architecture and Urbanism*, Tokyo
AW	*Architektur und Wohnform*, Stuttgart
B	*Bouw*, Rotterdam
BC	*Border Crossings*, Winnipeg
Bel	*Belle*, Sydney
BRW	*Business Review Weekly*, Sydney
Bu	*NSW Builder*, Sydney
Bull	*The Bulletin*, Sydney
BW	*Bauen und Wohnen*, Zürich
Cal	*Calli*, Mexico
COD	*Corporate & Office Design*, Sydney
CR	*Constructional Review*, Sydney
D	*Domus*, Milan
DBZ	*Deutsche Bauzeitschrift*, Gütersloh
Det	*Detail*, Munich
DJ	*Design Journal*, Seoul
HB	*Home Beautiful*, Sydney
I	*Interiors*, New York
ID(NY)	*Interior Design*, New York
ID(Sy)	*Interior Design*, Sydney
Inf	*Informes*, Madrid
Int	*Interbuild*, London
ITC	*L'industria italiana del cemento*, Rome
K	*Kindaikenchiku*, Tokyo
L	*Lichtbericht*, Lüdenscheid
LAD	*L'Architecture d'aujourdhui*, Paris
LM	*La Maison*, Brussels
MA	*Mode*, Sydney
MD	*Moebel Interior Design*, Stuttgart
NA	*Nuestra Arquitectura*, Buenos Aires
ob	*obras*, Madrid
RIBA J	*RIBA Journal*, London
RIBA Tr	*Transactions RIBA*, London
SC	*Studio Collections*, Sydney
SD	*Space Design*, Tokyo
TA	*Techniques & Architecture*, Paris
Vis	*Vision*, Hong Kong
VL	*Vogue Living*, Sydney
W	*Werk*, Zürich
WA	*World Architecture*, London
Zod	*Zodiac*, Milan

Articles by Harry Seidler

Perspective 61, Students' Arch'l Soc., U. Manitoba ('61); *MD* Jun. '64, pp. 272–4 (urban renewal); *MD* Dec. '65, pp. 576–7 (furniture); *ArSA* Aug. '81, pp. 21 41; *AA* Sep. '82, pp. 58–60; *VL* Apr/May '83 (lighting Australian embassy); *RIBA Tr* Vol. 3 No. 1 ('83–4), pp. 4–11; *Bel* Sep./Oct. '85, p. 155; *Vis* No. 26 (Jun. '86), pp. 47–50; *AR* Oct. '88 (Riverside Centre); *Weekend Australian* newspaper July 29–30 '89 Arts, p. 12 (Pei's Louvre); *Bull* Oct. 24 '89, pp. 60–4; *AB* Apr. '90, pp. 12–13 (facadism); *Bull* Mar. 20 '90, pp. 116–8 (facadism)

Selected Analytical Writings on Harry Seider since 1973

ABERCROMBIE, Stanley, 'Australian Embassy Paris', 1 Nov. '78 pp. 70–5
'Four by Seidler', *ID*(NY) May '90, pp. 210–23 (Penthouse, Hannes House, Capita Offices and Restaurant)
ADAMS, Brian, 'Harry Seidler's Sydney', *MA* Feb. '88, pp. 59–62
BOYD, Robin, 'Australia Square', *AF* Apr. '69, pp. 26–35
BRASH, Nick, 'Reflections of a Master Builder', *The Regent Magazine*, Hong Kong, 7th edn '84, pp. 26–35
CALLISTER, Winsome, 'Harry Seidler 1948–1990', *Agenda 12*, Melbourne, Aug. '90, pp. 8–9
CLEREHAN, Neil, 'Australian Superspans', *AP* Feb. '73, pp. 48–51 (Trade Group Offices)
DREW, Philip, 'Sydney Seidler', *AAQ*, Vol. 6 No. 1 '74, pp. 46–57 (general review from 1949 to 1974)
'Harry Seidler: Australian Embassy, Paris', *A+U* No. 100 Jan. '79, pp. 85–94
'The New Australian Embassy in Paris', *SD* Feb. '81, pp. 25–8
'Ethic and Form', *SD* Feb. '81, pp. 75–90
'A Building that takes its identity from not-so-plain geometry', *AIA* Aug. '82 (Ringwood)
'The Hong Kong Club Seidler Baroque', *Vis* No. 6 '83, pp. 66–71
'Secular Geometry – Ringwood Cultural Centre', *A* May '84, pp. 45–7
'Secular Geometry', *A+U* No. 170 Nov. '84, pp. 42–4 (Ringwood)
'All the glisten of Paradise', introduction, Exhibition Catalogue, Harry Seidler 1948–85, pp. 2–4
'Harry Seidler's Baroque Sinfonia for Hong Kong', *Vis* No. 26 '86, pp. 42–4
'Curviform Counterpoint', *AA* Jul. '86, pp. 49–50 (Hong Kong Club)
'Seidler Breaks the Tower Mould', *BRW* 21 Apr. '89, pp. 167–8 (Capita)
'Vast', *SC* April/May '89, pp. 170–2 (Lin Utzon Interview – Capita)
'Harry Seidler – Mastering the Mechanical', *WA* No. 7 '90, pp. 32–9
'Harry Seidler – A Humanist in Architecture Dreaming of Paradise on Earth', *DJ* No. 42 (1991), pp. 18–23 (assorted buildings)
FARRELLY, Elizabeth: 'Harry Seidler is a Modernist', *ID*(Sy) No. 18, '89
'Capita Centre', *AR* Aug. '91
'The unreconstructed Modernist', *Bull* 17 Sep. '91, p. 86
FRAMPTON, Kenneth: 'Structure and Meaning', *WA* No. 7, '90
GERAN, Monica: 'The Hong Kong Club', *ID*(Sy) Jul. '87, pp. 236–41
HALE, Brian: 'Going with the Flow', *COD* Autumn/Winter '87 (Riverside Centre)
IRACE, Fulvio: 'Grattacieli a Hong Kong', *Abit* Apr. '86
JOHNSON, Donald: 'Bauhaus, Breuer, Seidler: An Australian Synthesis', *Australian Journal of Art*, Sydney, Vol. 1 '78, pp. 65–81
KAUN, Anne: 'Aus-schnitt-Lich, Australien', *AAk* Apr. '90, pp. 42–6
KEYTE, Michael: 'Australian Embassy, Paris' *AR* Oct. '78
MARLIN, William: 'A Paris Accord', *ARec* Nov. '78
NECHANSKY, Conny: 'Harry Seidler', *AAk* Dec. '84, pp. 58–9
SAUNDERS, David: 'Homes for the Bureaucrats', *AA* Jul. '76 (Trade Group Offices)
SHARP, Dennis: Editorial, *WA* No. 7, '90
STACKHOUSE, John: 'Seidler's Marvel of Technology', *Bull* 16 Oct. '84, pp. 68–71 (Grosvenor Place)
STANNARD, Bruce, 'The trouble with Harry', *Bull* 17 Sep. '91, pp. 82–5 (Social Portrait)
TANNER, Howard: 'Harry Seidler: Beyond Local Horizons', *AB* No. 9, '87
TOWNDROW, Jennifer: 'Seidler's Poetic Geometry', *RIBA J*, Jul. '89, pp. 40–5

WALTER, Betsy: 'A Profile of Harry Seidler, Boots and Branches', *Bel* July/Aug. '79 (Australian Embassy and Glen Street Offices)
'Harry Seidler, a Private Collection', *Bel* Nov./Dec. '82 (Rose Seidler House, H.& P. Seidler House, L. Basser House)
'From Federation to Today: the changing face of Australian Homes', *Bel* Jan./Feb. '85, p. 94 (Rose Seidler House)
'Sydney's Ultimate Apartment', *MA* Apr. '89 (Penthouse)
'Capita', *COD* Spring/Summer '89
YOUNG, Richard: 'Harry goes Gold', *AA* Feb./Mar. '77, pp. 29–31

Periodical Articles

ABC Apartments (Proj): *CR* May '91, pp. 16–23
Amenities & Workshop Bldg: *A* Jan. '57, pp. 20–1
Apartments, Broadbeach: *AA* Nov. '83, pp. 42–3
——, **Earlwood**: *DBZ* Feb. '69, pp. 205–6
——, **NSW Housing Commission**: *Int* Oct. '64, pp. 18–9; *A* Oct. '65, pp. 24–5; *CR* Aug. '67, pp. 9–13
——, **Rushcutters Bay**: *AR* Jul. '61, pp. 12–5; *A* Oct. '63, pp. 12–3; *BW* Jun. '66, pp. 231–5; *DET* Jun. '68, pp. 1186–90; *LAD* Feb./Mar. '67
Arlington Apartments: *BW* Feb. '69, pp. 56–8; *CR* Jun. '69, pp. 38–41
Australian Embassy: *BW* Sep. '75, pp. 373–6; *A+U* May '76, pp. 23–7; *AR* Oct. '78, p. 210–24; *AA* Nov. '78, pp. 45–50; *BW* Nov. '78, pp. 453–60; *CR* Nov. '78, pp. 10–23; *L* Nov. '78, pp. 2–19; *D* Nov. '78, pp. 20–7; *MD* Nov. '78, pp. 42–7; *I* Nov. '78, pp. 70–5; *ARec*, Nov. '78, pp. 103–12; *LAD* Dec. '78, pp. 27–31; *A+U* Jan. '79, pp. 85–94; *Bel* Jul./Aug. '79, pp. 134–45; *ITC* Nov. '79, pp. 649–74; *SD* Feb. '81, pp. 24–8
Australia Square II: *DBZ* Oct. '63, pp. 858–60; *AA* Feb. '64, pp. 19–25; *D* Apr. '65, pp. 34–7; *CR* Sep. '66, pp. 10–7; *BW* Jan. '67, pp. 34–40; *ITC* Mar. '69, pp. 253–70; *AF* Apr. '69, pp. 26–35; May '69, pp. 101–7; *AW* Jul. '70, pp. 238–43; *Inf* Feb. '71, pp. 3–14; *DBZ* Apr. '74, pp. 607–10
Basser House: *A* May '61, pp. 20–21
Bland House: *CR* Aug. '84 pp 30–3; *A+U* Nov. '84, pp. 59–62
Blues Point Tower Apartments: *A* Jan. '59; *BW* Mar. '60, pp. 101–3; *AR* Jul. '63, pp. 12–4; *BW* Nov. '63, pp. 454–7; *DBZ* Jul. '64, pp. 524–9
Bowling Club: *A* Sep. '57; *A* Nov. '60, pp. 12–3; *DBZ* Sep. '63, pp. 731–3
Capita Centre: *A+U* Mar. '86, pp. 16–7; *TA* Jun./Jul. '87, pp. 90–3; *BRW* Apr. '89, pp. 167–8; *COD* Spring/Summer '89, pp. 26–31; *AR* Aug. '91, p. 49–54
CIBA Admin. & Warehouse Building: *A* Aug. '86, pp. 22–3; *MD* Oct. '64, pp. 495–7
City Centre Planning (Proj): *DBZ* Jul. '72, pp. 1255–6
City Council Apartments (Comp): *A* Oct. '59
Condominium Apartments: *AA* Apr. '71, pp. 191–9
Dr Fink House: *A* Apr. '49; *AR* Nov. '52, pp. 337–8; *A* Feb. '53
Eros House: *CR* Feb. '72, pp. 20–5
Exhibition Pavilion: *DBZ* Sep. '76, pp. 1089–90; *A+U* Oct. '76, pp. 43–44
Exley House: *A* Mar. '60, pp. 16–7, 32
Fairfield Municipal Library: *CR* May '76, pp. 46–51; *AA* Jan. '79, pp. 24–5
Gissing House: *MD* Feb. '73, pp. 74–7
Grosvenor Place: *AA* Sep. '84; *Bull* 16 Oct. '84, pp. 68–71; *A+U* Feb. '85, p. 18; *Australian Business*, Sydney, Dec. '88, pp. 116–8; *SD* Feb. '89, pp. 62–6
Group Housing, Campbell: *Int* Aug. '65, pp. 20–3; *AA* Jun. '72, pp. 302–5
——, **Garran**: *AA* Jun. '72, pp. 314–9
——, **Kurnell**: *A* Dec. '56; *BW* Sep. '57, pp. 326–8
Hannes House: *L* Nov. '84, pp. 16–7; *D* Jul./Aug. '85, pp. 39–40; *Bel* Sep./Oct. '85, pp. 198–201; *Bu* Jun. '86, pp. 266–73; *VL* Oct. '85, pp. 264–73; *MD* Feb. '86, pp. 63–7; *Abit* Apr. '87, pp. 156–65; *A+J* Aug. '86, pp. 123–30
Harry & Penelope Seidler House: *AA* Apr. '68, pp. 313–8; *AR* Jun. '68, pp. 422–6; *D* Aug. '68; *BW* Nov. '68, pp. 389–401; *Inf* Dec. '70, pp. 3–8
Harry Seidler Offices: *AJ* Oct. '73, pp. 895–9; *AP* Nov. '73, pp. 38–43; *CR* Nov. '73; *MD* Dec. '73, pp. 28–31; *AA* Dec. '73, pp. 74–7; *BW* Jan. '74, pp. 28–30; *ITC* Apr. '79, pp. 253–62; *Bel* Jul./Aug. '79, pp. 134–45
Heyden House: *A* Mar. '60, pp. 16–7, 32

Hillside Housing: *MD* Sep. '82, pp. 25–31; *AA* Sep. '82, pp. 52–7; *CR* Nov. '82, pp. 24–31; *AIT* May '83, pp. 34–6; *A + U* Nov. '84, pp. 45–52
Hilton Hotel: *COD* Autumn/Winter '87, pp. 160–3; *AA* Jul. '88, p. 704; *A + U* Dec. '88, pp. 77–84
Hong Kong Club & Offices: *CR* Aug. '81, pp. 12–7; *Vis 6* '83, pp. 24–69; *Vis 26* '86, pp. 20–45; *CR* Feb. '86, pp. 18–27; *Abit* Apr. '86, pp. 254–61; *AA* Jul. '86, pp. 42–8; *A + U* Sep. '86, pp. 71–80; *AJ* Oct. '86, pp. 63–8; *ITC* Dec. '86, pp. 868–85; *ID*(NY) Jul. '87, pp. 236–41; *AW* Mar. '87, pp. 7–8
Horwitz Office Building: *BW* Jul. '56, pp. 230–1
International Trade Centre *(Proj)*: *DBZ* Jul. '72, pp. 1255–6
Ithaca Gardens Apartments II: *A* Feb. '61, pp. 20–1; *LAD* Feb. '61; *ARec* Mar. '61, pp. 204–5; *BW* Jul. '61, pp. 263–6; *AD* Dec. '61, pp. 560–2; *DBZ* May '62, pp. 705–8
J. Meller House: *A* Dec. '61, pp. 26–7
Kalowski House: *A* Jan. '60
L. Basser House: *MD* Sep. '82, pp. 32–7; *L* Nov. '82, pp. 166–88; *Bel* Nov./Dec. '82; *AIT* Jan./Feb. '83, pp. 16–9
Landmark Tower: *TA* Jun./Jul. '87, pp. 94–7
Lend Lease House Offices: *BW* Oct. '62, pp. 412–6; *B* Sep. '63, p. 1243; *MD* Apr. '64, pp. 188–9; *DBZ* Feb. '65, pp. 165–8
Lessing House: *A* Aug. '61, pp. 10–1; *MD* May '64, pp. 244–5
Luursema House: *DBZ* Oct. '62, pp. 1547–8
Marcus Seidler House: *A* Jan. '50; *A* Apr. '54, pp. 20–5; *NA* Feb. '55, pp. 40–1
McMahons Point Development *(Proj)*: *A* Feb. '58, pp. 16–7; *MD* Mar. '58, pp. 69–73
Merson House: *CR* Aug. '84, pp. 26–9; *A + U* Nov. '84, pp. 53–8
Mid-City Shopping Centre: *CR* Aug. '82, pp. 34–9; *AA* Jan. '83, pp. 48–53; *MD* Feb. '83, pp. 20–1; *BU* Jul. '83, pp. 356–65; *BW* Nov. '83, pp. 4–6
MLC Centre: *CR* Feb. '74, pp. 2–15; *CR* Aug. '76, pp. 28–33; *A + U* Oct. '76, pp. 34–42; *AR* Mar. '77, pp. 145–6; *MD* May '77, pp. 38–41; *CR* Oct. '79, pp. 54–9; *A + U* Oct. '80, pp. 514–27; *A + U* Oct. '80, pp. 115–20; *L* Mar. '81, pp. 22–7; *ArSA* Aug. '81, pp. 20–5; *AIT* Nov./Dec. '82, pp. 538–47; *ITC* Dec. '82, pp. 893–918
Monahan House: *MD* Mar. '65, p. 30; *AW* Apr. '70, pp. 111–3
Newton House *(Proj)*: *A* Dec. '55
Muller House: *A* Jun. '64, pp. 14–5; *MD* Dec. '64, pp. 608–11
Navy Weapons Workshop: *CR* Aug. '82, pp. 23–5; *CR* Aug. '86, pp. 12–19; *AA* Jan. '87, pp. 60–3; *Bu* Feb. '87, pp. 26–33; *Det* May/Jun. '88, pp. 291–6; *ITC* Nov. '90, pp. 896–907
NSW Government Stores: *Int* Sep. '65, pp. 18–22; *BW* May '66, pp. 202–3; *AA* Apr. '72, pp. 184–93
Office Extension & Penthouse: *SD* Feb. '89, pp. 62–6; *MA* Apr. '89, pp. 72–9; *ID*(Sy) No. 18, '89, pp. 70–83; *AA* Jun. '89, pp. 68–72; *L* Sep. '89, p. 2–5; *CR* Aug. '90, pp. 10–17; *MD* Feb. '90, pp. 70–3; *HB* Oct. '90, pp. 12–17; *D* Dec. '90, pp. 76–9
Olympic Stadium *(Comp)*: *LAD* Sep. '54, p. 76
Olympic Swimming Pool *(Comp)*: *LAD* Sep. '54, p. 77
Paspaley House, Darwin: *A* May '62, pp. 14–5
Printers Union Bldg: *A* Dec. '59; *DBZ* Apr. '69, pp. 589–90
RAIA Convention Exhibition & Model House: *A* May '55
Ringwood Cultural Centre: *CR* Aug. '80, pp. 40–5; *L* Mar. '81, pp. 18–21; *AIA* Aug. '82, p. 65; *AA* Mar. '84, pp. 44–7; *A + U* Nov. '84, pp. 37–44
Riverside Development Stage I: *A + U* Oct. '85, pp. 16–8; *COD* Autumn/Winter '87, pp. 102–5; *CR* Feb. '88, pp. 10–9; *AR* May '85, pp. 88–91; *A + U* Dec. '88, pp. 65–76; *AAk* Oct. '88, pp. 82–5; *L* Sep. '89, p. 6–7; *ITC* Oct. '89, pp. 571–85
Rose House, Turramurra: *NA* Feb. '55, pp. 42–3; *BW* Mar. '56, pp. 73–5
Rose Seidler House: *AR* Scp. '51, pp. 150–1; *AR* Nov. '51, pp. 306–9; *A* Nov. '51; *I* Dec. '51, pp. 82–5; *BW* Oct. '52, pp. 238–40; *NA* Feb. '55, pp. 36–9; *Die Kunst*, Munich, No. 2 '57, pp. 72–5; *Bel* Jan.-Feb. '85, p. 94
Shell Headquarters: *CR* Nov. '89, pp. 10–19
Ski Lodge: *A* Feb. '63, pp. 17–9; *D* Jul. '63, pp. 18–23; *MD* Aug. '63, pp. 387–9; *BW* Jun. '64, pp. 245–7; *DBZ* Sep. '65, pp. 1457–62
Studio-Apartment: *A* Feb. '49, pp. 28–9
Sussman House: *A* Apr. '54, pp. 26–9; *A* Nov. '53
Sydney Cove Redevelopment: *MD* Apr. '65, p. 115; *DBZ* May '67, pp. 707–8
Sydney University Student Hostel *(Proj)*: *A* Sep. '50
T. Meller House: *A* May '50; *A* May '54; *AR* May '54, pp. 317–21; *NA* Mar. '55, pp. 70–5; *BW* Apr. '55, pp. 97–100
Torin Co Factory (Marcel Breuer): *AA* Jul. '77, pp. 42–5
Trade Group Offices: *AP* Feb '73, pp. 48–51; *CR* May '75, pp. 12–7; *AA* Jun./Jul. '76, pp. 62–5; *A + U* Oct. '76, pp. 21–33; *BW* Sep. '76, pp. 317–28; *D* Sep. '77, pp. 6–10; *ITC* Feb. '84, pp. 84–103
Two Exhibition Houses: *A* Nov. '62, pp. 18–9
Tyree House *(Proj)*: *A* Jul. '58
Universal House *(Proj)*: *MD* Mar. '58, pp. 92–3
Waks House I: *A* Jan. '49, pp. 38–9; *A* Nov. '51; *I* Dec. '51, pp. 85–8
Waks House II: *A* Jun. '61, pp. 12–3; *LAD* Sep. '62, pp. 32–3; *BW* Dec. '62, pp. 516–9
Waverley Art Gallery: *CR* Aug. '81, pp. 44–9
Waverley Civic Centre: *CR* Aug. '85, pp. 20–9; *A + U* Jan. '86, pp. 109–16; *AA* Jul. '88, pp. 75–7; *ITC* Nov. '88, pp. 661–79
Weinreich House: *MD* Mar. '65, p. 29; *DBZ* Jul. '69, pp. 1333–4
Welfare Centre for the Aged: *DBZ* Aug. '69, pp. 1499–500
Yarralumla Group Houses: *CR* Nov. '86, pp. 56–61; *AA* Jan. '87, pp. 64–5; *Bu* Jun. '87, pp. 313–9; *TA* Jun./Jul. '87, pp. 86–9; *A + U* Oct. '87, pp. 38–41
General Writing: *A* Mar. '55; *A* Aug. '56, pp. 86–92; *AR* Aug.' 56, pp. 84–92; *LAD* No. 73 '57, pp. 102–5; *Zod 3* '60; *MD* Jul. '61; *A&A* Jul.'62, pp. 28–49; *Ob* No. 99 '63, pp. 7–14; *LM* Jun. '65, pp. 184–93; *Cal* No. 24 '66, pp. 44–53; *AAQ* Vol. 6 No. 1 '74, pp. 47–58; *AA* Feb./Mar. '77, pp. 29–31; *AR* Sep. '78, p. 128, 135–6, 154; *Bel* Jul./Aug. '79, pp. 134–45; *SD* Feb. '81; *AA* Sep. '82, pp. 48–57; *A + U* Nov. '84, pp. 37–62; *AAk* Dec. '84, pp. 58–9; *AB* No. 9, '87, pp. 4–9; *BC* Oct. '88, pp. 26–34; *SD* Feb. '89, pp. 62–6; *RIBA J* Jul. '89, pp. 40–5; *AAk* Apr. '90, pp. 42–3; *ID*(NY) May '90, pp. 210–23; *WA* No. 7, '90, pp. 31–53; *AAk* Sep. '90, pp. 107–15; *DJ* No. 42 '91

Popular Press / Magazines

Adams, Brian, 'Harry Seidler's Sydney', *MA* Feb. '88, pp. 59–62
Hawley, Janet, 'Seidler and what makes Harry wild', Saturday Extra, *The Age* newspaper, Melbourne, 23 Nov. '85, pp. 1–2
Hayes, Babette, 'The Experts . . . The Architect', *Bel*, Sep.–Oct. '83, p. 34
——, 'Cooling Systems – Pools', *Bel*, Sep.–Oct. '83, pp. 154–5
Iatrou, Chris, and George Metaxas, 'Directions in Australian Architecture', *Vive La Vie*, Melbourne, Vol. 3 '88, pp. 38–9 (Seidler's opinion)
King, Stephanie, 'The Best Office of the Year', *Australian Business*, Sydney, Dec. '88, pp. 116–8 (IEL floor – Grosvenor Place)
McGregor, Craig, 'Thoroughly Modernist Harry', Good Weekend, *Sydney Morning Herald*, 2 Jun. '90, pp. 18–24 (social portrait)
Ruskin, Pamela, 'Man on the move', *Signature – Diners Club*, Aust., Feb./Mar. '72
Schofield, Louise, 'Seidler energises designs', Property Section, *Weekend Australian* newspaper, 20–21 Oct. '90, p. 11 (energy conservation)
Stanley-Hill, Colin, 'At home with the master modern', *HB* Oct. '90, pp. 12–17 (penthouse)
Stannard, Bruce, 'The trouble with Harry', *Bull* 17 Sep. '91, pp. 82–5
Sudjic, Deyan, 'When the Best Men Didn't Win – Architects Competition', *Blueprint*, London, Jun. '88, p. 55 (Hong Kong Shanghai Bank)
'En plein bois', *Connaissance Des Arts*, Paris, Mar. '66
'Modern Ideas in Unusual Home', *Womans Day & Home*, Sydney, May '52, p. 33 (Rose Seidler House)

Seidler Interviews

De Berg Tapes, National Library, Canberra, '72
ArSA Aug. '81, pp. 20–5
SC Sep./Oct. '84, pp. 26–9
Graphics (Sydney) Feb. '87, pp. 1–3
BC Fall '88, pp. 26–34
Australian Concrete Construction (Sydney) May '90
AAk Sep. '90, pp. 107–15

Credits

Foremost among the photographers whose images appear in this book, Max Dupain's extensive work must be acknowledged.

The early work was photographed by my late brother, Marcell. It was from him that I learned about photography and its importance to architecture. He introduced me to Max Dupain. In recent years, when Max was unable to travel, John Gollings stepped in to photograph the buildings in Hong Kong, Melbourne and Brisbane. The majority of the personal photos were taken by my wife and partner, Penelope.

Credit is more than due to the engineering professionals who worked closely with me to select the best structural forms and technical means. My collaboration with Pier Luigi Nervi, one of the famous twentieth-century names in structures, has already been mentioned. From 1950 there was Peter Miller, and, from 1960 on, his associates Alan Milston, John Ferris and Aldis Birzulis.

The Sydney Opera House controversy, and Ove Arup's part in it, is long past. In recent years Harry Seidler & Associates worked with his partners, Sir Jack Zunz and the fine Sydney team led by Peter Thompson.

These days energy planning and conservation are being given the increased attention they deserve. My own commitment caused me to place a greater reliance on mechanical engineers. Their advice has had a substantial impact in shaping both the overall forms, in addition to the smaller details, of my architecture in recent years. David Norman's and Don Thomas's teams are just some of the many dedicated professionals who have helped me in this area.

'... For forty years now, Max has recorded models and buildings. With zest and an innate selectivity of vision he appraised the visual strength of each form. His great skill exceeded the simple recording of fact. His eye transmuted the world in front of his lens to art, seizing the essence of each object with a mastery of technique and consummate sense for arranging the elements in his compositions. But chiefly, he responded to the Australian light. Light is his medium: his images celebrate its moods, its subtle gradations and luminescence...'

Collaborators

Through the decades spanned by the work in this book, many young people came and worked with me. Some have remained loyal collaborators for thirty years or longer. Others began as students, then left my office to become experienced professionals on their own.

To them, for their single-mindedness, their dedication to the task, and the deep satisfaction that is the reward of effective teamwork, I will always be grateful.

Most of the team in 1991

Architectural staff
Marsoedi Adisasmita 1959–60
Tim Anthios 1985–86
Garth Armstrong 1984–
John F Baker 1970–71, 73–74
John Baker 1989
Plamen Bassarov 1983–88
Alison Bean 1989–
Allan Beaven 1980–84
Michael Boyle 1958
Ian Breden 1962–63
Daniel Brown 1985–89
Brian Bunting 1963–66
Mark Edwards Butler 1980–
Sergio Buzzolini 1961–63
Tony Camilleri 1980–
Tony Caro 1972–
Louise Chapman 1984–
Ron Clinton 1959–60
Juan Contreras 1979–80
Andrew Currie 1985–89
John Curro 1983–
Frank D'Arcy 1952–53, 61–63
Geoff Danks 1959–65
John Daubney 1967–72
Michael Davies 1967–75
Renato Dettore 1979–85
Kate Dewhirst 1990–
Mark Dunbabin 1987–89
Ian Dunlop 1985–88
Michael Dunn 1987–88
Robin Dyke 1969–73
David Earle 1963
Jeremy Edmiston 1983–91

Dean Edwards 1984–
Henry Feiner 1973–76, 82–
Horst Flügel 1960
David Forbes 1964–68
Don Gazzard 1950–53
Joshua George 1985–89
Colin Griffiths 1954–81
Natasha Guilbaud 1987–88
Ian Guthrie 1975–76
Fred Heilpern 1959–68
Hans Helle 1959–62
George Henderson 1972–
Peter Hirst 1960–
Greg Holman 1980–
George Hrusovsky 1985–87
Peter Hrusovsky 1987–88
Vladimir Ivanov 1987–
Graham Jahn 1977–78, 80–81
Russel Jones 1986
Mark Jones 1985–86
Peter Justin 1971–76
Kiyoshi Kaneko 1984–85
Anne Kaun 1986
Yoji Kurisu 1984–
Volker Langbein 1970–76
Fotoulla Lazaridis 1982
Harry Levine 1982–85
Alan Logan 1975–76
Brendan Macfarlane 1982–83
Peter Makeig 1949–50
Alan McCallum 1986–87
Graham McDonald 1970–72, 80–
Dirk Meinecke 1984–

Anthony Moorhouse 1989–
Leonard Morgan 1973–76
Paul Northgrave 1972
Peter O'Loghlen 1984–85
Tim O'Sullivan 1983–87
Dimitri Pedashenko 1964–76
Lanfranco Palmitessa 1988–89
Kon Pavlov 1980–84
Elizabeth Peet 1985–88
Ken Quinlam 1950–51
Robert Regala 1953–54
Jutta Ress 1984–85
Roger Richardson 1961–63
Remo Riva 1971–72
Karl Romandi 1967–68
Jane Schneider 1980–82
Brian Scott 1982–83
Paul Seaberg 1987–
Harry Seidler 1948–
Penelope Seidler 1963–
Marie-Louise Sendes 1982–
Mark Sheldon 1975
Timothy Shiu 1988–
Reg Smith 1972–73
Carlos Sogari 1987–88
Michael Spicer 1987
Grant Spork 1985–87
Arief Suhadi 1987–
Thomas Tang 1985–
Nicholas Tesdorf 1973–76
Anthony Thistleton-Smith 1990–91
Robert Thorne 1970–71
Peter Torresan 1973–75, 80–87

Stephen Trstenjak 1988–
Jackie Urford 1985–
Furio Valich 1972–76
Les Westman 1963
Gilbert Williams 1980–
Robert Wilson 1972–75
John Wyndham 1965–66
Stephen Yee 1987–88
Peter Yip 1985–
Yow Sze Wun 1963
Raymond Yuen 1985–87

Secretarial staff
Joan Adler 1982–88
Robyn Atkinson 1958–60
Jill Bannerman 1971–78
Lynne Edwards 1987–89, 91–
Elizabeth Jobe 1961–65, 68–70
Carmel Kaveney 1974–76, 78–80
Kay Knowles 1966–68
Donna Koeppl 1988–91
Beth Marks 1970–71
Diane McPeak 1983–88
Diane Monro 1960–61
Jennifer Pettit 1984–
Susan Schultz 1973–74
Helen Stewart 1980–83

Bold type indicates Associates in Design